Perception, Knowledg

This collection of essays by eminent philosopher Fred Dretske brings together work on the theory of knowledge and philosophy of mind spanning thirty years. The two areas combine to lay the groundwork for a naturalistic philosophy of mind.

The fifteen essays focus on perception, knowledge, and consciousness. Together, they show the interconnectedness of Dretske's work in epistemology and his more contemporary ideas on philosophy of mind, shedding light on the links that can be made between the two. The first part of the book argues the point that knowledge consists of beliefs with the right objective connection to facts; two essays discuss this conception of knowledge's implications for naturalism. The second part articulates a view of perception, attempting to distinguish conceptual states from phenomenal states. A naturalized philosophy of mind, and thus a naturalized epistemology, is articulated in the third part.

This collection will be a valuable resource for a wide range of philosophers and their students, and will also be of interest to cognitive scientists, psychologists, and philosophers of biology.

Fred Dretske is Professor Emeritus in Philosophy at Stanford University and is currently senior research scholar at Duke University. He is the author of four other books.

CAMBRIDGE STUDIES IN PHILOSOPHY

General editor ERNEST SOSA (Brown University)

Advisory editors:

JONATHAN DANCY (University of Reading)
JOHN HALDANE (University of St. Andrews)
GILBERT HARMAN (Princeton University)
FRANK JACKSON (Australian National University)
WILLIAM G. LYCAN (University of North Carolina at Chapel Hill)
SYDNEY SHOEMAKER (Cornell University)
JUDITH J. THOMSON (Massachusetts Institute of Technology)

RECENT TITLES:

Perception, Knowledge, and Belief

Selected Essays

FRED DRETSKE

Stanford University

CAMBRIDGE
UNIVERSITY PRESS

PUBLISHED BY THE PRESS SYNDICATE OF THE UNIVERSITY OF CAMBRIDGE
The Pitt Building, Trumpington Street, Cambridge, United Kingdom

CAMBRIDGE UNIVERSITY PRESS
The Edinburgh Building, Cambridge CB2 2RU, UK   http://www.cup.cam.ac.uk
40 West 20th Street, New York, NY 10011–4211, USA   http://www.cup.org
10 Stamford Road, Oakleigh, Melbourne 3166, Australia
Ruiz de Alarcón 13, 28014 Madrid, Spain

First published 2000

Typeface Bembo 10.5/13 pt.   *System* DeskTopPro/UX [BV]

A catalog record for this book is available from the British Library.

Library of Congress Cataloging in Publication Data
Dretske, Fred I.
Perception, knowledge, and belief : selected essays / Fred
Dretske.
p.   cm. – (Cambridge studies in philosophy)
ISBN 0–521–77181–1. – ISBN 0–521–77742–9 (pbk.)
1. Knowledge, Theory of.   2. Philosophy of mind.   I. Title.
II. Series.
BD161.D73   2000
121'.092—dc21   99–15973
                                                                CIP

ISBN 0 521 77181 1 hardback
ISBN 0 521 77742 9 paperback

Transferred to digital printing 2003

Contents

Preface

These fifteen essays span almost thirty years – from 1970 (Epistemic Operators) to 1999 (The Mind's Awareness of Itself). They record a growing preoccupation with the mind's material constitution. I think of them as steps, sometimes very halting and uncertain steps, toward philosophical naturalism about the mind.

I began by worrying about very traditional epistemological questions. What makes a belief that something is F into knowledge that it is F? What makes an F-like experience a perception of an F? As the concept of information began to dominate my thinking about epistemology (circa 1980), I pursued naturalistic answers to these questions without pausing to ask what makes a belief a belief or an experience an experience. Knowledge was analyzed as information-caused belief. Perception was identified with (a particular kind of) information-carrying experience. In *Knowledge and the Flow of Information* (1981) I had argued that semantic information – what information (news, message) a signal carries – can be understood as an objective, a completely natural, commodity. It was as acceptable in a materialistic metaphysics as was the statistical construct of information employed by communications engineers. I therefore had, or so I thought, a naturalized epistemology. Knowledge and perception were merely specialized informational states in certain living organisms. I soon realized, however, that as long as I had no acceptable (i.e., naturalistic) account of belief, I had no acceptable account of knowledge. Until I could say what an experience was, I had no materialistic recipe for perception. If perception of an F is an information (about F)-rich experience, what, exactly, is an experience? If knowledge is information-caused belief, what, then, is a belief? Until I had answers to these questions, I had no answers to questions I expected an adequate epistemology to provide – for example, do machines (e.g., computers and robots) *know* things? Do measuring instruments and sensing devices (e.g., thermostats and pressure gauges) *perceive* the conditions they provide information about? What about animals? Does a frog *see* the flies it catches? Does it know they are flies? That will depend, of course, on whether the information the frog so obviously gets about the flies is embodied in beliefs and experiences.

Naturalism in philosophy – as I understand it – has the goal of articulating the application conditions of puzzling concepts (like *knowledge* and *perception*) so that empirical (scientific) methods can be used to answer questions we have about the things to which we apply these concepts. Until we reach this point of clarity in what we are talking about, there is a suspicion that we – philosophers – do not really know what we are talking about – thus the (seemingly) endless philosophical debates about (for example) skepticism. Naturalism in epistemology is merely the attempt to get clear *enough* about what we mean when we talk about knowledge and perception to be able to tell – in ways a biologist or an experimental psychologist would recognize as scientifically respectable – whether what we are saying is true or not.

It was for this reason that I came to view my information-based naturalization of knowledge and perception as inadequate. It left belief and experience as part of the mix, and I had no naturalistic recipe for either of these ingredients. Until I knew what a belief was, I could not say whether machines or frogs knew or perceived anything. I could not assess the skeptic's claim that we cannot know to be true most (all?) the things we believe to be true. Until I could say what an experience was, I had no defensible way of denying (or affirming) that robots actually perceive the obstacles they so expertly avoid. Even a lowly thermostat picks up and uses (to control the furnace) information about temperature. So why doesn't this qualify as perception and cognition? Because the instrument doesn't have experiences and beliefs? Just what are these? I had, furthermore, no grounds for saying (what we all believe) that in everyday perception what we experience (perceive) are rocks, trees, and (other) people and not (as some philosophers claim) something altogether different – mental representations (ideas) of these external objects. It was a growing awareness of these lacunae in my epistemology that drove me into philosophy of mind. One can certainly do epistemology without doing the philosophy of mind, but one cannot hope to naturalize the one without naturalizing the other.

This shift was gradual. Early essays on knowledge (1 and 2) are more concerned to argue that knowledge consists of belief with the right objective connection to the facts (a connection I later described in informational terms). By completely eschewing such traditional (but, to my mind, unhelpful) concepts as justification, evidence, and reasons, the hope was to make knowledge (like, say, weight or marital status) something more accessible to empirical methods. Assuming we could determine the presence of an appropriate belief, was it connected to the facts in the right way? Essays 1 and 3 are attempts to specify this "right" way. "Epistemic Operators" (Essay 2) is included because of its much-discussed argument against skepticism. Essays 4 and 5 are more explicit in the way they describe this conception of knowledge and its implications for the naturalistic project.

The essays in Part Two, Perception and Experience, cover twenty years. Essay 6 articulates a view of perception I first advanced in *Seeing and Knowing* (1969) and that I have defended against a variety of objections (e.g., Virgil Aldrich in Essay 6, Dan Dennett in Essay 8, and David Armstrong and others in Essay 7). Essays 9 and 10 attempt to describe the nature of conscious experience and its evolutionary function. Collectively, these five essays are my best effort to distinguish conceptual states – belief, judgment, and knowledge – from phenomenal states – sensations, experiences, and feelings. One cannot believe, judge, or know (conceptual states) that an animal is an armadillo without understanding what an armadillo is – without, in this way, having the concept *armadillo* – but one can see, feel, taste, and be aware (conscious) of an armadillo while being completely ignorant of what armadillos are or of what they look (taste, feel) like. For a naturalization project, then, there are really two problems about the mind: what sorts of material states are phenomenal states (today this is often referred to as the *hard* problem of consciousness) and what sorts of material states are conceptual states? Some philosophers have thought to deny that there are two problems – thereby making the naturalization of conscious experience a more tractable problem – by identifying experience with a special kind of judgment. I think this is a profound mistake. It makes things easier, but only by suppressing one of the most baffling – but, at the same time, one of the most distinctively mental – aspects of our conscious lives. The essays in this part are my effort to insist on and further clarify this important distinction.

Part Three, Thought and Intentionality, are my latest efforts to articulate and defend a naturalized philosophy of mind and, thus, a naturalized epistemology. In Essay 11 I argue that information (not just the signals that carry it) can do some real causal work in the world. This is, I believe, a first step in understanding how the mind (the chief consumer of information) can be causally efficacious in the world and how information can direct its activities. Only by understanding this, I feel, can one appreciate the role that reasons play in the explanation of behavior. I return to this theme again in Essay 15 by comparing the way beliefs explain the behavior of animals to the way money explains the behavior of vending machines. Essay 12 is a blunt – I'm sure some will find it crude – expression of my naturalistic philosophy of mind.

Part One

Knowledge

1

Conclusive Reasons

Conclusive reasons have a modal as well as an epistemic character. In having conclusive reasons to believe that P is the case one's epistemic credentials are such as to eliminate the possibility of mistake. This, at least, is how I propose to understand them for the remainder of this essay. Letting the symbol "$\langle\rangle$" represent the appropriate modality (a yet to be clarified sense of *possibility*), I shall say, then, that R is a conclusive reason for P if and only if, given R, $\sim \langle\rangle \sim$ P (or, alternatively, $\sim \langle\rangle$ (R. $\sim$ P)). This interpretation allows us to say of any subject, S, who believes that P and who has conclusive reasons for believing that P, that, given these reasons, he *could not be wrong* about P or, given these reasons, *it is false that he might be mistaken* about P.

Suppose, then, that

(1) S knows that P and he knows this on the basis (simply) of R entails
(2) R would not be the case unless P were the case.[1]

The latter formula expresses a connection between R and P that is strong enough, I submit, to permit us to say that if (2) is true, then R is a conclusive reason for P. For if (2) is true, we are entitled not only to deny that, given R, not-P *is* the case, but also that, given R, not-P *might* be the case. That is to say, (2) eliminates R and not-P as a possible

Reprinted From *Australasian Journal of Philosophy* 49, (1) (1971) 1–22, by permission of the publisher. An early version of this essay was read to the Philosophy Department at The University of Illinois, Chicago Circle. More recently it was read at The University of North Carolina's Colloquium in Philosophy, with Professor Robert Sleigh commenting.

1 I shall be using "R" and "P" to replace a variety of related grammatical units. Depending on the sentential context, they sometimes serve as noun phrases, sometimes as full indicative sentences, sometimes for appropriate transformations of the indicative.

(joint) state of affairs and, when we are *given* R, it eliminates not-P as a possible state of affairs. This is so because (2) entails the falsity of

(3) Although R is the case P might not be the case.

If we express (3) as "Given R, $\langle \rangle \sim P$," then (2) entails that it is false that, given R, $\langle \rangle \sim P$ that is equivalent to, given R, $\sim \langle \rangle \sim P$; and this is precisely the required feature of conclusive reasons given previously. Hence, when (2) is true, R is a conclusive reason for P.

What follows is an amplification of the preceding sketch – hence, an argument for the view that in those cases where knowledge that P rests on evidence, grounds, or reasons, when the question "How does S know?" can sensibly be asked and answered, the evidence, grounds, or reasons must be conclusive. Anything short of conclusive reasons, though it may provide one with justified true beliefs, fails to give the kind of support requisite to knowledge. I shall also urge that the possession of conclusive reasons to believe, properly qualified, is also a sufficient condition for knowledge.

1. KNOWING P ON THE BASIS OF R: THE CONNECTION BETWEEN (1) AND (2)

Suppose S, in order to assure himself that his child's temperature is normal (no fever), places a thermometer in the child's mouth, extracts it after several minutes, and observes a reading of 98.6°F. In remarking to the doctor that his child's temperature is normal, S is asked how he knows. S responds, naturally enough, by saying, "I just took his temperature." Let us assume, then, that we have an instantiation of (1):

(1a) S knows that his child's temperature is normal, and he knows this on the basis of the (normal) reading on the thermometer (which he has just placed in the child's mouth, etc.).

Can one consistently affirm (1a) and deny the corresponding instantiation of (2)?

(2a) The thermometer would not have read 98.6°F unless the child's temperature was normal.

If it is not already obvious that one cannot consistently affirm (1a) and deny (2a), I think it can be made obvious by considering the kind of thing that would show (2a) to be false. For example, if Charles, familiar with the particular thermometer in question, should say, "Oh, I know

4

that thermometer; it is fairly accurate for temperatures below 98° but it sticks at 98.6 for almost any higher temperature," we have been given solid grounds for rejecting (2a). Simultaneously, however, we have been given solid grounds for rejecting (1a). If it is *that* kind of thermometer, then if S's only basis for thinking his child's temperature normal is a 98.6 reading on it, then he does not *know* that his child's temperature is normal. It *might* be normal, of course, but if S knows that it is, he must have more to go on than the reading on this (defective) thermometer.

Other attempts to show (2a) to be false have the same effect; they immediately undermine R (the reading on the thermometer) as an adequate basis for someone's knowing that the child's temperature is normal (P). For in rejecting (2a) we reject the thermometer as a reliable device for discovering whether a person's temperature is normal, and knowledge is not acquired by relying on what is unreliable in precisely those respects in which we rely on it.

We frequently purport to know things on the basis of testimony. James has a large stamp collection and, after giving a detailed description of it, invites S to his home to see it. S declines, but he later refers to James's stamp collection in conversation. It is easy enough to imagine circumstances in which it would be natural for someone to ask S how he knew, what reasons he had for thinking that James had such a collection. And it is just as easy to imagine S, in response to such a query, referring to his conversation with James. Let us assume, then, that

(1b) S knows that James has a stamp collection, and he knows this on the basis of James's description (and invitation)

is true. I am not now concerned to argue that one can know something of this sort in this way; the question is, rather, whether (2b) must be true *if* (1b) is true.

(2b) James would not have said he had a stamp collection, described it in such detail, and issued an invitation unless he had a stamp collection.

If James is the sort of fellow about which (2b) cannot be truly asserted, then he is not the sort of fellow who can be trusted on such matters as this. If James is the sort of fellow who sometimes says such things as a joke, who would (or might) concoct such elaborate stories for his own amusement (or whatever), who would (or might) whimsically issue an invitation of this sort under totally false pretexts, then, despite the fact that he is (by hypothesis) telling the truth on this occasion, his testimony is hardly the sort on which one can rest a claim to know. In denying

5

(2b) one is conceding that James would, or might, have said what he did without possessing a stamp collection, and in the light of this concession one cannot go on to insist that, nonetheless, S *knows* he has a stamp collection on the basis, simply, of what James said.

Gilbert Harman contrasts two cases, *the lottery case* and *the testimony case*.[2] Although S, say, has only one among thousands of tickets in a lottery and, hence, has an extremely slender chance of winning, we naturally reject the idea that S could know that he was going to lose on the basis of a correct probability estimate (well over 99.9%) of his losing. Even if S correctly predicts that he is going to lose, we would deny that he knew he was going to lose if the *only* basis he had for this belief was the fact that his chances of winning were so slight.[3] Harman compares this case with the situation in which we often seem prepared to say that S knows that P when he is told that P is the case by some other person (testimony case). Although probability estimates are not altogether appropriate here, we do know that people sometimes lie, sometimes they are honestly mistaken, and so on. There always seems to be a chance that what a person tells us is not the case, however sincere or credible he may appear, and the order of magnitude of this chance seems to be comparable to the chance that we might win in some appropriate lottery situation. Why, then, are we prepared to say that we know in the one case but not in the other? Harman has some revealing remarks to make about these cases, but I mention them only to bring out their relevance to the present discussion. For I think this contrast strengthens the view that (2) is normally accepted as a necessary consequence of (1), that when we are unwilling to endorse the corresponding instantiation of (2) we are unwilling to talk of anyone knowing that P is the case on the basis of the evidence expressed by R. In many testimony situations we are, I believe, willing to affirm (2): the person would not have said it unless it was so. In the lottery case, however, the connection between R and P expressed by this subjunc-

---

2 "Knowledge, Inference, and Explanation," in *American Philosophical Quarterly*, July 1968.

3 Of course S may have said "I know I am going to lose" and he may say now, after he has lost, "I knew I was going to lose," but these expressions are normally accepted without epistemological quibbling because they are taken as little more than expressions of resignation or despair. With this use of the verb "to know," one can know one is going to lose and *still* spend a dollar for a ticket and a chance at the prize—a fact about human beings that is puzzling if they believe they know (in any epistemologically relevant sense) that they are going to lose.

tive conditional fails to be realized, and it fails no matter how great the probabilities become. Adjusting the wording of (2) to suit the example in question[4] we have

(2c) If S were going to win the lottery, his chances of winning would not be $1/m$ (m being the number of tickets sold).

Whatever (finite) value we give to m, we know this is false since someone whose chances of winning are $1/m$ *will* win, and since there is nothing special about S that would require him to have a better chance of winning than anyone else in order to win, we reject (2c) as false. Hence, we reject the idea that S can know he is going to lose on the basis of the fact that his chances of losing are $(m - 1)/m$.

Alvin Goldman, in developing a causal account of knowledge, constructs a situation in which S is said to know that a nearby mountain (I will call it M) erupted many years ago. He knows this on the basis of the presence of solidified lava throughout the countryside surrounding the mountain.[5] According to Goldman, a necessary condition for S's knowing that M erupted many years ago on the basis of the present existence and distribution of the lava is that there be a causal connection between the eruption of the mountain and the present existence and distribution of the lava. I do not wish to dispute this claim at the moment since the view I am advancing is even stronger: viz. that a necessary condition for S to know that M erupted on this basis is that

---

4 The wording of (2) will sometimes have to be adjusted to suit the particular instantiation in question. The chief factors determining this adjustment are the relative temporal locations of R, P, and the time of utterance and also the causal connections, if any, that are believed to hold between R and P. The particular wording I have given (2) is most appropriate when P is some state of affairs antecedent to (or contemporaneous with) both R and the time of utterance. This, of course, is the result of the fact that (2) is most often used when P is some state of affairs causally responsible for the present condition R. When P is a future state we might express (2) as: R would not be the case unless P were going to happen. For example, he would not have registered unless he were going to vote. I do not wish to preclude the possibility of knowing that something *will* occur on the basis of present evidence by restricting the wording of (2). The difficulty, of course, is that when P is some future state, the subjunctive relating it to R generally becomes somewhat questionable. We prefer to say, in our more cautious moods, that if he were not *planning* to vote, he would not have registered (acknowledging, thereby, the fact that contingencies may interfere with the execution of his plans). But in the same cautious moods we prefer to say, not that we know he is going to vote (because he registered), but that we know he plans or intends to vote.

5 "A Causal Theory of Knowing," *Journal of Philosophy*, June 22, 1967, p. 361.

(2d) The lava would not be here, and distributed in this manner, unless M
   erupted

is true. (2d) is a stronger claim than that the eruption of M is causally
connected with the present existence and distribution of the lava. (2d)
requires, in addition, that M's eruption be necessary for the present state
of affairs. To illustrate, consider the following embellishment on Goldman's example. Not far from M is another mountain, N. The geology
of the area is such that at the point in time at which M erupted
something, so to speak, was bound to give; if M had not erupted, N
would have. Furthermore, the location of N is such that if it, rather than
M, had erupted, the present distribution of lava would have been, in all
respects relevant to S's taking it as a reason for believing M erupted, the
same. In such circumstances Goldman's necessary condition is satisfied,
but mine is not. (2d) is false; it is false that the lava would not be here,
and distributed in this fashion, unless M had erupted. For if, contrary to
the hypothesis, M had not erupted, N would have, leaving the very
same (relevant) traces.

In such circumstances I do not think we could say that S knew that
M erupted on the basis of the present existence and distribution of lava.
For, by hypothesis, *this* state of affairs would have obtained whether M
erupted or not and, hence, there is nothing about this state of affairs that
favors one hypothesis (M erupted) over a competing hypothesis (N
erupted). S is still correct in supposing that M did erupt, still correct in
supposing that it was M's eruption that is causally responsible for the
present existence and distribution of lava, but he does not know it was
M that erupted – not unless he has some additional grounds that preclude N. If he has such additional grounds, call them Q, then we can
say that he knows that M erupted and he knows this on the basis of R
and Q. In this case, however, the corresponding instantiation of (2) is
also satisfied: R *and* Q would not be the case unless M erupted. As
things stand, the most that S could know, on the basis simply of the
present existence and distribution of lava, is that *either M or N erupted*.
(2) permits us to say this much, and no more, about what can be known
on the basis of lava flow.

The case becomes even clearer if we exploit another of Harman's
examples.[6] Harold has a ticket in a lottery. The odds against his winning

---

6 In "Knowledge, Inference, and Explanation," pp. 168–169. I have adapted the example
   somewhat.

are 10,000 to 1. The prize, call it an X, is something that Harold does not now have nor could he reasonably expect to obtain one by means other than winning the lottery. Enter a philanthropic gentleman, Rockaford, who decides to give Harold an X if (as seems likely) he should fail to win one in the lottery. Things go as one would expect; Harold holds a losing ticket. Rockaford keeps his word and gives Harold an X. S, familiar with the preceding circumstances but unaware of whether Harold won or lost in the lottery, finds Harold with his newly acquired X. S infers that Harold received his X from Rockaford. He concludes this because he knows that the only other way Harold might have acquired an X is by winning the lottery and the odds against that happening are enormous. The following conditions are satisfied: (a) Harold received his X from Rockaford; (b) S believes that Harold received his X from Rockaford; (c) S is warranted in believing this since the chances of his having received it in any other way are negligible; (d) Rockaford's generous gift of an X to Harold is the (causal?) explanation of Harold's present possession of an X; and, finally (e) S correctly reconstructs (to use Goldman's language) the causal chain of events that brought about Harold's possession of an X. Yet, why does it seem clear (at least to myself – and apparently to Harman) that S does *not* know that Rockaford gave Harold his X. Because

(2e) Harold would not have an X unless Rockaford gave him one

is plainly false.[7] If Rockaford had not given him an X, it would have been because Harold already possessed one as a winner in the lottery. Hence, Harold would possess an X even if Rockaford had not given him one. It is not true that R would not be the case *unless* P; hence, not true that S knows that P on the basis of R.[8]

(2), therefore, expresses something stronger than a causal relationship be-

---

7 There is a way of reading (2e) that makes it sound true – viz., if we illicitly smuggle in the fact that Harold *has lost* the lottery. That is, (2e') "Harold, having lost the lottery, would not have an X unless Rockaford had given him one" is true. But this version of (2) makes R, the reason S has for believing Rockaford gave him an X, not only Harold's possession of an X but also *his having lost the lottery*. This, by hypothesis, is not part of S's reason; hence, not properly included in (2e). (2e) must be read in something like the following fashion: Harold would not have an X, whatever the outcome of the lottery, unless Rockaford had given him one. With this reading it is clearly false.

8 It is difficult to say whether this is a counterexample to Goldman's analysis. I think it satisfies all the conditions he catalogs as sufficient for knowledge, but this depends on how strictly Goldman intends the condition that S must be warranted in inferring that P is the case from R.

tween R and P. It should be pointed out, however, that it expresses something that is, in certain important respects, weaker than a universal association between states or conditions similar to R and states or conditions similar to P. When "R" and "P" are expressions that stand for particular conditions or states of affairs, as will often be the case when we know one thing on the basis of something else, (2) expresses a connection between more *determinate* states of affairs than those described by talking about states similar to R and P. If someone remarks, midway through a poker hand, that if his neighbor had not folded (dropped from the game) he (the speaker) would have been dealt a royal flush, he is obviously not maintaining that *whenever* his neighbor remains in the game, he (the speaker) is rewarded with a royal flush. Rather, he is talking about *this* hand (already holding four cards to the royal flush), *this particular* distribution of cards in the remainder of the deck, *this particular* seating arrangement, and so on. He is not saying that his neighbor's remaining in the game is, quite generally, sufficient for his receipt of a royal flush. Rather, he is saying that *in the particular circumstances which in fact prevailed on this occasion*, circumstances that include such things as card distribution, arrangement of players, and so on, an occurrence of the first sort (neighbor remains in game) will invariably be followed by one of the second sort (his receipt of a royal flush). One cannot falsify his claim by showing that he would not have received a royal flush, despite his neighbor's remaining in the game, if the card distribution in the deck had been different from what it in fact was. For his claim was a claim about the inevitable sequence of events *with that distribution of cards.*

Statements such as (2), then, even when R and P are expressions for particular states of affairs, express a general uniformity, but this general uniformity is not that whenever a state similar to R is the case, then a state similar to P will also be (or have been) the case. The uniformity in question concerns the relationship between states similar to R and P *under a fixed set of circumstances.* Whenever (a state such as) R *in circumstances C* then (a state such as) P where the circumstances C are defined in terms of those circumstances that actually prevail on the occasion of R and P. But does C include *all* the circumstances that prevail on the occasion in question or only *some* of these? Clearly not all the circumstances since this would trivialize every subjunctive conditional of this sort. Even if we restrict C to only those circumstances logically independent of R and P we still obtain a trivialization. For, to use Goldman's mountain example (as embellished), C would still include the fact that N did not erupt (since this is logically independent of both R and P), and this is obviously one of the circumstances *not* held fixed when we say that the lava would not be here unless M erupted. For in asserting his subjunctive we mean to be asserting something that would be *false* in the situation described (N would have erupted if M had not), whereas if we hold this circumstance (N did not erupt) fixed, the uniformity between the presence of lava and M's eruption would *hold*.

I think that our examples, not to mention an extensive literature on the subject,[9] point the way to a proper interpretation of C. The circumstances that are assumed constant, that are tacitly held fixed, in conditionals such as (2), are those circumstances prevailing on the occasion in question (the occasion on and between which the particular states R and P obtain) that are logically and causally independent of the state of affairs expressed by P.[10] When we have a statement in the subjunctive that (unlike (2)) is counterfactual (the antecedent gives expression to a state of affairs that does or did not obtain), then C includes those circumstances prevailing on the occasion that are logically and causally independent of the state of affairs (or lack of such state) expressed by the *antecedent* of the conditional. In our poker game, for example, we can say that S's statement (I would have got a royal flush if my neighbor had stayed in the game) *fixes* that set of circumstances that are logically and causally independent of his neighbor's staying in the game (i.e., the antecedent since the statement is counterfactual). Hence, if there is another player in the game (whose presence or absence affects the cards dealt to S) who would have dropped out if S's neighbor had not dropped

---

9 I am not proposing a solution to the problem to which Nelson Goodman (*Fact, Fiction and Forecast*, Chapter I), Roderick Chisholm ("The Contrary-to-Fact Conditional," *Mind*, 55, 1946), and others addressed themselves in trying to specify the "relevant conditions" associated with counterfactuals. I shall use the notion of "causality" in my treatment, a device that both Goodman and Chisholm would regard as question-begging. I am not, however, attempting to offer an extensionalist analysis of the subjunctive conditional; I am merely trying to get clear in what way such conditionals are stronger than the statement of a causal relationship between R and P and yet (in one sense) weaker than a statement of the universal association between states similar to R and P.

10 This characterization of the circumstances "C" has interesting and, I believe, significant repercussions for subjunctives having the form of (2) in which R expresses some present (or past) state of affairs and P expresses some future state of affairs. Although I lack the space to discuss the point here, I believe an important asymmetry is generated by a shift in the relative temporal locations of R and P. I also believe, however, that this asymmetry is faithfully reflected in the difference between knowing what *will* happen on the basis of present data and knowing what *did* happen on the basis of present data. In other words, I feel that an asymmetry in (2), arising from a shift in the relative temporal locations of R and P, helps one to understand the difference we all feel between knowing, on the one hand, what did happen or is happening and, on the other hand, what will happen.

out, then this person's remaining in the game is *not* held fixed, not included in C, because it is causally connected to the state of affairs expressed by the antecedent in S's statement. Therefore, we can show S's statement to be false if we can show that such a circumstance prevailed, and it is along these lines that one would surely argue in attempting to show S that he was wrong, wrong in saying that he would have received a royal flush if his neighbor had stayed in the game.

On the other hand, one cannot show that S's statement is false by showing that, were the cards differently arranged in the remainder of the deck, he would not have received his royal flush; for the arrangement of cards in the remainder of the deck (unlike the presence or absence of our other player) is (presumably) independent of S's neighbor's departure from the game. Hence, it is one of the conditions held fixed, included in C, by S's statement, and we are not allowed to consider alterations in it in assessing the general implication of S's statement.

Or consider our original thermometer example. Recall, the statement in question was: "The thermometer would not have read 98.6° unless the child's temperature was normal." Suppose someone responds, "Oh, it would have (or might have) if the thermometer was broken." It is important to understand that one can grant the truth of this response without abandoning the original assertion; for the original assertion had, as its general implication, *not* a statement expressing a uniform relationship between states of affairs similar to the child's temperature (normal body temperature) and states of affairs similar to the thermometer reading (a reading of 98.6), but, rather, a uniformity between such states *under a fixed set of circumstances.* And, if I am right, this fixed set of circumstances includes *the actual state of the thermometer* (defective or accurate); it is one of those circumstances prevailing on the occasion in question that is causally and logically independent of the child's temperature. Hence, this circumstance cannot be allowed to vary as it is in the preceding response by the words "if the thermometer was broken." To determine the truth of the original assertion, we must suppose that the thermometer is accurate (or defective) *whatever the actual condition is.* If, therefore, the thermometer was not broken or otherwise defective on that occasion, then the suggestion that it would (or might) have read the same despite a feverish child if it were broken or defective is, although quite true, irrelevant to the truth of the statement: "It would not have read 98.6 unless the child's temperature was normal."

One final important feature of (2). I have said that, generally speaking, the placeholders "R" and "P" represent expressions designating *specific* states of affairs or conditions. When this is so, (2) still has a general implication, but the general implication, expressing a uniform relationship between states of affairs similar to R and P, *has its scope restricted* to situations in which the circumstances C (as specified earlier) obtain. Since we are talking about specific states of affairs in most instantiations of (2), it becomes extremely important to observe the sorts of referring expressions embodied within both "R" and "P." For example, when I say, "John would not have said it was raining unless it was raining," I am talking about *John* and about a *particular utterance* of his. *Someone else* might have said this without its being true; John may have said *something else* without its being true. Nonetheless, *John* would not have said *it was raining* unless it was. An incurable liar about most things, John has a pathological devotion to accuracy on matters concerning the weather. In such a case, although John is, admittedly, a most unreliable informant on most matters, we can say that he would not have said it was raining unless it was so. This is only to say that the referring expressions to be found in "R" and "P" *help to define the scope* of the implied generalization. Recall, the implied generalization was about states of affairs *similar* to (the particular states) R and P. Similar in what respect? The sorts of referring expressions to be found within "R" and "P" help us to answer this question. In the case of John, the general implication involved not *a person's saying something* (under circumstances C), not *John's saying something* (under circumstances C), but John's saying something about the weather (under circumstances C).

2. THE POSSIBILITY OF MISTAKE: THE CONNECTION BETWEEN (2) AND (3).

Taking a cue from the fact that (2) expresses some form of necessary relationship between R and P, I have (in my opening remarks) expressed (2) as: Given R, $\sim \langle\rangle \sim$ P (or, alternatively, $\sim \langle\rangle$(R. $\sim$ P)). I think the full justification for expressing (2) in this fashion lies in the fact that (2) and (3) are contradictories, and since (3) may be rendered as

(3) Given R, $\langle\rangle \sim$ P (or, alternatively, $\langle\rangle$(R. $\sim$ P)

(2) may be represented as "Given R, $\sim \langle\rangle \sim$ P."

To see that this is so, it should be noticed that in denying the connection between R and P expressed by (2) we do not commit ourselves to anything as strong as

(4) R would be the case even though not-P were the case.

(4) is the *contrary* of (2), not its contradictory, since both (2) and (4) may turn out false.[11] For example, suppose S asserts,

(2g) I would have won the lottery if I had bought two tickets (instead of only one).

We may deny the truth of this contention without committing ourselves to the truth of

(4g) You would have lost even if you had bought two tickets.

All that is intended in denying (2g) is that the purchase of two tickets is connected with winning in the alleged manner, that the purchase of two tickets would have assured him of winning. Its failing to be connected in the manner alleged is, however, quite consistent with *his winning* with two tickets. What we commit ourselves to in denying (2g) is

(3g) You *might* have lost even with two tickets.

(3g) asserts what (2g) denies; viz. that even with two tickets it is *still* a matter of chance; the possibility of losing is *not* eliminated by holding two tickets instead of one.

As a matter of common practice, of course, we often employ something similar to (4) in denying (2). This is understandable enough since the truth of (4) does entail the falsity of (2). The point I am driving at, however, is that we need not affirm anything as strong as (4) in denying (2); all we are required to affirm is that R and not-P *might* both be the case or that, even though R is given, P *might not* be the case. That is to say, the proper expression for the negation of (2) is (3); and if we understand (3) as affirming "Given R, $\langle\rangle \sim$ P" (alternatively $\langle\rangle$(R. $\sim$ P)), then we are justified in representing (2) as "Given R, $\sim \langle\rangle \sim$ P" (alternatively, $\sim \langle\rangle$(R. $\sim$ P)). If someone says, "James would not have come without an invitation," we can deny this without supposing that James would have come without an invitation. For suppose we know that if James had not received an invitation, he would have flipped a coin to decide whether to go or not. In such a case, it is not true that he would not have come without an invitation, but neither is it true

---

11 A point that Goodman acknowledges in a footnote: "Literally a semifactual and the corresponding counterfactual are not contradictories but contraries, and both may be false." *Fact, Fiction and Forecast*, p. 32, note 2.

that he would have come without an invitation. The fact is that *he might have come* (depending on the outcome of the toss) without an invitation.

Before proceeding there is an important ambiguity that must be eliminated. There is a use of the word "might" (and related modal terms) that gives expression to the speaker's epistemic state in relation to some situation. It is a use of the word "might" that is naturally followed by a parenthetical "for all I know." For example, in saying, "He might win the election," the speaker is most naturally understood as expressing the fact that he does not know whether he will win the election or not, that he has no (or there are no) very convincing grounds for supposing he will lose. This use of the word can properly be deployed even when the state of affairs in question is *physically* or *logically* impossible. S, for instance, may concede the premises of our valid argument but, nonetheless, ignorant of its validity, insist that the conclusion might (for all he knows) be false even though the premises are true.

Contrasted with this epistemic use of the modal terms is what we might call an *objective* sense of these terms, a sense of the term "could" (for example) in which if R entails P then, independent of what S knows about the logical relationship between R and P, it is false to say that R and not-P could (or might) both be the case. Moreover, if we accept the results of modern physics, then in this objective sense of the term S's statement that there are objects that *can* travel faster than the speed of light is false, and it is false even though, *for all he knows*, there are objects that can. In this objective sense one is making a remark about the various possibilities for the occurrence, or joint occurrence, of events or the coexistence of states of affairs, and in this sense ignorance of what is the case is no guarantee that one's statements about what *might* or *could* be the case are true. The possibilities must actually be as one alleges. When S (knowing that James had an invitation to come) asserts that James, being the sort of fellow he is, might (even) have come without an invitation, he is making a remark *about James* and what James is inclined to do or capable of doing. He is obviously not registering some fact about his ignorance of whether or not James possesses an invitation.

The modal term appearing in (3) is meant to be understood in the objective sense. (3) is meant to be a statement about the possibilities for the joint realization of two states of affairs (R and not-P) independent of what the speaker happens to know about the actual realization of P (R being given). Drawing from our discussion in the preceding section, we can say that if (2) is true, if R would not be the case unless P were the case, then *in these circumstances* (specified earlier) P is a state of affairs

15

that is necessary to the realization of R. Hence, in these circumstances it is false to say that R and not-P might both be the case or that, given R, not-P might be the case, and it is false whether or not anyone appreciates the fact that it is false.

We have here a more or less *particularized* impossibility; (3), as well as (2), is tied to the circumstances, C, specified earlier. Nothing else but (a state such as) P could have brought about (a state such as) R *in these circumstances*. Often, of course, our statements about what could be the case, about what is possible, are broader in scope. They do not restrict themselves to the particular set of circumstances prevailing on some specific occasion. They are statements to the effect that, whatever the circumstances on this occasion happened to be, there are (nonetheless) circumstances in which a state relevantly similar to R is, or might easily be, brought about without a state relevantly similar to P. S may admit, for example, that the thermometer would not have read 98.6 unless the child's temperature was normal – hence, concede that it would be false to say that in these circumstances (given the thermometer reading) the child might (nonetheless) have a fever. Yet, he may go on to insist that one *can* get a normal reading on a thermometer with a feverish child. One can do so when one has a defective thermometer, when the child is sucking an ice cube, and so on. That is, one *can* have R without P in *other* circumstances. These "general" possibilities are, however, quite consistent with the "particularized" impossibilities expressed by (3). Most genuine impossibilities can be made possible by enlarging the frame of reference, by relaxing the conditions tacitly taken as fixed in the original statement of impossibility. I can't swim the English Channel; this despite the fact that I could *if* I had trained since a boy, been endowed with the requisite endurance, and so on.

If I may summarize the argument up to this point in preparation for the following section: (1) entails (2), if S knows that P, and he knows this on the basis (simply) of R, then R would not be the case unless P were the case. Furthermore, (2) gives expression to a connection between R and P that permits us to say that when R is given, in the kinds of circumstances that actually prevailed on the occasion in question, the possibility of not-P is eliminated. The sense of the word "possible" that is operative here is, I submit, the *same* sense of this word that is operating in our strongest statements about what is physically possible; the difference between the possibility expressed in (3) and other, apparently stronger, statements of what is possible and impossible is simply a shift in the set of circumstances that is taken as fixed. The impossibility expressed by (3) is an impossibility relative to those circumstances, C, held fixed in (2), and it is this fact that makes (3) the contradictory of (2) and, hence, that makes its negation a logical consequence of (1).

3. CONCLUSIVE REASONS

Let us call R a conclusive reason for P if and only if R would not be the case unless P were the case.[12] This makes logically conclusive reasons (LCR) a subclass of conclusive reasons. Conclusive reasons depend, simply, on the truth of (2); LCR require that the truth of (2) be demonstrable on purely logical and definitional grounds. When the conditional is true, but not logically true, we can speak of the conclusive reasons as being *empirically conclusive* (ECR).

Of course, R may *be* a conclusive reason for believing P without anyone believing P, much less having R as his reason for believing. I shall say, therefore, that S *has conclusive reasons*, R, for believing P if and only if:

(A) R is a conclusive reason for P (i.e., (2) is true),
(B) S believes, without doubt, reservation, or question, that P is the case and he believes this on the basis of R,
(C) (i) S knows that R is the case or
    (ii) R is some experiential state of S (about which it may not make sense to suppose that S *knows* that R is the case; at least it no longer makes much sense to ask *how* he knows).

With only minor embellishments, to be mentioned in a moment, I believe that S's having conclusive reasons for believing P is *both* a necessary and a sufficient condition for his knowing that P is the case. The appearance of the word "know" in this characterization (in (Ci)) does not render it circular as a characterization of knowledge since it can be eliminated by a recursive application of the three conditions until (Cii) is reached.

If S has conclusive reasons for believing P, then it is *false* to say that, given these grounds for belief, and the circumstances in which these grounds served as the basis for his belief, *S might be mistaken about P.* Having conclusive reasons, as I have just defined it, not only implies that P is the case, it not only implies that S believes that P is the case,

---

12 Recall footnote 5 concerning the particular wording of (2); I intend those remarks to apply to this definition of "conclusive reasons."

but it also implies that, in the circumstances in which he came to believe that P, his basis for believing that P was sufficiently secure to eliminate the possibility of his being mistaken about P. This goes a long way toward capturing everything that philosophers have traditionally required of knowledge. Indeed, in certain respects it goes beyond it in requiring a stronger connecton between one's reasons or grounds and what one believes (on the basis of these reasons or grounds) than has normally been demanded by those wishing to preserve our ordinary knowledge claims from skeptical criticism.[13] Since, however, I have already argued for the necessity of (A), for R's being a conclusive reason for P, I shall concentrate on the question of whether or not S's having a conclusive reason for believing P is sufficient for his knowing that P.

Several preliminary points must be mentioned briefly. It may be thought that in arguing for the impossibility of mistake as a necessary condition for knowing that P, I have been wasting my time. It may be thought that if S knows that P, then P *cannot* be false since S's knowing that P entails P; hence, S *cannot* be mistaken in believing that P. In answer to this objection it should be pointed out that the impossibility of mistake that I have been talking about is an impossibility that arises in virtue of a *special connection* between S's reasons, R, and what he consequently believes, P. It is not the trivial impossibility of being wrong about something that (by hypothesis) you know. When philosophers

---

13 It is this stronger connection that blocks the sort of counterexample that can be generated to justified-true-belief analyses of knowledge. Gettier's (and Lehrer's) examples, for instance, are directed at those analyses that construe knowledge in terms of a *degree* of justification that is compatible with being justified in believing something false (both Gettier and Lehrer mention this feature at the beginning of their discussion). The counterexamples are then constructed by allowing S to believe that P (which is false) *with the appropriate degree of justification*, letting P entail Q (which is true), and letting S believe that Q on the basis of its logical relationship to P. We have, then, a case where S truly believes that Q *with the appropriate degree of justification* (this degree of justification is allegedly preserved through the entailment between P and Q), but a case where S does *not know* that Q (since his means of arriving as it were so clearly defective). On the present analysis, of course, the required connection between S's evidence and P is strong enough to *preclude* P's being false. One cannot have *conclusive* reasons for believing something that is false. Hence, this sort of counter-example cannot be generated. Part of the motivation for the present analysis is the conviction (supported by Gettier-like examples) that knowledge, if it embodies an evidential relation at all, must embody a strong enough one to eliminate the *possibility* of mistake. See Edmund Gettier's "Is Justified True Belief Knowledge?" *Analysis*, 23.6, June 1963, and Keith Lehrer, "Knowledge, Truth and Evidence," *Analysis*, 25.5, April 1965. I should also mention here that these same sorts of considerations seemed to move Brian Skyrms toward a similar analysis; see especially pp. 385–386 in his "The Explication of 'X knows That P'," *The Journal of Philosophy*, June 22, 1967.

concern themselves with the possibility of mistake in putative cases of knowledge, they are not concerned with the possibility of mistake that is trivially avoidable by saying that *if* you do know that P, then you cannot be mistaken about P. They are concerned, rather, with that possibility as it exists in relation to one's evidence or grounds for believing P, and *that* is the possibility with which (2) is concerned.

The point may be put in another way. Both

I. R would not be the case unless P were the case
R is the case

and

II. R ⊃ P (when it is *not* true that R would not be the case unless P)
R

constitute conclusive grounds, logically conclusive grounds, for believing P. Neither set of premises would be true unless P were true, and this fact is in both cases demonstrable on purely logical and definitional grounds. But the significant difference between I and II is that in I, but *not* in II, the second premise *alone* turns out to be a *conclusive* reason (ECR). If we were searching for conclusive reasons to believe P, then in the second case we would require as our reasons *both premises*, and this would require that we knew that both premises were true (see clause (C) in having conclusive reasons). In case I, however, the second premise alone is a conclusive reason and, hence, to have conclusive reasons it is required *only that we know that R is the case*. We need not (as in case II) know that the first premise is true. All that is required in case I for R alone to be a conclusive reason is that the first premise be true; there is nothing that requires S to know that the first premise is true in order to have R as his conclusive reason for believing P. For if the first premise is true (regardless of whether S knows it is true or not), then (3) is false; hence, the possibility of S's being mistaken about P has been successfully avoided – and it has been successfully avoided *whether or not S knows it has been avoided*.

In speaking of conclusive reasons I do not wish to suggest that in having R as a conclusive reason S must be in a position to *give R* as his reason. R may simply be a certain experience that S has undergone and, having undergone this experience, come to the belief that P was the case on the basis of (as a result of) this experience. He may find it difficult, or impossible, to give verbal expression to R. He may have forgotten R. Or R may consist in something's looking a particular way

19

to him that he finds difficult to describe. Still, if the way the thing looks to S is such that it would not look that way unless it had the property Q, then its looking that way to S is a conclusive reason for S's believing that it has the property Q; and if S believes that it is Q *on this basis*, then he has, in the way the thing looks to him, a conclusive reason for believing it Q.

Also, there are a number of things that people commonly profess to know (Sacramento is the capital of California, the earth is roughly spherical) for which there is no definite piece of evidence, no single state of affairs or easily specifiable set of such states, that even approximates a conclusive reason. In such cases, although we can cite no single piece of data that is clinching and, hence, are at a loss for conclusive reasons when asked to give reasons (or when asked "How do you know?") we, nonetheless, often enough have conclusive reasons in a vast spectrum of experiences that are too diverse to admit of convenient citation. Countless experiences converge, so to speak, on the truth of a given proposition, and this variety of experience may be such that although one *may* have had any *one* of these experiences without the proposition in question being true, one *would not* have had *all* of them unless what one consequently believes was true. The fallibility of source A and the fallibility of source B does not automatically entail that when A and B *agree* about P's being the case, that, nonetheless, P might still be false. For it may be that A and B *would not* both have indicated that P was the case unless P was the case, although neither A nor B, taken by themselves, provide conclusive reasons for P. For example, although any single newspaper account may be in error on a particular point, several independent versions (wire services, of course, tend to eliminate this independence) may be enough to say that we know that something is so *on the basis of the newspaper accounts*. All of them would not have been in such close agreement unless their account was substantially correct.[14]

Finally, I do not wish to suggest by my use of the word "reason" that

---

14 The fact that all newspapers sometimes print things that are false does not mean that we cannot know that something is true on the basis of a single newspaper account. The relevant question to ask (as in the case of a person's testimony – see Section 1) is not whether *newspapers* sometimes print false stories, not even whether *this newspaper* sometimes prints false stories, but whether *this newspaper* would have printed *this story* if it were not true. The *Midville Weekly Gazette's* story about dope addiction on the campus may not correspond with the facts, but would *The Times* have printed this story about the president's visit to Moscow if it were not true?

when S has conclusive reasons for believing P, S has *reasoned* his way to the conclusion that P is the case from premises involving R or that S has consciously used R as a reason in arriving at the belief that P. I am inclined to think (but I shall not now argue it) that when one knows that P, on whatever basis this might be, little or no reasoning is involved. I would prefer to describe it as follows: sometimes a person's conviction that P is the case can be traced to a state of affairs (or cluster of situations) that satisfies the three conditions defining the possession of conclusive reasons. When it can be so traced, then he knows; when it cannot be so traced, then we say he does not know, although he may be right about P's being the case. Of course, his belief may be *traceable* to such a source without our being able to trace it. In such a case we are mistaken in saying that he does not know.

Turning now to the question of whether having conclusive reasons to believe, as defined by (A)–(C), constitutes a sufficient condition for knowledge, I shall mention and briefly respond to what I consider to be the most serious objections to this proposal.

There is, first, a tendency to conflate knowing that P with knowing that one knows that P. If this is done then conditions (A)–(C) will immediately appear insufficient since they do not describe S as knowing or having any basis for believing that R, his basis for believing P, constitutes an adequate basis, much less a conclusive basis, for believing P. Even if one does not go this far, there is still a tendency to say that if S knows that P, then S must at least *believe* that he knows that P is the case. If one adopts this view then, once again, conditions (A)–(C) appear inadequate since they do not describe (nor do they entail) that S believes he knows that P is the case. I see no reason, however, to accept either of these claims. We naturally expect of one who knows that P that he believe that he knows, just as we expect of someone who is riding a bicycle that he believe he is riding one, but in neither case is the belief a *necessary* accompaniment. The confusion is partially fostered, I believe, by a failure to distinguish between what is implied in knowing that P and what is implied (in some sense) by someone's *saying* he knows that P. Consider, however, cases in which we freely ascribe knowledge to agents in which it seems quite implausible to assign the level of conceptual sophistication requisite to their believing something about knowledge, believing something about their epistemic relation to the state of affairs in question. A dog may know that his master is in the room, and I (at least) want to say that he can know this in a straightforward sense without (necessarily) possessing the conceptual understanding that seems to be required to say of him that he believes he knows this, believes that he has good reasons, or believes *anything* about his epistemic relation to the fact that his master is in the room.[15] Yet, it seems perfectly natural to say of a dog that he knows (sometimes) when his master is in the room. And this is not, let me add, simply a matter of the dog's being right about something. For if we knew that the dog thought his master was in the room on the basis, say, of certain sounds and smells (sounds and smells that were, generally speaking, a reliable sign of his master) when these sounds and smells were totally unrelated to his master's presence in the room *on this occasion*, we would not say the dog knew even if he happened to be right about his master's being in the room. Imagine a blind dog's being "taken in" by a thief in his master's clothing while the master lies unconscious in the corner. The dog, taken in as he is by the thief, certainly thinks his master is in the room, and he is right (although, of course, he is wrong about this man's being his master). But just as clearly, the dog does not know that his master is in the room. We require conclusive reasons even in the case of animals. Would the dog have smelled what he did, and heard what he did, if his master was not in the room? If he *would have*, or *might have*, then he doesn't know.[16]

15 This seems to be the essence of Arthur Danto's argument (against Hintikka) that "S knows that P" does not entail "S knows that S knows that P" in "On Knowing that We Know," *Epistemology: New Essays in the Theory of Knowledge*, Avrum Stroll (ed.), 1967, pp. 49–51.
16 Robert Sleigh has suggested an interesting modification of this case – one that would appear to cause difficulty. Suppose that the dog *is* taken in by the thief but, in addition, circumstances are such that the thief *would not* be in the room *unless* the dog's master was also there. It may be a bit difficult to imagine circumstances of this sort, but other examples (not involving animals as the knowers) can easily be manufactured (Chisholm's example of a man mistaking a sheep dog for a sheep in a field works nicely when the further condition is added that the dog would not be there unless there were some sheep in the field). With such a modification it would seem that the dog has conclusive reasons for believing his master present since it would not have heard and smelled what it did unless his master was present. But does the dog know that his master is present? I think it natural to read this situation in such a way that the dog believes that his master is in the room *because* he mistakenly believes that this man (the thief) is his master. If read in this way, of course, there is no difficulty since the dog's basis for believing that his master is present is obviously defective – it is not true, nor does the dog know, that this man is his master. If, however, we read this case in such a way that the dog simply takes the sounds and smells as a sign of his master's presence (without misidentifying anyone), then the dog *does* have conclusive reasons (he would not have smelled and heard what he did unless his master was present), but I should want to say that in this case *he knows* that his master is present. I do not think that this is an excessively strained interpretation. It seems to me quite similar to situations in which we know that something is so on the basis of some indicator or sign (e.g., an instrument reading) but are ignorant as to the mechanism *in*

Furthermore, consider a skeptic who talked himself into believing that his grounds for believing in an external world were not sufficiently good to truly say he *knew* there was an external world and, hence, no longer believed, positively disbelieved, that he knew there was an external world. I think that as long as he continued to believe (without doubt, reservation, or question) that there was an external world, and continued to believe it on the same basis as we do, he would know there was an external world (assuming here that *we* know it) *whatever* he happened to believe about what he knew.[17]

The remarks I have just made about believing that one knows apply, a fortiori, to knowing that one knows. One qualifies for knowledge when one has conclusive reasons for believing; one need not, in addition, know that one has conclusive grounds. To know that one has conclusive reasons, empirically conclusive reasons, means that one knows that (A) is true and this, in turn, means that one has logically conclusive reasons (see case I earlier). Knowing that one knows is a form of inoculation against skeptical challenges to the quality of one's empirically conclusive reasons; one *knows* that R would not be the case unless P were the case. Lacking such inoculation, however, one still knows. One is simply less prepared to defend (justify) the *claim* to knowledge; but inability to justify the truth of what one claims is seldom, if ever, a refutation of the truth of what one claims, and this applies to knowledge claims as well as to any other.

There is a certain type of counterexample that exploits this confusion, and I would like to mention it at this point to further clarify the intent of conditions (A)–(C). Suppose S, for a perfectly silly reason, or by sheer accident, comes to the true belief that (a state such as) R is a conclusive reason for believing that (a state such as) P is or was the case. Happening upon a state such as R in the appropriate circumstances, then, he believes that P is the case on the basis of R. Doesn't he now have *conclusive reasons* for believing P? But isn't it equally obvious that he does *not* know that P is the case? Yes and no. Yes, he does have conclusive reasons (as I have defined this). No, it is not obvious that he does not know that P

---

virtue of which that indicator or sign is a reliable (conclusive) index of what we purport to know.

17 Examples such as this, along with other, more systematic considerations, convince me that not only should we not require that S believe he has conclusive reasons in order to know, but also that we should not require that he not believe he does not have conclusive reasons. If a person's believing that he knows is compatible with his not knowing, why shouldn't a person's believing that he does not know be compatible with his knowing?

is the case. I believe that this objection trades on the very confusion we have just discussed; that is, it mistakenly supposes that if S does not know that R is conclusive for P (has no legitimate basis for believing this), then S does not know that P is the case (has no legitimate basis for believing this). Or, what I think amounts to the very same thing, it fallaciously concludes that S (given his basis for belief) might be wrong about P from the fact that S (given his basis for belief) might be wrong about R's being conclusive for P. Or, to put it in still another way, it incorrectly supposes that if it is, either wholly or in part, accidental that S is right about R's being conclusive for P, then it is also, either wholly or in part, accidental that he is right about P's being the case. Such inferences are fallacious and, I believe, they are fallacious in the same way as the following two examples: (a) Concluding that it was sheer luck (chance), a mere accident, that the declarer made his bid of seven spades because it was sheer luck (chance), a mere accident, that he was dealt thirteen spades; (b) Concluding that the window was broken accidentally because the man who threw the brick through it came by the belief that bricks break windows in an accidental (silly, unreasonable, or what have you) way.

Sometimes the stage is set for a nonaccident in a purely accidental way. In the preceding case it *is* accidental that S knows that P on the basis of R, but this does not make it accidental that he is right about P – for he believes P on the basis of R, and R simply would not be the case unless P were the case. Given R, it is not at all accidental that he is right about P. What *is* accidental is that he was correct in believing that R was a conclusive reason for P, but all this shows is that he does not know that R is conclusive for P, does not know that he knows that P. And with this much I am in full agreement.[18]

Skeptical arguments have traditionally relied on the fact that S in purporting to know that P on the basis of R, was conspicuously unable to justify the quality of his reasons, was hopelessly incapable of providing satisfactory documentation for the truth of (A). The conclusion fallaciously drawn from this was that S did not know that P was true (simply)

---

18 In speaking of "accidentality" in this connection I have in mind Peter Unger's analysis of knowledge in terms of its not being at all accidental that the person is right (see his "An Analysis of Factual Knowledge," *Journal of Philosophy*, March 21, 1968). That is, I want to claim that any S satisfying conditions (A)–(C) is a person of whom it is true to say that it is not at all accidental that he is right about P's being the case, although it may be accidental that this is no accident (it may be accidental that he *has* conclusive reasons, that he has reasons in virtue of which it is not at all accidental that he is right about P).

on the basis of R. Clearly, however, all that follows from the fact that S has little or no grounds for thinking (A) true is that he lacks satisfactory grounds for thinking he knows that P is true. It does not follow that he does not know that P is true. Knowing that P is the case on the basis of R involves knowing that R is the case (and believing P on that basis) *when (A) is true*. It is the truth of (A), not the fact that one knows it true, that makes R conclusive for P.

There is another respect in which traditional skeptical arguments have been on the mark. One way of expressing my argument is to say that the familiar and (to some) extremely annoying challenge, "Couldn't it be an illusion (fake, imitation, etc.)?" or "Isn't it possible that you are dreaming (hallucinating, etc.)?" is, in a certain important respect, quite proper and appropriate *even when there is no special reason to think you are dreaming, hallucinating, confronting a fake and so on*. For our knowledge claims do entail that the evidence or grounds one has for believing *would not* have been available if what one consequently believes (and claims to know) were false; hence, they do entail that, given one's evidence or grounds, *it is false that one might be mistaken* about what one purports to know. (1) does entail the falsity of (3); hence, (1) can be shown to be false not only by showing that S *is* dreaming or hallucinating or whatever, but also by showing that he might be, that his experience or information on which he bases his belief that P can be had in such circumstances as these without P being the case. It is not in the propriety or relevance of these challenges that skepticism has gone awry. On the contrary, the persistent and continuing appeal of skepticism lies in a failure to come to grips with this challenge, in a refusal to acknowledge its legitimacy and, hence, *answer it*. It simply will not do to insist that in concerning himself with the possibility of mistake a skeptic is setting artificially high standards for knowledge and, therefore, may be ignored when considering ordinary knowledge claims. (1) does imply that (3) is false, and it seems to me quite a legitimate line of argument for the skeptic to insist that if (3) is true, if you might be dreaming or whatever, then (1) is false – you do not know, on the basis of your present visual, auditory, and other experiences, what you purport to know.

I think there are several confusions to be found in traditional skepticism, but one of them is not that of insisting that to know that P on the basis of R, R must *somehow* preclude the possibility of not-P. The confusions lie elsewhere. If one interprets the "might" (or "could") of (3) too narrowly (as simply "logically possible") then, of course, (3) will, in almost all interesting cases, turn out true and (therefore) (1) false.

Even if one liberalizes the interpretation of (3), and thinks of it as representing some form of physical impossibility, as I have, there is still the tendency to think of this physical impossibility in its most general sense, as the impossibility of violating some natural law that holds *in all circumstances* and not, as I have argued, the impossibility of having R with not-P in the particular circumstances that in fact prevail on the occasion in question. The most subtle confusion, however, is the one mentioned in the preceding paragraphs – the fallacy of supposing that in knowing that P we must somehow be able to justify the fact that we know that P. Doubtless we should have some justification for (1) if we assert it, but our lack of such a justification reflects *not on the truth* of what we have said, but *on the propriety of our saying it*. What would show that we did not know that P on the basis of R is the truth of (3), not our incapacity to show it false (by showing (2) true for instance). For if (2) is true, then, in answer to the skeptic's question, "Couldn't you be hallucinating?" or "Might it not be a fake or imitation of some sort?" the correct response, whether or not we *know* it to be correct, whether or not we can *show* it to be correct, is "No!"

Still, even if one should accept the arguments up to this point, there are genuine difficulties with taking as a sufficient condition for knowledge the possession of conclusive reasons to believe. I shall not try to absorb these difficulties in this essay; I have tried to do so with respect to a more restricted set of cases (visual perception) in another place.[19] Whether these complications can be handled in the much more general type of situation I have been discussing I leave open – only suggesting the lines along which I think they can be satisfactorily handled. The two examples I present do not affect my argument that the possession of conclusive reasons is a *necessary* condition for knowledge.

S, upon inspecting an immersed chemical indicator, declares that the solution in which it is immersed is a base. He believes (correctly) that the indicator is the sort that turns from yellow to blue only when immersed in a base. The indicator is Thymol Blue and would not have turned from yellow to blue (in these conditions) unless the solution were a base. The following three conditions are satisfied:

(A') The indicator's change in color (yellow to blue) is a conclusive reason for believing that the solution is a base.

---

19 *Seeing and Knowing* (Chicago, 1969), Chapter III.

(B') S believes that the solution is a base, and he believes this on the basis of the indicator's change in color.

(C') S knows that the indicator changed from yellow to blue (he saw it change – saw *that* it changed).

I have said that these three conditions were sufficient for knowledge. Does S know that the solution is a base? Before answering this question the reader should be informed that there is another chemical indicator, Bromophenal Blue, that also turns from yellow to blue but *only when* immersed in an *acid*. S, however, is quite unaware of the existence of other such indicators. He merely assumes that *a* yellow indicator turning blue is a positive test for a base. S's ignorance on this point does not alter the fact that the preceding three conditions are satisfied. Yet, despite the satisfaction of these conditions, I find it (in some cases) most implausible to say he knows that the solution is a base. Whether he knows or not depends in a crucial way on our understanding of condition (B'). The indicator's change in color, although it is a conclusive reason, has its conclusiveness, so to speak, restricted in scope to the range of cases in which Thymol Blue is the indicator (or, if this laboratory uses only Thymol Blue, in which the indicator is *from* this laboratory or of the sort used in this laboratory). What is a conclusive reason for believing the solution to be a base is that a *Thymol Blue* indicator (or an indicator from this laboratory) changed from yellow to blue when immersed in it, *not* simply that *an* (unspecified) chemical indicator changed from yellow to blue. The fact that *this* indicator *happens to be* Thymol Blue is what accounts for the truth of (A'). Since, however, it is a Thymol Blue indicator's (or some other appropriately specified indicator's) color transformation that is conclusive, we must (see condition (B')) require that S's basis for believing the solution to be a base be that *a Thymol Blue indicator* (or *such-and-such indicator*) changed from yellow to blue. He need not, once again, know that a Thymol Blue's color transformation (or such-and-such indicator's transformation) *is conclusive*, but he must be exploiting those things about the indicator's transformation *in virtue of which it is conclusive*. In some cases an A's being B is a conclusive reason for believing P only in virtue of the fact that it is, in particular, an A (or, say, something that is Q) that is B; in such cases we must understand condition (B) as requiring that S's basis for believing P include not only the fact that this (something or other) is B, but also that this something or other is, in particular, *an A* (or something that is Q). And this requires of us in addition that we understand

27

condition (C) that in such a way that S not only know that R is the case, know (let us say) that A is B, but also know that it is, in particular, an A that is B.[20]

One further example to illustrate a distinct, but closely related, difficulty. Suppose K is behaving in such a way that it is true to say that he would not be behaving in that way unless he was nervous. Suppose S purports to know that K is nervous and, when asked how he knows this, replies by saying, "From the way he is behaving." Once again, our three conditions are satisfied or can easily be assumed to be satisfied. Yet, if we suppose that the distinctive thing about K's behavior is that he is doing B_1 while performing B_2, then if S is relying on B_1 (or B_2) alone, we should not say that he knows that K is nervous. It is quite true that the basis for S's belief (that K is nervous) is K's behavior, and in this (relatively unspecified) sense we might say that S is relying on the significant aspects of the situation, but the fact is that the crucial aspects (those aspects that make K's behavior conclusive) are more specific than those on which S is relying in purporting to know. We must insist, therefore, that S's basis for believing P be as specific in regard to the relevant aspects of R as is necessary to capture the distinctive (i.e., conclusive, those figuring essentially in the satisfaction of (2)) features of the situation.

I think both of the preceding qualifications can be summarized by saying that when one has conclusive reasons, then this is sufficient for knowing that P is the case when those reasons are properly specific, both with regard to what it is that displays the particular features on which one relies and on the particular features themselves. A complete state-

---

20 This type of restriction is required for the sort of example discussed in my article "Reasons and Consequences," Analysis, April 1968. In this article I argued that one could know that the A is B (e.g., the widow was limping) while having little, if any, justification for believing that it was, in particular, a widow who was limping (hence, one could know that the widow was limping without knowing that it was a widow who was limping). Since, however, the statement "The widow is limping" implies "There is (or it is) a widow who is limping," I took this as showing that S can know that P, know that P entails Q, and yet not know that Q. On the present analysis of conclusive reasons, of course, P is a conclusive reason for Q (since P entails Q) and anyone who believed Q on the basis of P should (on this analysis) know that Q. The restriction being discussed in the text blocks this result by requiring S to know those things in particular about P that make it conclusive for Q. In this example S must know that it is a widow who is limping since it is this aspect of his conclusive reason (the widow is limping) in virtue of which it functions as a conclusive reason for believing that there is a widow who is limping. I am indebted to Bruce Freed for clarification on this point.

ment of these restrictions is, however, far beyond the scope of this essay. Suffice it to say that the possession of conclusive reasons for believing is a necessary condition for knowledge and, properly qualified along the lines suggested here, also (I think) sufficient.

2

Epistemic Operators

Suppose Q is a necessary consequence of P. Given only this much, it is, of course, quite trivial that if it is true that P, then it must also be true that Q. If it is a fact that P, then it must also be a fact that Q. If it is necessary that P, then it is necessary that Q; and if it is possible that P, then it must also be possible that Q.

I have just mentioned four prefixes: "it is true that," "it is a fact that," "it is necessary that," and "it is possible that." In this essay I shall refer to such affixes as *sentential operators* or simply *operators*; when affixed to a sentence or statement, they operate on it to generate another sentence or statement. The distinctive thing about the four operators I have just mentioned is that, if Q is a necessary consequence of P, then the statement we get by operating on Q with one of these four operators is a necessary consequence of the statement we get by operating on P with the same operator. This may be put more succinctly if we let "O" stand for the operator in question and "O(P)" for the statement we get by affixing the operator "O" to the statement "P." We can now say that the preceding four operators share the following property: if P entails Q, then O(P) entails O(Q). I shall call any operator having this property a *penetrating operator* (or, when emphasis is required, a *fully*

Reprinted from *The Journal of Philosophy* 67(24), 1007–1023 (1970), by permission of the publisher. Versions of this essay were read to the philosophy departments of several universities in the United States and Canada during the year 1969–1970. I profited greatly from these discussions. I wish especially to thank Paul Dietl, who helped me to see a number of points more clearly (perhaps still not clearly enough, in his opinion). Finally, my exchanges with Mr. Don Affeldt were extremely useful; I am much indebted to him in connection with some of the points made in the latter portions of the article.

penetrating operator). In operating on *P* these operators penetrate to every necessary consequence of *P*.

We are now in a position to ask ourselves a preliminary question. The answer to this question is easy enough, but it will set the stage for more difficult questions. Are all sentential operators fully penetrating operators? Are all operators such that if *P* entails *Q*, then O(*P*) entails O(*Q*)? If *all* operators are penetrating operators, then each of the following statements must be true (when *P* entails *Q*):

(1) You cannot have a reason to believe that *P* unless you have a reason to believe that *Q*.
(2) You cannot know that *P* unless you know that *Q*.
(3) You cannot explain why *P* is the case unless you can explain why *Q* is the case.
(4) If you assert that *P*, then you assert that *Q*.
(5) If you hope that *P*, then you hope that *Q*.
(6) If it is strange (or accidental) that *P*, then it must be strange (or accidental) that *Q*.
(7) If it was a mistake that *P*, then it was a mistake that *Q*.

This list begins with two epistemic operators, "reason to believe that" and "know that." Since I shall be concerned with these later in the essay, let me skip over them now and look at those appearing near the end of the list. They will suffice to answer our opening question, and their status is much less problematic than that of some of the other operators.

"She lost" entails "Someone lost." Yet, it may be strange that she lost, not at all strange that someone lost. "Bill and Susan married each other" entails that Susan got married; yet, it may be quite odd that (strange that, incredible that) Bill and Susan married each other but quite unremarkable, not at all odd that, Susan got married. It may have been a mistake that they married each other, not a mistake that Susan got married. Or finally, "I hit the bull's-eye" entails that I either hit the bull's-eye or the side of the barn; and although I admit that it was lucky that (accidental that) I hit the bull's-eye, I will deny that it was lucky, an accident, that I hit either the bull's-eye or the side of the barn.

Such examples show that not all operators are fully penetrating. Indeed, such operators as "it is strange that," "it is accidental that," and "it is a mistake that" fail to penetrate to some of the most elementary logical consequences of a proposition. Consider the entailment between

31

"*P. Q*" and "*Q*." Clearly, it may be strange that *P* and *Q*, not at all strange that *P*, and not at all strange that *Q*. A concatenation of factors, no one of which is strange or accidental, may itself be strange or accidental. Taken by itself, there is nothing odd or suspicious about Frank's holding a winning ticket in the first race. The same could be said about any of the other races: there is nothing odd or suspicious about Frank's holding a winning ticket in the *n*th race. Nonetheless, there is something very odd, very suspicious, in Frank's having a winning ticket in *n* races.

Therefore, not only are these operators *not* fully penetrating, they lie, as it were, on the other end of the spectrum. They fail to penetrate to some of the most elementary consequences of a proposition. I shall refer to this class of operators as *nonpenetrating* operators. I do not wish to suggest by this label that such operators are totally impotent in this respect (or that they are all uniform in their degree of penetration). I mean it, rather, in a rough, comparative, sense: their *degree of penetration* is less than that of any of the other operators I shall have occasion to discuss.

We have, then, two ends of the spectrum with examples from both ends. Anything that falls between these two extremes I shall call a *semipenetrating operator*. And with this definition I am, finally, in a position to express my main point, the point I wish to defend in the rest of this essay. It is, simply, that all epistemic operators are semipenetrating operators. There is both a trivial and a significant side to this claim. Let me first deal briefly with the trivial aspect.

The epistemic operators I mean to be speaking about when I say that all epistemic operators are semipenetrating include the following:

(a) *S* knows that . . .
(b) *S* sees (or can see) that . . .
(c) *S* has reason (or a reason) to believe that . . .
(d) There is evidence to suggest that . . .
(e) *S* can prove that . . .
(f) *S* learned (discovered, found out) that . . .
(g) In relation to our evidence it is probable that . . .

Part of what needs to be established in showing that these are all semipenetrating operators is that they all possess a degree of penetration greater than that of the nonpenetrating operators. This is the trivial side of my thesis. I say it is trivial because it seems to me fairly obvious that if someone knows that *P* and *Q*, has a reason to believe that *P* and *Q*, or can prove that *P* and *Q*, he thereby knows that *Q*, has a reason to believe that Q, or can prove (in the appropriate epistemic sense of this term) that Q. Similarly, if S knows that Bill and Susan married each other, he (must) know that Susan got married (married someone). If he knows that P is the case, he knows that P or Q is the case (where the "or" is understood in a sense that makes "P or Q" a necessary consequence of "P"). This is not a claim about what it would be appropriate to say, what the person himself thinks he knows or would say he knows. It is a question, simply, of what he knows. It may not be appropriate to *say* to Jim's wife that you know it was either her husband, Jim, or Harold who sent the neighbor lady an expensive gift *when you know it was Harold*. For, although you do know this, it is misleading to say you know it – especially to Jim's wife.

Let me accept, therefore, without further argument that the epistemic operators are not, unlike "lucky that," "strange that," "a mistake that," and "accidental that," nonpenetrating operators. I would like to turn, then, to the more significant side of my thesis. Before I do, however, I must make one point clear lest it convert my entire thesis into something as trivial as the first half of it. When we are dealing with the epistemic operators, it becomes crucial to specify whether the agent in question knows that P entails Q. That is to say, P may entail Q, and S may know that P, but he may not know that Q *because*, and perhaps *only* because, he fails to appreciate the fact that P entails Q. When Q is a simple logical consequence of P we do not expect this to happen, but when the propositions become very complex, or the relationship between them very complex, this might easily occur. Let P be a set of axioms, Q a theorem. S's knowing P does not entail S's knowing Q just because P entails Q; for, of course, S may not know that P entails Q, may not know that Q is a *theorem*. Hence, our epistemic operators will turn out *not* to be penetrating because, and perhaps *only* because, the agents in question are not fully cognizant of all the implications of what they know to be the case, can see to be the case, have a reason to believe is the case, and so on. Were we all ideally astute logicians, were we all fully apprised of all the necessary consequences (supposing this to be a well defined class) of every proposition, perhaps then the epistemic operators would turn into fully penetrating operators. That is, assuming that if P entails Q, we *know* that P entails Q, then every epistemic operator is a penetrating operator: the epistemic operators penetrate to all the *known* consequences of a proposition.

It is this latter, slightly modified, claim that I mean to reject. Therefore, I shall assume throughout the discussion that when Q is a necessary consequence of P, every relevant agent *knows that it is*. I shall be dealing with only the *known consequences* (in most cases because they are immediate and obvious consequences). What I wish to show is that, even under this special restriction, the epistemic operators are *only* semi-penetrating.

I think many philosophers would disagree with this contention. The conviction is that the epistemic worth of a proposition is hereditary under entailment, that whatever the epistemic worth of P, *at least* the same value must be accorded the known consequences of P. This conviction finds expression in a variety of ways. Epistemic logic: if S knows that P, and knows that P entails Q, then S knows that Q. Probability theory: if A is probable, and B is a logical consequence of A, then B is probable (relative to the same evidence, of course). Confirmation theory: if evidence e tends to confirm hypothesis h, then e indirectly confirms all the logical consequences of h. But perhaps the best evidence in favor of supposing that most philosophers have taken the epistemic operators to be fully penetrating is the way they have argued and the obvious assumptions that structure their arguments. Anyone who has argued in the following way seems to me to be assuming the thesis of penetrability (as I shall call it): if you do not know whether Q is true or not, and P cannot be true unless Q is true, then you (obviously) do not know whether P is true or not. A slightly more elaborate form of the same argument goes like this: if S does not know whether or not Q is true, then for all he knows it might be false. If Q is false, however, then P must also be false. Hence, for all S knows, P may be false. Therefore, S does not know that P is true. This pattern of argument is sprinkled throughout the epistemological literature. Almost all skeptical objections trade on it. S claims to know that this is a tomato. A necessary consequence of its being a tomato is that it is not a clever imitation that only looks and feels (and, if you will, tastes) like a tomato. But S does not know that it is *not* a clever imitation that only looks and feels (and tastes) like a tomato. (I assume here that no one is prepared to argue that anything that looks, feels, and tastes like a tomato to S *must be* a tomato.) Therefore, S does not know that this is a tomato. We can, of course, reply with G. E. Moore that we certainly *do* know it is a tomato (after such an examination) and since tomatoes are not imitations we know that this is not an imitation. It is interesting to note that this reply presupposes the same principle as does the skeptical objection: they both assume that if S knows that this is a P, and knows that every P is a Q, then S knows that this is a Q. The only difference is that the skeptic

34

performs a modus tollens, Moore a modus ponens. Neither questions the principle itself.

Whether it be a question of dreams or demons, illusions or fakes, the same pattern of argument emerges. If you know this is a chair, you must know that you are not dreaming (or being deceived by a cunning demon), since its being a (real) chair entails that it is not simply a figment of your own imagination. Such arguments assume that the epistemic operators, and in particular the operator "to know," penetrate to all the known consequences of a proposition. If these operators were not penetrating, many of these objections might be irrelevant. Consider the following exchange:

> S: How strange! There are tomatoes growing in my apple tree.
> K: That isn't strange at all. Tomatoes, after all, are physical objects and what is so strange about physical objects growing in your apple tree?

What makes K's reply so silly is that he is treating the operator "strange that" as a fully penetrating operator: it cannot be strange that there are tomatoes growing in the apple tree unless the consequences of this (e.g., there are objects growing in your apple tree) are also strange. Similarly, it *may not* be at all relevant to object to someone who claims to know that there are tomatoes in the apple tree that he does not know, cannot be absolutely sure, that there are really any material objects. Whether or not this is a relevant objection will depend on whether or not this particular consequence of there being tomatoes in the apple tree is one of the consequences to which the epistemic operators penetrate. What I wish to argue in the remainder of this essay is that the traditional skeptical arguments exploit precisely those consequences of a proposition to which the epistemic operators do not penetrate, precisely those consequences that distinguish the epistemic operators from the fully penetrating operators.

In support of this claim let me begin with some examples that are, I think, fairly intuitive and then turn to some more problematic cases. I shall begin with the operator "reason to believe that," although what I have to say could be said as well with any of them. This particular operator has the added advantage that if it can be shown to be only semipenetrating, then many accounts of knowledge, those that interpret it as a form of justified true belief, would also be committed to treating "knowing that" as a semipenetrating operator. For, presumably, "knowing that" would not penetrate any deeper than one's "reasons for believing that."

Suppose you have a reason to believe that the church is empty. *Must* you have a reason to believe that it is a church? I am not asking whether you generally have such a reason. I am asking whether one can have a reason to believe the church empty without having a reason to believe that it is a church that is empty. Certainly your reason for believing that the church is empty is not *itself* a reason to believe it is a church; or it *need not* be. Your reason for believing the church to be empty may be that you just made a thorough inspection of it without finding anyone. That is a good reason to believe the church empty. Just as clearly, however, it is not a reason, much less a good reason, to believe that what is empty is a church. The fact is, or so it seems to me, I do not have to have *any* reason to believe it is a church. Of course, I would never *say* the church was empty, or that I had a reason to believe that the church was empty, unless I believed, and presumably had a reason for so believing, that *it was* a church that was empty, but this is a presumed condition of my *saying* something, not of my having a reason to believe something. Suppose I had simply assumed (correctly as it turns out) that the building was a church. Would this show that I had no reason to believe that the church was empty?

Suppose I am describing to you the "adventures" of my brother Harold. Harold is visiting New York for the first time, and he decides to take a bus tour. He boards a crowded bus and immediately takes the last remaining seat. The little old lady he shouldered aside in reaching his seat stands over him glowering. Minutes pass. Finally, realizing that my brother is not going to move, she sighs and moves resignedly to the back of the bus. Not much of an adventure, but enough, I hope, to make my point. I said that the little old lady realized that my brother would not move. Does this imply that she realized that, or knew that, *it was my brother* who refused to move? Clearly not. We can say that S knows that X is Y without implying that S knows that *it is X* that is Y. We do not *have* to describe our little old lady as knowing that *the man* or *the person* would not move. We can say that she realized that, or knew that, *my brother* would not move (minus, of course, this pattern of emphasis), and we can say this because saying this does not entail that the little old lady knew that, or realized that, it was my brother who refused to move. She knew that my brother would not move, and she knew this despite the fact that she did not know something that was necessarily implied by what she did know – viz., that the person who refused to move was my brother.

I have argued elsewhere that to see that *A* is *B*, that the roses are wilted for example, is not to see, not even to be able to see, that they are roses that are wilted.[1] To see that the widow is limping is not to see that it is a widow who is limping. I am now arguing that this same feature holds for all epistemic operators. I can know that the roses are wilting without knowing that they are roses, know that the water is boiling without knowing that it is water, and prove that the square root of 2 is smaller than the square root of 3 and, yet, be unable to prove what is entailed by this – viz., that the number 2 *has* a square root.

The general point may be put this way: there are certain presuppositions associated with a statement. These presuppositions, although their truth is entailed by the truth of the statement, are not part of what is *operated on* when we operate on the statement with one of our epistemic operators. The epistemic operators do not *penetrate* to these presuppositions. For example, in saying that the coffee is boiling I assert that the coffee is boiling, but in asserting this I do not assert that *it is* coffee that is boiling. Rather, this is taken for granted, assumed, presupposed, or what have you. Hence, when I say that I have a reason to believe that the coffee is boiling, I am not saying that this reason applies to the fact that it is coffee that is boiling. This is *still* presupposed. I may have such a reason, of course, and chances are good that I do have such a reason or I would not have referred to what I believe to be boiling *as coffee*, but to have a reason to believe the coffee is boiling is not, thereby, to have a reason to believe it is coffee that is boiling.

One would expect that if this is true of the semipenetrating operators, then it should also be true of the nonpenetrating operators. They also should fail to reach the presuppositions. This is exactly what we find. It may be accidental that the two trucks collided, but not at all accidental that it was two trucks that collided. Trucks were the only vehicles allowed on the road that day, and so it was not at all accidental or a matter of chance that the accident took place between two trucks. Still, it was an accident that the two trucks collided. Or suppose Mrs. Murphy mistakenly gives her cat some dog food. It need not be a mistake that she gave the food to *her* cat, or *some* food to *a* cat. This was intentional. What was a mistake was that it was dog food that she gave to her cat.

Hence, the first class of consequences that differentiate the epistemic operators from the fully penetrating operators is the class of consequences associated with the presuppositions of a proposition. The fact

---

1 *Seeing and Knowing* (Chicago: University Press, 1969), pp. 93–112, and also "Reasons and Consequences," *Analysis* (April 1968).

that the epistemic operators do not penetrate to these presuppositions is what helps to make them semipenetrating. And this is an extremely important fact. For it would appear that if this is true, then to know that the flowers are wilted I do not have to know that they are flowers (that are wilted) and, therefore, do not have to know all those consequences that follow from the fact that they are flowers, real flowers, that I know to be wilted.

Rather than pursue this line, however, I would like to turn to what I consider to be a more significant set of consequences – "more significant" because they are the consequences that are directly involved in most skeptical arguments. Suppose we assert that x is A. Consider some predicate, "B," that is incompatible with A, such that nothing can be both A and B. It then follows from the fact that x is A that x is not B. Furthermore, if we conjoin B with any other predicate, Q, it follows from the fact that x is A that x is not-(B and Q). I shall call this type of consequence a *contrast consequence*, and I am interested in a particular subset of these; for I believe the most telling skeptical objections to our ordinary knowledge claims exploit a particular set of these contrast consequences. The exploitation proceeds as follows: someone purports to know that x is A, that the wall is red, say. The skeptic now finds a predicate "B" that is incompatible with "A." In this particular example we may let "B" stand for the predicate "is white." Since "x is red" entails "x is not white" it also entails that x is not-(white and Q) where "Q" is any predicate we care to select. Therefore, the skeptic selects a "Q" that gives expression to a condition or circumstance under which a white wall would appear exactly the same as a red wall. For simplicity we may let "Q" stand for "cleverly illuminated to look red." We now have this chain of implications: "x is red" entails "x is not white" entails "x is not white cleverly illuminated to look red." If "knowing that" is a penetrating operator, then if anyone knows that the wall is red he must know that it is not white cleverly illuminated to look red. (I assume here that the relevant parties know that if x is red, it cannot be white made to look red.) He must know that this particular contrast consequence is true. The question is: do we, generally speaking, know anything of the sort? Normally we never take the trouble to check the lighting. We seldom acquire any *special* reasons for believing the lighting normal, although we can talk vaguely about there being no reason to think it unusual. The fact is that we habitually take such matters for granted, and although we normally have *good* reasons for making such routine assumptions, I do not think these reasons are sufficiently good, not without special precautionary checks in the particular case, to say of the particular situation we are in that we *know* conditions are normal. To illustrate, let me give you another example – a silly one, but no more silly than a great number of skeptical arguments with which we are all familiar. You take your son to the zoo, see several zebras, and, when questioned by your son, tell him they are zebras. Do you know they are zebras? Well, most of us would have little hesitation in saying that we did know this. We know what zebras look like, and, besides, this is the city zoo and the animals are in a pen clearly marked "Zebras." Yet, something's being a zebra implies that it is not a mule and, in particular, not a mule cleverly disguised by the zoo authorities to look like a zebra. Do you know that these animals are not mules cleverly disguised by the zoo authorities to look like zebras? If you are tempted to say "Yes" to this question, think a moment about what reasons you have, what evidence you can produce in favor of this claim. The evidence you *had* for thinking them zebras has been effectively neutralized, since it does not count toward their *not* being mules cleverly disguised to look like zebras. Have you checked with the zoo authorities? Did you examine the animals closely enough to detect such a fraud? You might do this, of course, but in most cases you do nothing of the kind. You have some general uniformities on which you rely, regularities to which you give expression by such remarks as "That isn't very likely" or "Why should the zoo authorities do that?" Granted, the hypothesis (if we may call it that) is not very plausible, given what we know about people and zoos. But the question here is not whether this alternative is plausible, not whether it is more or less plausible than that there are real zebras in the pen, but whether *you know* that this alternative hypothesis is false. I don't think you do. In this I agree with the skeptic. I part company with the skeptic only when he concludes from this that, therefore, you do not know that the animals in the pen are zebras. I part with him because I reject the principle he uses in reaching this conclusion – the principle that if you do not know that Q is true, when it is known that P entails Q, then you do not know that P is true.

What I am suggesting is that we simply admit that we do *not* know that some of these contrasting "skeptical alternatives" are *not* the case, but refuse to admit that we do not know what we originally said we knew. My knowing that the wall is red certainly entails that the wall is red; it also entails that the wall is not white and, in particular, it entails that the wall is not white cleverly illuminated to look red. But it does not follow from the fact that I know that the wall is red that I *know* that

39

it is not white cleverly illumin⁣ted to look red. Nor does it follow from the fact that I know that those animals are zebras that I know that they are not mules cleverly disguised to look like zebras. These are some of the contrast consequences to which the epistemic operators do not penetrate.

Aside from asserting this, what arguments can be produced to support it? I could proceed by multiplying examples, but I do not think that examples alone will support the full weight of this view. The thesis itself is sufficiently counterintuitive to render controversial most of the crucial examples. Anyone who is already convinced that skepticism is wrong and who is yet troubled by the sorts of skeptical arguments I have mentioned will, no doubt, take this itself as an argument in favor of my claim that the epistemic operators are only semipenetrating. This, however, hardly constitutes an argument against skepticism. For this we need *independent* grounds for thinking that the epistemic operators do not penetrate to the contrast consequences. So I shall proceed in a more systematic manner. I shall offer an analogy with three other operators and conclude by making some general remarks about what I think can be learned from this analogy. The first operator is "explains why" or, more suggestively (for the purposes of this analogy):

(A) R is the reason (explanatory reason) that (or why) . . .

For example, the reason S quit smoking was that he was afraid of getting cancer. The second operator has to do with reasons again, but in this case it is a reason that tends to *justify* one in doing something:

(B) R is a reason for . . . (S to do Y).[2]

For example, the fact that they are selling the very same (type of) car here much more cheaply than elsewhere is a reason to buy it here rather than elsewhere. The status of this as a reason will, of course, depend on a variety of circumstances, but situations can easily be imagined in which this would be a reason for someone to buy the car here. Finally, there is a particular modal relationship which may be construed as a sentential operator:

(C) R would not be the case unless . . .

---

2 Unlike our other operators, this one does not have a propositional operand. Despite the rather obvious differences between this case and the others, I still think it useful to call attention to its analogous features.

For example, he would not have bid seven no-trump unless he had all four aces. I shall abbreviate this operator as "$R \rightarrow \ldots$"; hence, our example could be written "he bid seven no-trump $\rightarrow$ he had all four aces."

Each of these operators has features similar to those of our epistemic operators. If one retraces the ground we have already covered, one will find, I think, that these operators all penetrate deeper than the typical nonpenetrating operator. If R explains why (or is the reason that) P and Q are the case, then it explains why (is the reason that) Q is the case.[3] If I can explain why Bill and Harold are always invited to every party, I can explain why Harold is always invited to every party. From the fact that it was a mistake for me to quit my job it does not follow that it was a mistake for me to do something, but if I had a reason to quit my job, it does follow that I had a reason to do something. And if the grass would not be green unless it had plenty of sunshine and water, it follows that it would not be green unless it had water.

Furthermore, the similarities persist when one considers the presuppositional consequences. I argued that the epistemic operators fail to penetrate to the presuppositions; the preceding three operators display the same feature. In explaining why he takes his lunch to work, I do not (or need not) explain why he goes to work or why he works at all. The explanation may be obvious in some cases, of course, but the fact is, I need not be able to explain why he works (he is *so* wealthy) to explain why he takes his lunch to work (the cafeteria food is *so* bad). The reason the elms on Main Street are dying is *not* the reason there are elms on Main Street. I have a reason to feed my cat, no reason (not, at least, the same reason) to have a cat. And although it is quite true that he would not have known about our plans if the secretary had not told him, it does not follow that he would not have known about our plans if *someone other than the secretary* had told him. That is, (He knew about our plans) $\rightarrow$ (The secretary told him) even though it is *not* true that (He knew about our plans) $\rightarrow$ (It was the secretary who told him). Yet, the fact that *it was the secretary* who told him is (I take it) a presupposi-

---

3 One must be careful not to confuse sentential conjunction with similar-sounding expressions involving a relationship between two things. For example, to say Bill and Susan got married (if it is intended to mean that they married *each other*), although it entails that Susan got married, does not do so by *simplification*. "Reason why" penetrates through logical simplification, *not* through the type of entailment represented by these two propositions. That is, the reason they got married is that they loved each other; that they loved each other is not the reason Susan got married.

tional consequence of the fact that *the secretary* told him. Similarly, if George is out to set fire to the first empty building he finds, it may be true to say that George would not have set fire to the church unless it (the church) was empty yet false to say that George would not have set fire to the church unless *it was a church*.

I now wish to argue that these three operators do not penetrate to a certain set of contrast consequences. To the extent that the epistemic operators are similar to these operators, we may then infer, by analogy, that they also fail to penetrate to certain contrast consequences. This is, admittedly, a weak form of argument, depending as it does on the grounds there are for thinking that the preceding three operators and the epistemic operators share the same logic in this respect. Nonetheless, the analogy is revealing. Some may even find it persuasive.[4]

(A) The pink walls in my living room clash with my old green couch. Recognizing this, I proceed to paint the walls a compatible shade of green. This is the reason I have, and give, for painting the walls green. Now, in having this explanation for why I painted the walls green, I do not think I have an explanation for two other things, both of which are entailed by what I do have an explanation for. I have not explained why I did not, *instead* of painting the walls green, buy a new couch or cover the old one with a suitable slip cover. Nor have I explained why, instead of painting the walls green, I did not paint them white and illuminate them with green light. The same effect would have been achieved, the same purpose would have been served, albeit at much greater expense.

I expect someone to object as follows: although the explanation given for painting the walls green does not, by itself, explain why the couch was not changed instead, it nonetheless succeeds as an explanation for why the walls were painted green only insofar as there is an explanation for why the couch was not changed instead. If there is no explanation for why I did not change the couch instead, there has been no real, no complete, examination for why the walls were painted green.

I think this objection wrong. I may, of course, have an explanation for why I did not buy a new couch: I love the old one or it has

---

4 I think that those who are inclined to give a causal account of knowledge should be particularly interested in the operator "$R \rightarrow \ldots$" since, presumably, it will be involved in many instances of knowledge ("many," not "all," since one might wish to except some form of immediate knowledge – knowledge of one's own psychological state – from the causal account). If this operator is only semipenetrating, then any account of knowledge that relies on the relationship expressed by this operator (as I believe causal accounts must) will be very close to giving a semipenetrating account of "knowing that."

sentimental value. But then again I may not. It just never occurred to me to change the couch; or (if someone thinks that its not occurring to me *is* an explanation of why I did not change the couch) I may have thought of it but decided, for what reasons (if any) I cannot remember, to keep the couch and paint the walls. That is to say, I cannot explain why I did not change the couch. I thought of it but I did not do it. I do not know why. Still, I *can* tell you why I painted the walls green. They clashed with the couch.

(B) The fact that they are selling Xs so much more cheaply here than elsewhere may be a reason to buy your Xs here, but it certainly need not be a reason to do what is a necessary consequence of *buying* your Xs here – viz., not *stealing* your Xs here.

(C) Let us suppose that S is operating in perfectly normal circumstances, a set of circumstances in which it is true to say that the wall he sees would not (now) look green to him unless it was green (if it were any other color it would look different to him). Although we can easily imagine situations in which this is true, it does not follow that the wall would not (now) look green to S if it were white cleverly illuminated to look green. That is,

(i) The wall looks green (to S) → the wall is green.
(ii) The wall is green *entails* that the wall is not white cleverly illuminated to look green (to S).

are both true; yet, it is *not true* that

(iii) The wall looks green (to S) → is not white cleverly illuminated to look green (to S).

There are dozens of examples that illustrate the relative impenetrability of this operator. We can truly say that A and B would not have collided if B had not swerved at the last moment and yet concede that they would have collided without any swerve on the part of B if the direction in which A was moving had been suitably altered in the beginning.[5]

---

5   The explanation for why the modal relationship between R and P (R → P) fails to carry over (penetrate) to the logical consequences of P (i.e., R → Q where Q is a logical consequence of P) is to be found in the set of circumstances that are taken as *given*, or *held fixed*, in subjunctive conditionals. There are certain logical consequences of P that, by bringing in a reference to circumstances tacitly held fixed in the original subjunctive (R → P), introduce a possible variation in these circumstances and, hence, lead to a *different framework* of fixed conditions under which to assess the truth of R → Q. For instance, in the last example in the text, when it is said that A and B would not have collided if B had

43

The structure of these cases is virtually identical with the one that appeared in the case of the epistemic operators, and I think that by looking just a little more closely at this structure we can learn something very fundamental about our class of epistemic operators and, in particular, about what it means to know something. If I may put it this way, within the context of these operators no fact is an island. If we are simply rehearsing the facts, then we can say that it is a fact that Brenda did not take any dessert (although it was included in the meal). We can say this without a thought about what sort of person Brenda is or what she might have done had she ordered dessert. However, if we put this fact into, say, an explanatory context, if we try to explain this fact, it suddenly appears within a network of related facts, a network of possible alternatives that serve to define *what it is that is being explained*. What is being explained is a function of two things – not only the fact (Brenda did not order any dessert), but also the range of relevant alternatives. A relevant alternative is an alternative that might have been realized in the existing circumstances if the actual state of affairs had not materialized.[6] When I explain why Brenda did not order any dessert by saying that she was full (was on a diet, did not like anything on the dessert menu), I explain why she did not order any dessert *rather than, as opposed to, or instead of* ordering some dessert and *eating it*. It is this competing possibility that helps to define what it is that I am explaining when I explain why Brenda did not order any dessert. Change this

---

not swerved at the last moment, the truth of this conditional clearly takes it *as given* that A and B possessed the prior trajectories they in fact had on the occasion in question. *Given* certain facts, including the fact that they were traveling in the direction they were, they would not have collided if B had not swerved. Some of the logical consequences of the statement that B swerved do not, however, leave these conditions unaltered – e.g., B did not move in a perfectly straight line in a direction 2° counterclockwise to the direction it actually moved. This consequence "tinkers" with the circumstances originally taken *as given* (held fixed), and a failure of penetration will usually arise when this occurs. It *need not be true* that A and B would not have collided if B had moved in a perfectly straight line in a direction 2° counterclockwise to the direction it actually moved.

6   I am aware that this characterization of "a relevant alternative" is not, as it stands, very illuminating. I am not sure I can make it more precise. What I am after can be expressed this way: if Brenda *had* ordered dessert, she *would not* have thrown it at the waiter, stuffed it in her shoes, or taken it home to a sick friend (she has no sick friend). These are not alternatives that *might* have been realized in the existing circumstances if the actual state of affairs had not materialized. Hence, they are not relevant alternatives. In other words, the "might have been" in my characterization of a relevant alternative will have to be unpacked in terms of counterfactuals.

contrast, introduce a different set of relevant alternatives, and you change what it is that is being explained and, therefore, what counts as an explanation, even though (as it were) the same fact is being explained. Consider the following contrasts: ordering some dessert and throwing it at the waiter; ordering some dessert and taking it home to a sick friend. With these contrasts none of the preceding explanations are any longer explanations of why Brenda did not order dessert. Anyone who really wants to know why Brenda did not order dessert and throw it at the waiter will not be helped by being told that she was full or on a diet. This is only to say that, within the context of explanation and within the context of our other operators, the proposition on which we operate must be understood as embedded within a matrix of relevant alternatives. We explain why P, but we do so within a framework of competing alternatives A, B, and C. Moreover, if the possibility D is not within this contrasting set, not within this network of relevant alternatives, then even though not-D follows necessarily from the fact, P, which we do explain, we do not explain why not-D. Although the fact that Brenda did not order dessert and throw it at the waiter follows necessarily from the fact that she did not order dessert (the fact that is explained), this necessary consequence is not explained by the explanation given. The only contrast consequences to which this operator penetrates are those that figured in the original explanation as relevant alternatives.

So it is with our epistemic operators. To know that x is A is to know that x is A within a framework of relevant alternatives, B, C, and D. This set of contrasts, together with the fact that x is A, serves to define what it is that is known when one knows that x is A. One cannot change this set of contrasts without changing what a person is said to know when he is said to know that x is A. We have subtle ways of shifting these contrasts and, hence, changing what a person is said to know *without changing the sentence that we use to express what he knows.* Take the fact that Lefty killed Otto. By changing the emphasis pattern we can invoke a different set of contrasts and, hence, alter what it is that S is said to know when he is said to know that Lefty killed Otto. We can say, for instance, that S knows that *Lefty* killed Otto. In this case (and I think this is the way we usually hear the sentence when there is no *special* emphasis) we are being told that S knows the identity of Otto's killer, that *it was Lefty* who killed Otto. Hence, we expect S's reasons for believing that Lefty killed Otto to consist in facts that single out Lefty as the assailant *rather than* George, Mike, or someone else. On the other hand, we can say that S knows that Lefty *killed* Otto. In this case we are being told that S knows *what Lefty did to Otto*; he killed him *rather than* merely injuring him, killed him *rather than* merely threatening him, and so on. A good reason for believing that Lefty *killed* Otto (rather than merely injuring him) is that Otto is dead, but this is not much of a reason, if it is a reason at all, for believing that *Lefty* killed Otto. Changing the set of contrasts (from "Lefty rather than George or Mike" to "killed rather than injured or threatened") by shifting the emphasis pattern changes what it is that one is alleged to know when one is said to know that Lefty killed Otto.[7] The same point can be made here as we made in the case of explanation: the operator will penetrate *only* to those contrast consequences that form part of the network of relevant alternatives structuring the original context in which a knowledge claim was advanced. Just as we have not explained why Brenda did not order some dessert and throw it at the waiter when we explained why she did not order some dessert (although what we have explained – her not ordering any dessert – entails this), so also in knowing that Lefty *killed* Otto (knowing that what Lefty did to Otto was kill him) we do not *necessarily* (although we may) know that *Lefty* killed Otto (know that *it was Lefty* who killed Otto). Recall the example of the little old lady who knew that my brother would not move without knowing that it was my brother who would not move.

The conclusions to be drawn are the same as those in the case of explanation. Just as we can say that within the original setting, within the original framework of alternatives that defined what we were trying to explain, we *did explain* why Brenda did not order any dessert, so also within the original setting, within the set of contrasts that defined what it was we were claiming to know, we *did know* that the wall was red and *did know* that it was a zebra in the pen.

To introduce a novel and enlarged set of alternatives, as the skeptic is inclined to do with our epistemic claims, is to exhibit consequences of what we know, or have reason to believe, that we may not know, may not have a reason to believe; but it does not show that we did not know, did not have a reason to believe, whatever it is that has these

---

7 The same example works nicely with the operator "$R \rightarrow \ldots$" It may be true to say that Otto would not be dead unless Lefty *killed* him (unless what Lefty did to him was kill him) without its being true that Otto would not be dead unless *Lefty* killed him (unless it was Lefty who killed him).

consequences. To argue in this way is, I submit, as much a mistake as arguing that we have not explained why Brenda did not order dessert (within the original, normal, setting) because we did not explain why she did not order some and throw it at the waiter.

3

The Pragmatic Dimension of Knowledge

Knowing that something is so, unlike being wealthy or reasonable, is not a matter of degree. Two people can both be wealthy, yet one can be wealthier than the other; both be reasonable, yet one be more reasonable than the other. When talking about people, places, and topics (*things* rather than facts), it makes sense to say that one person knows something *better than* another. He knows the city better than we do, knows more Russian history than any of his colleagues, but doesn't know his wife as well as do his friends. But *factual* knowledge, the knowledge *that* something is so, does not admit of such comparisons.[1] If we both know that today is Friday, it makes no sense to say that you know this better than I. A rich man can become richer by acquiring more money, and a person's belief (that today is Saturday, for example) can be made more reasonable by the accumulation of additional evidence, but if a person already knows that today is Friday, there is nothing he can acquire that will make him know it better. Additional evidence will not promote him to a loftier form of knowledge – although it may make him *more certain* of something he already knew. You can boil water beyond its boiling point (e.g., at 300° F) but you are not, thereby, boiling it better. You are simply boiling it at a higher temperature.

In this respect factual knowledge is *absolute*. It is like being pregnant: an all-or-nothing affair. One person cannot be *more* pregnant or pregnant

---

Reprinted from *Philosophical Studies* 40 (1981), 363–378, copyright © 1981 by Kluwer Academic Publishers, with kind permission from Kluwer Academic Publishers.

1 I know we sometimes say things that suggest a comparison of this sort (e.g., No one knows better than I that there are a lot of mosquitoes in the Northwest Territories), but I take such constructions to be describing not better knowledge, but more direct, more compelling, kinds of evidence.

better than someone else. Those who view knowledge as a form of justified (true) belief typically acknowledge this fact by speaking not simply of justification, but of *full, complete,* or *adequate* justification. Those qualifications on the sort of justification required to know something constitute an admission that knowledge is, whereas justification is not, an absolute idea. For these qualifiers are meant to reflect the fact that there is a certain threshold of justification that must be equaled or exceeded if knowledge is to be obtained, and *equaling or exceeding this threshold* is, of course, an absolute idea. I can have a better justification than you, but my justification cannot be more adequate (more sufficient, more full) than yours. If my justification is complete in the intended sense, then your justification cannot be more complete.

Philosophers who view knowledge as some form of justified true belief are generally reluctant to talk about this implied threshold of justification. Just how much evidence or justification, one wants to ask, is *enough* to qualify as an adequate, a full, or a complete justification? If the level or degree of justification is represented by real numbers between 0 and 1 (indicating the conditional probability of that for which one has evidence or justification), any threshold less than 1 seems arbitrary. Why, for example, should a justification of 0.95 be good enough to know something when a justification of 0.94 is not adequate? And if one can know P because one's justification is 0.95 and know Q because one's justification is similarly high, is one excluded from knowing P and Q because the justification for their joint occurrence has (in accordance with the multiplicative rule in probability theory) dropped below 0.95?

Aside, though, from its arbitrariness, any threshold of justification less than 1 seems to be *too low.* For examples can easily be given in which such thresholds are exceeded without the justification being *good enough* (by ordinary intuitive standards) for knowledge. For example, if the threshold is set at 0.95, one need only think of a bag with 96 white balls and 4 black balls in it. If someone draws a ball at random from this bag, the justification for believing it to be white exceeds the 0.95 threshold. Yet, it seems clear (to me at least) that such a justification (for believing that a white ball has been drawn) is *not* good enough. Someone who happened to draw a white ball, and believed he drew a white ball on the basis of this justification, would not know that he drew a white ball.

Examples such as this suggest (although they do not, of course, prove) that the absolute, noncomparative character of knowledge derives from the absoluteness, or conclusiveness, of the justification required to know. If I know that the Russians invaded Afghanistan, you can't know this better than I know it because in order to know it I must already have an optimal, or conclusive, justification (a justification at the level of 1), and you can't do better than that. I have explored this possibility in other essays, and I do not intend to pursue it here.[2] What I want to develop in this essay is a different theme, one that (I hope) helps to illuminate our concept of knowledge by showing how this absolute idea can, despite its absoluteness, remain sensitive to the shifting interests, concerns, and factors influencing its everyday application. In short, I want to explore the way, and the extent to which, this absolute notion exhibits a degree of contextual relativity in its ordinary use.

To do this it will be useful to briefly recapitulate Peter Unger's discussion of absolute concepts.[3] Although he misinterprets its significance, Unger does, I think, locate the important characteristic of this class of concepts. He illustrates the point with the term *flat*. This, he argues, is an absolute term in the sense that a surface is flat only if it is *not at all bumpy or irregular.* Any bumps or irregularities, however small and insignificant they may be (from a practical point of view), mean that the surface on which they occur is not really flat. It may be *almost* flat, or *very nearly* flat, but (as both these expressions imply) it is not really flat. We do, it seems, compare surfaces with respect to their degree of flatness (e.g., West Texas is flatter than Wisconsin), but Unger argues that this must be understood as a comparison of the degree to which these surfaces approximate flatness. They cannot both be flat and, yet, one be flatter than the other. Hence, if A is flatter than B, then B (perhaps also A) is not really flat. Flatness does not admit of degrees, although a surface's nearness to being flat does, and it is this latter magnitude that we are comparing when we speak of one surface being flatter than another.

Unger concludes from this analysis that not many things are really flat. For under powerful enough magnification almost any surface will exhibit *some* irregularities. Hence, contrary to what we commonly say (and, presumably, believe), these surfaces are not really flat. When we describe them as being flat, what we say is literally false. Probably *nothing* is really flat. So be it. This, according to Unger, is the price we pay for having absolute concepts.

If knowledge is absolute in this way, then there should be similar

---

2 "Conclusive reasons," *Australasian Journal of Philosophy* (May 1971) and *Seeing and Knowing* (University of Chicago Press, 1969).
3 Peter Unger, "A defense of skepticism," *Philosophical Review* 80 (1971).

objections to its widespread application to everyday situations. Powerful magnification (i.e., critical inquiry) *should*, and with the help of the skeptic *has*, revealed "bumps" and "irregularities" in our evidential posture with respect to most of the things we say we know. There are always, it seems, possibilities that our evidence is powerless to eliminate, possibilities that until eliminated, block the road to knowledge. For if knowledge, being an absolute concept, requires the elimination of *all* competing possibilities (possibilities that contrast with what is known), then, clearly we seldom, if ever, satisfy the conditions for applying the concept.

This skeptical conclusion is unpalatable to most philosophers. Unger endorses it. Knowledge, according to him, is an absolute concept that, like flatness, has very little application to our bumpy, irregular world.

I have in one respect already indicated my agreement with Unger. Knowledge *is* an absolute concept (I disagree with him, however, about the source of this absoluteness; Unger finds it in the *certainty* required for knowledge; I find it in the *justification* required for knowledge). Unlike Unger, though, I do not derive skeptical conclusions from this fact. I will happily admit that *flat* is an absolute concept, and absolute in roughly the way Unger says it is, but I do not think this shows that nothing is really flat. For although nothing can be flat if it has *any* bumps and irregularities, what *counts* as a bump or irregularity depends on the type of surface being described. Something is empty (another absolute concept, according to Unger) if it has nothing in it, but this does not mean that an abandoned warehouse is not really empty because it has light bulbs or molecules in it. Light bulbs and molecules do not count as *things* when determining the emptiness of warehouses. For purposes of determining the emptiness of a warehouse, molecules (dust, light bulbs, etc.) are irrelevant. This isn't to say that, if we changed the way we used warehouses (e.g., if we started using, or trying to use, warehouses as giant vacuum chambers), they *still* wouldn't count. It is only to say that, given the way they are now used, air molecules (dust particles, etc.) don't count.

Similarly, a road can be perfectly flat even though one can *feel* and *see* irregularities in its surface, irregularities that, were they to be found on the surface of, say, a mirror would mean that the mirror's surface was not really flat. Large mice are not large animals and flat roads are not necessarily flat surfaces. The Flat Earth Society is certainly an anachronism, but it is not denying the existence of ant hills and gopher holes.

Absolute concepts depict a situation as being completely devoid of a certain sort of thing: *bumps* in the case of flatness and *objects* in the case of emptiness. The fact that there can be *nothing* of this sort present for the concept to be satisfied is what makes it an absolute concept. It is why if X is empty, Y cannot be emptier. Nonetheless, when it comes to determining what *counts* as a thing of this sort (a bump or an object), and hence what counts against a correct application of the concept, we find the criteria or standards peculiarly spongy and relative. What counts as a thing for assessing the emptiness of my pocket may not count as a thing for assessing the emptiness of a park, a warehouse, or a football stadium. Such concepts, we might say, are *relationally aboslute*; absolute, yes, but only relative to a certain standard. We might put the point this way: to be empty is to be *devoid of all relevant things*, thereby exhibiting, simultaneously, the absolute (in the word "all") and relative (in the word "relevant") character of this concept.

If, as I have suggested, knowledge is an absolute concept, we should expect it to exhibit this kind of *relationally* absolute character. This, indeed, is the possibility I mean to explore in this essay. What I propose to do is to use what I have called relationally absolute concepts as a model for understanding knowledge. In accordance with this approach (and in harmony with an earlier suggestion) I propose to think of knowledge as an evidential state in which *all relevant alternatives* (to what is known) *are eliminated*. This makes knowledge an absolute concept, but the restriction to *relevant* alternatives makes it, like *empty* and *flat*, applicable to this epistemically bumpy world we live in.

Why do this? What are the advantages? A partial catalog of benefits follows:

(1) A growing number of philosophers are able to find, or so they claim, a pragmatic, social, or communal dimension to knowledge.[4] A

---

4 I have in mind Harman's discussion in: *Thought* (Princeton, 1973) of evidence one does not possess, Goldman's barn example in "Discrimination and perceptual knowledge," *The Journal of Philosophy* 73.20 (1976), the sorts of examples appearing in various Defeasibility analyses of knowledge (see Keith Lehrer and Thomas Paxson, Jr., "Knowledge: Undefeated justified true belief," *Journal of Philosophy* 66.8 [1969] and Peter Klein, "A proposed definition of propositional knowledge," *Journal of Philosophy*, 68.16 [1971], Ernest Sosa's recommendation (in "How do you know?", *American Philosophical Quarterly* 11.2 [1974]) that we must depart from the traditional conception of knowledge by putting in relief the relativity of knowledge to an epistemic community (p. 117), and David Annis's "A contextualist theory of epistemic justification," *American Philosophical Quarterly*, 15.3 (1978), in which the basic model of justification (and presumably of knowledge) revolves around a person's being able to meet certain objections. The trend here, if this is a trend, seems to

variety of examples indicate, or seem to these philosophers to indicate, that knowledge depends not *just* on the evidential status of the knower vis-à-vis what is known, but also on such factors as the general availability, and proximity, of (misleading) counterevidence, on the sorts of things that are commonly taken for granted by others in the relevant community, on the interests and purposes of speakers (in claiming to know) and listeners (in being told that someone knows), and the importance or significance of *what* is known or someone's knowing it. I, personally, happen to think that most of these examples show nothing of the kind. These factors affect not *whether* something is known, but whether it is reasonable to *say* you know or to *think* you know. But, for the moment, I do not want to argue the point. I merely wish to point out that insofar as knowledge *is* a function of such pragmatic, social, or communal factors, the present approach to its analysis can absorb this relativity without compromising the absoluteness of knowledge itself. The social or pragmatic dimension to knowledge, if it exists at all, has to do with what *counts* as a relevant alternative, a possibility that must be evidentially excluded, in order to have knowledge. It does not change the fact that to know, one must be in a position to exclude *all* such possibilities. It does not alter the fact that one must have, in this sense, an optimal justification – one that eliminates every (relevant) possibility of being mistaken.

(2) Secondly, this approach to the analysis of knowledge helps to avoid the proliferation of *senses* that sometimes threatens to engulf epistemological discussions. We don't have different senses of the verb "to know" – a strong sense here, a weak sense there – but *one* sense with different applications. We don't have two senses of the word "empty" – one for pockets and one for warehouses. We have one sense (or meaning) with a difference in what counts as a thing.

(3) Thirdly, we get a better perspective from which to understand the persisting and undiminished appeal of skeptical arguments. Most philosophers have experienced the futility of trying to convince a devoted skeptic, or just a newly converted freshman, that we *do* know there are tables and chairs *despite* the possibility of dreams, hallucinations, cunning demons, and diabolical scientists who might be toying with our

be toward the kind of relativity espoused by Thomas Kuhn in his *The Structure of Scientific Revolutions* (Chicago, 1962).

brain on Alpha Centuri (Nozick's example). Somehow, in the end, we seem reduced to shrugging our shoulders and saying that there are certain possibilities that are just too remote to worry about. Our evidence isn't good enough to eliminate these wilder hypotheses because, of course, these wild hypotheses are carefully manufactured so as to *neutralize* our evidence. But dismissing such hypotheses as too remote to worry about, as too fanciful to have any impact on our ordinary use of the verb "to know," is merely another way of saying that for purposes of assessing someone's knowledge that this is a table, certain alternative possibilities are simply not relevant. We are doing the same thing (or so I submit) as one who dismisses chalk dust as irrelevant, or too insignificant, to worry about in describing a classroom as empty. What it is important to realize, especially in arguments with the skeptic, is that the impatient dismissal of his fanciful hypotheses is not (as he will be quick to suggest) a mere *practical* intolerance, and refusal to confront, decisive objections to our ordinary way of talking. It is, rather, a half-conscious attempt to exhibit the *relationally* absolute character of our cognitive concepts.

(4) Finally, this approach to the analysis of knowledge gives us the kind of machinery we need to handle the otherwise puzzling examples that are becoming more frequent in the epistemological literature. Consider yet one more example (one *more* because this one, I think, combines elements of several of the more familiar examples). An amateur bird-watcher spots a duck on his favorite Wisconsin pond. He quickly notes its familiar silhouette and markings and makes a mental note to tell his friends that he saw a Gadwall, a rather unusual bird in that part of the Midwest. Since the Gadwall has a distinctive set of markings (black rump, white patch on the hind edge of the wing, etc.), markings that no other North American duck exhibits, and these markings were all perfectly visible, it seems reasonable enough to say that the bird-watcher *knows* that yonder bird is a Gadwall. He can see that it is.

Nevertheless, a concerned ornithologist is poking around in the vicinity, not far from where our bird-watcher spotted his Gadwall, looking for some trace of Siberian grebes. Grebes are ducklike water birds, and the Siberian version of this creature is, when it is in the water, very hard to distinguish from a Gadwall duck. Accurate identification requires seeing the birds in flight since the Gadwall has a white belly and the Grebe a red belly – features that are not visible when the birds are in the water. The ornithologist has a hypothesis that some Siberian grebes have been migrating to the Midwest from their home in Siberia, and he and his research assistants are combing the Midwest in search of confirmation.

Once we embellish our simple story in this way, intuitions start to diverge on whether our amateur bird-watcher does indeed know that yonder bird is a Gadwall duck (we are assuming, of course, that it *is* a Gadwall). Most people (I assume) would say that he did *not* know the bird to be a Gadwall if there actually were Siberian grebes in the vicinity. It certainly sounds strange to suppose that he could give assurances to the ornithologist that the bird he saw was *not* a Siberian grebe (since he knew it to be a Gadwall duck). But what if the ornithologist's suspicions are unfounded? None of the grebes have migrated. Does the bird-watcher still not know what he takes himself to know? Is, then, the simple presence of an ornithologist, with his false hypothesis, enough to rob the bird-watcher of his knowledge that the bird on the pond is a Gadwall duck? What if we suppose that the Siberian grebes, because of certain geographical barriers, *cannot* migrate? Or suppose that there really are no Siberian grebes – the existence of such a bird being a delusion of a crackpot ornithologist. We may even suppose that, in addition to there being no grebes, there is no ornithologist of the sort I described, but that people in the area believe that there is. Or *some* people believe that there is. Or the bird-watcher's *wife* believes that there is and, as a result, expresses skepticism about his claim to know that what he saw was a Gadwall duck. Or, finally, although no one believes any of this, some of the locals are interested in whether or not our bird-watcher *knows* that there are no look-alike migrant grebes in the area.

Somewhere in this progression philosophers, most of them anyway, will dig in their heels and say that the bird-watcher really *does* know that the bird he sees is a Gadwall, and that he knows this despite his inability to justifiably rule out certain alternative possibilities. For example, if there are no look-alike grebes and no ornithologist of the sort I described, but the bird-watcher's wife believes that there are (a rumour she heard from her hairdresser), this does not rob him of his knowledge that the bird he saw was a Gadwall. He needn't be able to rule out the possibility that there are, somewhere in the world, look-alike grebes that have migrated to the Midwest in order to know that the bird he saw was a Gadwall duck. These other possibilities are (whether the bird-watcher realizes it or not) simply too remote.

Most philosophers will dig in their heels here because they realize that if they don't, they are on the slippery slope to skepticism with nothing left to hang on to. If false rumors about look-alike grebes and ornithologists can rob an expert bird-watcher of his knowledge that a bird seen in good light, and under ideal conditions, is a Gadwall duck, then similarly false rumors, suspicions, or even conjectures about deceptive demons or possible tricks will rob everyone of almost everything they know. One of the ways to prevent this slide into skepticism is to acknowledge that although knowledge requires the evidential elimination of all relevant alternatives (to what is known), there is a shifting, variable set of relevant alternatives. It may be that our bird-watcher does know the bird is a Gadwall under normal conditions (because look-alike grebes are not a relevant alternative) but does not know this if there is a suspicion, however ill founded it may be, that there exist look-alike grebes within migrating range. This will (or should) be no more unusual than acknowledging the fact that a refrigerator could truly be described as empty to a person looking for something to eat but *not* truly described as empty to a person looking for spare refrigerator parts. In the first case "empty" implies having no food in it; in the second it implies having no shelves, brackets, and hardware in it.

These, then, are some of the advantages to be derived from this approach to the analysis of knowledge. They are, however, advantages that can be harvested only if certain questions can be given reasonable answers: in particular (a) what makes a possibility relevant? (b) If, in order to know, one must rule out all relevant alternatives, how is this "elimination" to be understood? What does it take, evidentially, to "rule out" an alternative? (c) Is it possible, as this type of analysis suggests, for one to know something at one time and, later, not know it (due to the introduction of another relevant alternative) without forgetting it? (c) Can one make it easier to know things by remaining ignorant of what are, for others, relevant possibilities?

These, and many more questions, need answers if this framework for the analysis of knowledge is to be anything more than suggestive. Since I cannot here (or anywhere else, for that matter) provide answers to all these questions, I will try, in the time remaining, to fill in some of the large gaps.

Call the *Contrasting Set (CS)* the class of situations that are necessarily eliminated by what is known to be the case. That is, if S knows that P, then Q is in the CS (of P) if and only if, given P, necessarily not-Q. In our bird-watcher's example, the bird's being a Siberian grebe (or any kind of grebe at all) is in the CS of our bird-watcher's knowledge, or putative knowledge, that it is a Gadwall duck. So is its being an elephant, a hummingbird, a holographic image, or a figment of his imagination. Furthermore, let us call the set of possible alternatives that a person must be in a evidential position to exclude (when he knows that *P*) the *Relevancy Set (RS)*. In saying that he must be in a position to exclude these possibilities I mean that his evidence or justification for thinking these alternatives are *not* the case must be good enough to say he *knows* they are not the case. Items in the *CS* that are not in the *RS* I shall call *irrelevant alternatives*. These are items that, although their existence is incompatible with what is known to be the case, the knower *need not* (although he may) have a justification for thinking do not exist. Under normal conditions (the kinds of conditions that I assume prevail in the world today) the possibility of something's being a look-alike grebe, although it is a member of the contrasting set, is not a member of the *RS* of a bird-watcher's knowledge that what he sees is a Gadwall duck (in the kind of circumstances I described).[5] On the other hand, its being an eagle, a mallard, or a loon *are* members of the *RS* since if the bird-watcher could not eliminate these possibilities (sufficient unto knowing that it was not an eagle, a mallard, or a loon) on the basis of the bird's appearance and behavior, then he would not know that it was a Gadwall.

What we are suggesting here is that the *RS* is always a proper subset of the *CS* and, moreover, may not be the same *RS* from situation to situation even though what is known remains the same. The situation can be diagrammed as follows:

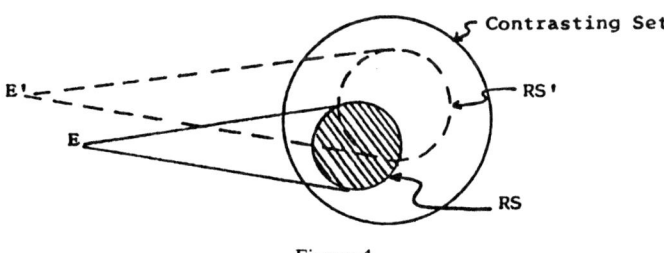

Figure 1

The solid lines indicate an *RS* and the corresponding piece of evidence that would be required to know with this *RS*. With a different *RS* (*RS'*), indicated by dotted lines, different evidence would be re-

5 Although there are grebes, and some of them look like ducks, there are (to the best of my knowledge) no Siberian grebes that look like Gadwall ducks. This part of my story was pure invention.

quired. If Siberian grebes are in the *RS*, then additional, more elaborate, evidence is required to know that yonder bird is a Gadwall than in the normal situation. Since the bellies are of different color, one might, for example, be able to tell that it was a Gadwall by watching it in flight. The point, however, is that something more would be needed than was available in the original, normal situation.

In terms of this kind of diagram, a skeptic could be represented as one who took $RS = CS$ in all cases. One's evidence must be comprehensive enough to eliminate all contrasting possibilities – there being no irrelevant alternatives.

Once the mistake is made of identifying *RS* with *CS*, the pressure (on non-skeptics) for lowering the standards of justification (requisite for knowing) becomes irresistible. For if in order to know that *P* one must be justified in rejecting *all* members of the *CS* (not just all members of the *RS*), then one can no longer expect very impressive levels of justification for what people know to be the case. If the evidence our bird-watcher has for believing the bird to be a Gadwall duck (wing markings, etc.) is also supposed to justify the proposition that it is *not* a look-alike grebe, then, obviously, the justification is nowhere near conclusive. What some philosophers seem inclined to conclude from this is that knowledge does not require conclusive evidence. The reasoning is simple: the bird-watcher knows it is a Gadwall; he doesn't have conclusive reasons (he can't exclude the possibility that it is a look-alike grebe); therefore knowledge does not require conclusive reasons. But this, I submit, is a fallacy, a misunderstanding of what needs to be conclusively excluded in order to know. Such reasoning is analogous to arguing that to be empty an object can have a few hundred things in it, and to conclude this on the basis of the undeniable fact that empty classrooms, warehouses, and buildings generally have at least a hundred things in them.

But what determines the membership of an *RS*? An *RS*, you will recall, is a set of situations each member of which contrasts with what is known to be the case and must be evidentially excluded if one is to know. Are there criteria for membership in this set? I'm now going to stick my neck out by saying what some of the considerations are that determine the membership of these sets. I do not expect much agreement.

(1) The first point has to do with the way we use contrastive focusing to indicate the range of relevant alternatives. I have discussed this phe-

nomenon in another place, so let me give just one example to illustrate the sort of thing I have in mind.[6] Someone claiming to know that Clyde *sold* his typewriter to Alex is not (necessarily) claiming the same thing as one who claims to know that Clyde sold his typewriter to *Alex*. The sentence we use to express what they know is the same, of course, but they reflect, and are designed to reflect, different *RS*s. A person who knows that Clyde *sold* his typewriter to Alex must be able to rule out the possibility that he *gave* it to him, or that he *loaned* it to him, or (perhaps) that he merely *pretended* to sell it to him. But he needs only a nominal justification, if he needs any justification at all, for thinking it was Alex to whom he sold it. He has to be right about its *being* Alex, of course, but he isn't claiming to have any special justification for thinking it was Alex rather than, say, his twin brother Albert. On the other hand, the person who knows that Clyde sold his typewriter to *Alex* is claiming to know that it wasn't Albert and is, therefore, expected to be in possession of evidence bearing on the identity of the recipient. But, in this second case, the knower needs only a nominal justification for the belief that Clyde *sold* him the typewriter rather than, say, loaned it to him. He certainly needn't be able to exclude the possibility that the entire transaction was a sham designed to fool the IRS.

(2) A second point, related to the first, is the way the subject term chosen to give verbal expression to what is known often functions to restrict the range of relevant alternatives.[7] Once again, an example will have to suffice. If I say that I could tell that your sister was amused by my funny story, I do not thereby claim to know that she is really your sister, really a human being (rather than a cleverly contrived robot), or really the sort of creature that could experience amusement. These possibilities, although certainly relevant to the truth of what I say, in the sense that if they were realized I would not know what I say I know, are not possibilities that I need be in an evidential position to exclude to know that your sister was amused by my joke. I was, as it were, *taking it for granted* that she was your sister (hence, a human being, a creature that could experience amusement), and I was claiming to know something about the thing so referred to. On the other hand, if I said that I could tell that the object in the corner (that happened to be your sister) was

---

6   In "Contrastive statements," *The Philosophical Review* (October 1972).
7   I tried to describe the way this works with perceptual claims in *Seeing and Knowing* (Chicago, 1969), pp. 93–112.

amused by my funny story, the possibility that it is a robot becomes a relevant alternative, one that I am (by this choice of words) accepting epistemic responsibility for excluding.

(3) Thirdly, in saying that we know we often reveal, either directly or indirectly, *how* we know. I could *see* that the tire was flat, could tell (by the way they *behaved*) that they were in love, *heard* them making plans to go, learned (from the *newspapers*) that the auto workers went out on strike, and used *my pocket calculator* to get the answer. The *way* we come to know, the channel (so to speak) over which we obtain our information, is, I submit, always the locus of irrelevant alternatives. Others can challenge the reliability of this channel (our visual system, our auditory system, the newspapers, the pocket calculator), and if it turns out unreliable in some way they will thereby have discredited our claim to knowledge. But others cannot discredit our claim to knowledge merely by pointing out that the channel over which we received our information *could be* unreliable or that we do not *know* it to be reliable. Possible malfunctions in the channel over which we receive information (combined with a resulting false message) are members of the *CS* but they are not members of the *RS*. To say that one can see, by the newspapers, that the auto workers are going on strike is to advance a knowledge claim (that the auto workers are going on strike) on the *assumption* of the newspapers' reliability. *If* the newspapers *are* a reliable source of such information, then the claimant does know what he says he knows, and he knows it in the way he says he knows it. One cannot undermine this claim by raising possibilities about deceptive newspaper stories or arguing that the claimant does not know that the newspapers, or this newspaper, is reliable. He never said he did know this. What he did say is that he knew the auto workers were going out on strike while simultaneously disclosing what he was taking for granted, which, *if true*, allowed him to know this.

I take the same to be true about our sensory systems when we come to know something by seeing, hearing, tasting, and touching. This is the function of our frequent indications (when advancing a knowledge claim) of the manner in which we came to know. We are, by this device, tipping off our listeners, helping them to identify which possibilities are irrelevant to what we are claiming to know.

(4) Fourthly, some people, I am sure, would insist that a pertinent factor influencing the size and membership of the *RS* is the importance (for the speaker and listeners) of what is known or of someone's know-

ing it. There is a difference between driving by a string of gasoline stations and driving in the middle of the desert. Running out of gas in the first case may be merely an inconvenience; in the latter case it may be a matter of life and death. This makes a difference between knowing (by glancing at your fuel gauge) that you still have some gas in your tank. The implications of being wrong in these two cases are much different – *so* different (some would claim) that additional precautions must be taken (to rule out certain possibilities) in the second case if one is to *know* that one still has some gasoline. And there is even a bigger difference between these cases and knowing that the coolant liquid surrounding the reactor on Three Mile Island is at a safe level by glancing at a similar kind of gauge. The fuel gauge (and associated mechanism) that suffices for knowing that you still have some gasoline (when driving in the city) is just not good enough for knowing that there is sufficient liquid coolant surrounding the reactor. This somewhat paradoxical fact (the fact, namely, that a particular instrument should be good enough to give knowledge in one place, not good enough in another) is to be explained, some would say, by the fact that as the stakes go up, the stakes associated with being right about what one purports to know, so does the size of the *RS*. There are *more* possibilities that must be eliminated in the nuclear power plant than must be eliminated in the automobile. In particular, a malfunction in the instrument itself must be guarded against in the dangerous situation. If it isn't, one doesn't know.

There is, I admit, some appeal to this point, but I think it mistaken. I see no reason why a standard automobile gauge, transplanted from the automobile to the nuclear power plant, functioning as the *only* indicator of the coolant level, should not, assuming it continues to function reliably (as reliably as it did in the automobile), be able to do precisely what the more expensive instruments do – viz., tell the operators that the coolant is at a safe level. I admit that the operators *should not* rely on a single gauge, and certainly not one manufactured under such casual quality control, but if they *do* rely on it, I don't see any basis for denying that they know. They should be nervous, but this nervousness is not to be explained by their failure to know what the coolant level is, but rather by their uncertainty as to when (due to gauge malfunction) they *stop* knowing it.

(5) Finally, we come to the difficult question, the question of when an alternative (not otherwise excluded as irrelevant by one of the considerations already discussed) is just *too remote* to qualify as relevant. In the case of our bird-watcher, some philosophers, thinking to turn the tables

on the skeptic (by drastically diminishing the *RS*), have suggested that an alternative becomes relevant only when there are positive reasons for thinking it is, or may be, realized. Doubt can also be irrational, and if there are no reasons to doubt, mere possibilities are irrelevant to whether what is believed is known.

This, obviously, is an overreaction. The Wisconsin lakes could be loaded with migrant Siberian grebes without the bird-watcher's having any reason to think that such look-alike birds actually existed. His lack of any reason to doubt, his ignorance of the possibility that what he sees is a grebe and not a Gadwall, is irrelevant. The mere possibility is in this case enough to show he doesn't know.

This shows that having a reason (evidence) to think *X* is a genuine possibility is not a necessary condition for *X*'s being a relevant alternative. Perhaps, though, it is sufficient. Perhaps, that is, a reasonable (justified) belief that yonder bird *might* be a look-alike grebe (whether or not this belief is true) is enough to make its being a look-alike grebe a relevant possibility.

But if a person really does believe that the bird could be a grebe, aside from the question of whether or not this belief is reasonable, he surely fails to have the kind of belief requisite to knowing it is a Gadwell. He certainly doesn't think he knows it is a Gadwall. I do not know exactly how to express the belief condition on knowledge, but it seems to me that anyone who believes (reasonably or not) that he *might* be wrong fails to meet it.[8] And so the present suggestion is irrelevant to our problem. It describes conditions in which the subject fails to know but only by robbing him of the belief requisite to knowledge.

It may be thought that the mere presence of evidence that one might be wrong, assuming this evidence does not affect one's willingness to believe, is enough to make the respect in which one (according to this evidence) might be wrong a relevant alternative. This has the unfortunate consequence that one can rob a person, indeed a whole community, of its knowledge by spreading a false rumor. I can, for example, tell the bird-watcher that I just met an ornithologist looking for migrant grebes. Once this message is relayed to the bird-watcher, even if he rejects it as a silly fabrication, he no longer knows that the bird he saw

---

8   We needn't suppose that for *S* to know that *P*, *S* must believe that he can't be wrong. But it does seem reasonable to insist that if *S* knows that *P*, he does not believe that he might be wrong. In other words, if the bird-watcher really believes that the bird he sees might be a grebe, then he does not know it is a Gadwall.

was a Gadwall duck. And, as a consequence, the whole community is robbed of its knowledge that their local pond was visited by a rather rare bird (a Gadwall duck). The mere fact that I have given them a reason to think that the bird could be a look-alike grebe,[9] whether or not they accept this as a reason, implies that, lacking evidence that it was not a grebe, they do not know it was a Gadwall.

Without dragging the dialectic out any longer, let me simply say what such considerations suggest to me. They suggest that the difference between a relevant and an irrelevant alternative resides not in what we happen to *regard* as a real possibility (whether reasonably or not), but in the kind of possibilities that actually exist in the objective situation. Whether or not our bird-watcher knows that the bird he sees is a Gadwall depends on whether or not, in some objective sense, it could be a look-alike grebe (or any other similar-looking creature). If, as a matter of fact, there are no look-alike grebes, that settles the matter. He knows it is a Gadwall. If there are grebes, but due to certain geographical barriers they are confined to their Siberian habitat, then, once again, the possibility of the bird's being a grebe, although remaining a logical possibility, is not a relevant possibility. They, the grebes, cannot migrate to the Midwest.

If, however, there are grebes and they can migrate, but just have not done so, the case becomes more ambiguous. I think, however, that we now have a genuine possibility, a relevant alternative. By hypothesis the bird-watcher does not know it is not a migrant grebe, and however improbable this possibility may be, there is nothing the bird-watcher has (either in the look of the bird or in general background information) that excludes the possibility that what he is looking at is a migrant grebe. He does not, therefore, know it to be a Gadwall. He will, no doubt, say he knows. And everyone else may agree and, as a result, think *they* know (having been told by someone who knows). But the truth lies elsewhere. It is, I suggest, tantamount to saying that the bottle is empty when there is a drop left. No one is going to quarrel with this description since all the relevant implications (e.g., we can't make another martini) are true. But the claim itself is false.

9 I assume here that my saying "There is an ornithologist in the area looking for migrant grebes, a species that looks very much like a Gadwall duck" is prima facie evidence that there *is* an ornothologist in the area looking for migrant grebes. If the bird-watcher ignores me (as we are assuming he does), he nonetheless has been given evidence that the bird he saw might have been a grebe.

4

The Epistemology of Belief

Believing is easy, knowing is hard. Believing is easy because it is just a way of saying something in the internal language of thought. No trick at all once you have the language. Talk is cheap. The real trick is getting things right or, even harder, securing some *guarantee* that one has got things right. This is knowledge and this is hard.

Such is the conventional contrast between knowledge and belief. Underlying this contrast is the idea that knowledge, unlike belief, requires special endowments. It takes something *more* to know because knowledge requires, besides mere belief, some reliable coordination of internal belief with external reality, and this coordination, being an extremely delicate matter, requires the exercise of special skills. If, though, one takes no thought for whether they are true or false, reliable or unreliable, then believing itself is mere child's play – a form of mental doodling. Witness the fact that the ignorant believe as effortlessly as the learned – indeed it seems, with far *less* effort. According to the conventional wisdom, then, the problem, at least for epistemology (but perhaps not for the philosophy of mind), is not one of understanding how we manage to *have* beliefs, but one of understanding the sources and extent of their reliability.

This picture, I submit, dominates philosophical thinking about knowledge and belief. It is what keeps epistemology a durable, if not exactly flourishing, industry. We can thank, or blame, Descartes for installing it as the centerpiece of philosophical debate about our cogni-

Reprinted from M. D. Roth and G. Ross, eds., *Doubting* (1990), pp. 183–194, copyright ca 1990 by Kluwer Academic Publishers, with kind permission from Kluwer Academic Publishers.

tive predicament. I think, though, that this picture distorts the episte-mological task by grossly underestimating the cognitive demands of simple belief. Knowing is hard, but believing is no piece of cake either. In fact, or so I wish to argue, believing something requires precisely the same skills involved in knowing. Anyone who believes something *thereby* exhibits the cognitive resources for knowing. There is, as we shall see, a gap between belief and knowledge, but it is not one that provides any comfort to the philosophical skeptic. If I may, for dramatic effect, over-state my case somewhat, if you can't know it, you can't believe it either.

1. REPRESENTATION AND MISREPRESENTATION

Let me organize my defense of this thesis by discussing representations in general and, in particular, the representational powers we typically assign to measuring instruments. I shall return to beliefs, a special kind of representation, in a moment.

Consider, first, a fairly crude altimeter, a device used for measuring altitude or height above sea level. It operates basically as a pressure gauge, responding to changes in air pressure as altitude varies. As the instrument ascends, the diminished air pressure allows a diaphragm, to which a pointer is attached, to expand. The expanding diaphragm moves the pointer across a scale calibrated in feet above sea level.

We can, of course, fool this instrument. We can place it in a chamber from which air has been pumped. The partial vacuum in the chamber will cause the instrument to register, say, 35,000 feet when it is, in fact, only a few hundred feet above sea level. The instrument, it seems, misrepresents its own altitude. It "says" it is at 35,000 feet when it is not. If altimeters had beliefs, this surely, would qualify as a false belief.

But have we really fooled the instrument? This depends on what we take it to be representing or saying. I said earlier that the instrument misrepresented its own altitude. But why suppose it is *altitude* that the instrument represents or, in this case, misrepresents? *We*, after all, are the ones who printed "feet above sea level" on the face of the instrument and called it an "altimeter." We are the ones making it "say" this. The instrument itself (if I may take its part for the moment) might object to this way of describing its representational efforts. It is, it might say, a device for representing pressure, and its representation of the pressure, even in a vacuum chamber, is perfectly accurate. It is making no mistake. No one is fooling it. It believes the pressure is 5 pounds per square inch and the pressure *is* 5 pounds per square inch. If anyone is making a mistake (the instrument concludes), it is we who assigned it a representational capacity beyond its actual powers. One could as well print "Gross National Product in Dollars" on its face and then complain that it misrepresented the state of the national economy.

It seems more reasonable to say that it is the instrument's job to register the pressure and that it is *our* job (the job of those who use the instrument) to see to it that a change in pressure is reliably correlated with altitude (or whatever other quantity we use the instrument to measure) – to see to it, in other words, that the instrument is used in conditions in which alterations in pressure carry information about the magnitudes we use the instrument to measure. If this is so, then the instrument is discharging its representational responsibilities in a perfectly satisfactory way. We aren't fooling the instrument; at most we are fooling ourselves.

Is the speedometer on a car misrepresenting the vehicle's speed if we jack up the car, engage the gears, and run the engine? The drive shaft and wheels will turn, and the speedometer will, accordingly, register (say) 30 mph. The car, of course, is stationary. Something is amiss, and if we have to place blame, the speedometer is the likely culprit. It is saying something false. Or is it? How do we decide what the speedometer is saying? Perhaps the speedometer is representing the only thing it is capable of representing, saying the only thing it knows how to say, namely, that the wheels are turning at a certain rate. The mistake, if a mistake is being made here at all, occurs in us, in what we *infer* must be true if what the speedometer says is true.

What, then, does a measuring instrument actually represent? Or, to put it more suggestively, what does the instrument really believe? Does the altimeter have altitude beliefs or merely pressure beliefs? Does the speedometer have vehicle-speed beliefs or merely wheel-rotation beliefs? Until we are in a position to answer these questions we cannot say *how*, or even *whether*, it is possible to "fool" the instrument. We cannot say whether, in situations like those described earlier the instruments are misrepresenting anything, whether it is even possible to make them "believe" something false.

It is time to stop describing instruments in such inappropriate ways. Although I think it sensible to speak of instruments representing the quantities they are designed to measure, I do not, of course, think they *say* or *believe* things. We cannot, literally, *fool* instruments. They don't make *mistakes*. I allowed myself to speak this way in order to reveal my overall strategy. So before moving on to a discussion of creatures to which it does make sense to attribute genuine cognitive states (like belief and knowledge), let me describe an intermediate case. Some may find it more realistic, and hence more convincing, than examples involving speedometers and altimeters.

A frog in its natural habitat will flick with its tongue at small, moving, dark spots. The neural mechanisms responsible for this response have, for fairly obvious reasons, been called "bug detectors." In the frog's natural habitat, all (or most) small, moving, dark spots are bugs, a staple item in the frog's diet. Psychologists (with presumably better intentions than I had with the altimeter) have removed frogs from their natural habitat, projected small, moving, dark *shadows* on a surface in front of the frogs, and observed the creatures' response. Not unexpectedly, the frogs "zap" the moving shadow.

What shall we say about this situation? Has the frog mistakenly identified the shadow as a bug? Is the frog misrepresenting its surroundings? Does the frog have a false belief, a belief to the effect that *this* (small, moving, dark spot) is a bug? Or shall we say that the frog (assuming for the moment that it *has* beliefs) does not have "bug" beliefs at all? Instead what it has are "small-moving-dark-spot" beliefs? Since the frog *usually* operates in circumstances (swamps, ponds, etc.) where small, moving, dark spots are bugs, natural selection has favored the development of a zapping reflex to whatever the frog perceives as a small, dark spot. If we take this latter view, then although psychologists can starve a frog in this artificial environment, they can't fool it. The frog never makes a mistake because it never represents, or *takes* things to be other than they are. It represents the shadow *as* a small, moving, dark spot, and this representation is perfectly correct. The frog goes hungry in this situation, not because it mistakenly sees dark spots as edible bugs, but because what it correctly sees as moving spots are not, in fact, edible bugs.

If we adopt this latter strategy in describing what the frog believes, then it becomes very hard, if not impossible, to fool the animal. If the frog has beliefs at all, it approaches infallibility in these beliefs. And this infallibility is achieved in the same way it was (or could be) achieved with the altimeter and speedometer – by tailoring the content of belief (representation) to *whatever* properties of the stimulus trigger the relevant response. If we are willing to be less ambitious in this way about what we describe the frog as believing, we can be correspondingly more ambitious in what we describe the frog as knowing.

But there is, surely, a truth of the matter. The frog either believes there is a bug in front of it or it doesn't. It isn't up to *us* to determine the content of the frog's beliefs in the way it may be up to us to say what an altimeter represents.[1] Before we create, by fiat, infallible frogs we had better look to those factors, whatever they are, that determine the content of a creature's beliefs. Only when we are clear about this can we proceed to questions about the reliability of these beliefs – to traditional epistemological questions. This, then, brings us to the question of how belief content is determined – to the question of learning.

2. LEARNING

Dolphins have an extremely sensitive sonar system that allows them to detect, and in some cases identify, objects in the water fifty feet away. They have, for example, been taught to identify cylinders at this distance. The identification occurs whether the cylinders in question are short and squat or long and narrow, solid or hollow, metal or wood, red, yellow or blue. Regardless of the object's value along these other dimensions, the dolphin can distinguish the cylinders from the noncylinders.

If a child of four achieved this level of discrimination, especially if its distinctive response to cylinders was the utterance of the *word* "cylinder," we would doubtless credit it (perhaps prematurely) with the concept of a cylinder and, hence, with the capacity for holding beliefs to the effect that something was a cylinder. There are those, however, who prefer to be less liberal with dolphins or, indeed, with any creature lacking a natural language. Since I do not think this issue is particularly relevant to the point I wish to make with this example, I will continue to speak of the dolphin as believing of the cylinders it picks out that they are cylinders.

Suppose, now, that when the dolphin is being taught to identify cylinders, the trainer uses *only* cylinders made of plastic. All the noncylinders, the cubes, spheres, pyramids, and so on, are made of some other material – wood, say. Since the dolphin reaches criterion (as the psychologists say) on plastic objects, responding positively to all and only plastic objects, can we say that the dolphin has learned to recognize *plastic objects*, that it now, when responding positively to X, has a belief

---

1 Some philosophers, I know, would deny this. I make the assumption, nonetheless, because (1) I believe it, and (2) it makes my argument that much more difficult and, therefore, that much more significant if correct.

to the effect that X is plastic? Does the dolphin now have some crude notion of *plasticity*?

Of course not. The reason we are prepared to credit the dolphin with the concept of a cylinder (and hence, with beliefs to the effect that *this* is a cylinder and *that* is not) is not *just* because it distinguishes cylinders from other shaped objects (for it does, with equal success, distinguish plastic from nonplastic objects) but because of our conviction that it was the *cylindricality* of these objects to which the creature was responding (and not their *plasticity*). The animal's sensitive sonar is capable (or so we believe) of picking up information about the shape of distant objects, and it was trained to respond in some distinctive way to *this* piece of information. There is no reason to think it was picking up, or responding to, information about the chemical constitution of these objects – to the fact that they were plastic. We could test this, of course. Merely place a wooden cylinder in the pool and observe the animal's response. A positive response would indicate that it was the cylindricality, not the plasticity, to which the animal developed a sensitivity. It was, as I prefer to put it (more about this later), information about the object's shape, not information about its chemical structure, that guided the animal's discriminatory behavior during learning. It is this fact that lies behind our unwillingness to credit the dolphin with the concept *plastic* and our willingness (or greater willingness) to credit it with the concept of cylindricality, even though (given the restricted learning conditions) it became as successful in distinguishing plastic from nonplastic objects as it did in distinguishing cylinders from noncylinders. Even if (cosmic coincidence) all and only cylinders were made of plastic, so that our trained dolphins could infallibly detect plastic objects (or detect them as infallibly as they detected cylinders), this would not have the slightest tendency to make us say that they had acquired the concept of plastic or could now have beliefs about the plasticity of objects. The level of sophistication to which we are willing to rise in describing the belief content of the dolphin is no *higher* than the kind of information about objects to which we believe it sensitive. The dolphin can have "cylinder" beliefs but not "plastic" beliefs because, as far as we know anyway, it has a sensory system that allows it to pick up information about the shape, but not the chemical structure, of objects at a distance.

It is important to understand what is happening when we make these judgements, what kinds of considerations shape our decisions about what level of conceptual sophistication to assign an animal (whether it be a frog, a dolphin, or a human child). The decision about what concept to assign a creature, and hence the decision about what sorts of beliefs we may attribute to it, are guided by our assessment of the sort of information the animal utilizes during learning to articulate, develop, and refine its discriminatory and classificatory repertoire. If we are talking about an instrument, something that doesn't learn, then its representational power, what it represents things as being, is a function of the information to which the instrument is sensitive. Since altimeters are not sensitive to information about the gross national product, no matter what I happen to write on the face of the instrument, an altimeter cannot represent or misrepresent the gross national product. But since the instrument is sensitive to information about pressure and, some would say, in some situations at least, to information about altitude, it is capable of both representing and misrepresenting these magnitudes.

This principle (the principle, namely, that the representational powers of a system are limited by its informational pickup and processing capabilities) underlies many of our judgments about the conditions in which someone can and cannot learn. Why can't you teach a normally endowed child her colors in the dark? Because information about the *color* of the objects is not therein made available for shaping the child's discriminatory and identificatory responses. Even if the child succeeds in picking out all the blue objects (in virtue of the fact, say, that all and only the blue ones are furry), she will not, by this procedure, learn the concept *blue*. She will not *believe* of the next furry blue object she finds that it is blue. The most she will believe is that it is furry. Even if we taught her to say "blue" every time she encountered a blue object in the dark, we would not, thereby, have given the child a *color* concept. We would merely have given her an eccentric way of expressing her concept of furryness.

The moral of the story is this: to learn what an *X* is, to acquire the capacity to represent something as an *X* (believe it to be an *X*), it is not enough to be shown *X*s and non-*X*s and to distinguish successfully between them. Unless the information that the *X*s are *X* is made available to the learner (or instrument), and it is *this* information that is *used* to discriminate and classify, the system will not be representing anything as an *X*. Even if some concept is acquired, and even if this concept *happens* to be coextensive with that of *X* (thus allowing the subject to distinguish successfully the *X*s from the non-*X*s), the concept acquired will not be that of an *X*. The subject will not be able to believe of *X*s that they are *X*. For the concept acquired during learning is determined by the kind of information to which the learner becomes sensitive, and if no information about the *X-ness* of objects is made available during learning (despite the availability of *X*s), no such concept can develop.

I have begun to talk more and more about information, so let me pause a moment to explain what I mean by this way of talking. I mean nothing very technical or abstract. In fact, I mean pretty much what (I think) we all mean in talking of some event, signal, or structure carrying (or embodying) information about another state of affairs. A message (i.e., some event, stimulus, or signal) carries information about *X* to the extent to which one could learn (come to know) something about *X* from the message. And, in particular, the message carries the information that *X* is a dingbat, say, if and only if one could learn (come to know) that *X* was a dingbat from the message. This does not mean that one *must* learn the *X* is a dingbat from a message that carries this information. One may not, after all, know the code. The message may be in Chinese. When I say that one *could* learn that *X* was a dingbat from the message I mean, simply, that the message has whatever reliable connection with dingbats is required to enable a suitably equipped but otherwise ignorant receiver to learn from it that *X* is a dingbat.[2]

I think it is this sense of the term "information" that is operative in a wide variety of ordinary contexts, and it is for this reason that I feel safe in saying that I am using the term as it is commonly used. We say that a pamphlet contains information about how to probate a will because we believe that someone could learn something about how to probate a will by consulting the pamphlet. Information booths are called information booths because the clerks working there either know, or can quickly find out, about matters of interest to the average patron. One can *come to know* by making inquiries at such places. Similarly, when scientists tell us that the pupil of the eye is a source of information about another person's feelings and attitudes, that a thunder signature contains information about the lightning channel that produced it, that the dance of a honey bee contains information as to the whereabouts of the nectar, or that the light from a star contains information about the chemical composition of that body, the scientists are clearly referring to information as something capable of yielding knowledge. And *what* information a signal carries is identified with what one could learn from it. This, I submit, is the very same sense of "information" in which we speak of books, newspapers, and authorities as containing, or having, information about a particular topic.

---

2 I assume here some kind of reliability account of knowledge or justification.

This is not intended to be a philosophically illuminating analysis of information. At least no epistemologist would find it of any special interest. Rather than telling us anything important about knowledge, it uses the concept of knowledge to tell us something about information. But this merely indicates that information is a member of that constellation of epistemic terms that can be interdefined in fairly trivial ways.[3] This, though, is unimportant for my present purposes. What is important is the epistemic character of the concept of information and its connection with knowledge. For if this connection is as I have expressed it, then the upshot of my argument so far can be expressed as follows: what *concept* a person acquires during learning, and hence what beliefs he is henceforth capable of holding, is restricted to the kind of information he is capable of picking up and processing. But, in virtue of the connection between information and knowledge, we now see that this is equivalent to saying that the beliefs a person is capable of holding as a result of learning are restricted to the sorts of things that that person (given his information-processing resources) is capable of knowing.

The argument is rather simple, so let me recapitulate. To learn what a dingbat is, and hence to acquire the conceptual resources necessary for believing that something is a dingbat, one must be exposed not only to dingbats, but also to the *information* that they are dingbats. Not only must this information be made available, it must be *picked up* and *used* by the learner to guide his discriminatory and identificatory responses if he is to be credited with the relevant concept. Since this is so, the learner cannot come to believe something is a dingbat unless he has the cognitive (i.e., information-processing) resources for knowing something is a dingbat.[4] Only someone who *can* know (or could know – the learner may have lost his capacity for picking up the required information) – that this is a dingbat can believe it to be a dingbat.

It should be emphasized that this is a thesis about the relationship between what is believed and what is, or can be, known, not a thesis

3 Although they can be interdefined in fairly trivial ways, they needn't be. In *Knowledge and the Flow of Information* (Bradford/MIT, 1981), I give an independent (of knowledge) analysis of information, thus making the concept available for the analysis of knowledge.

4 Obviously one can believe something is a dingbat when it is not a dingbat – hence, believe things that cannot be known (because they are not the case). I hope it is clear from the wording in the text that I am not denying this obvious fact. The thesis is, rather, that if one has the concept of a dingbat (hence, capable of holding beliefs to the effect that something is a dingbat), then that something is a dingbat is the *sort* of thing one can know.

about what, if anything, can be known or believed. The thesis is, in other words, quite independent of one's views about what if anything, dolphins, frogs, or people can know (or believe) to be the case. I have not said that frogs can (in their natural habitat) know when a bug flies by. Nor have I denied this (e.g., by saying that they could only know that there was a small, dark spot moving by). And for purposes of this essay, I don't particularly care what a dolphin can know, or believe, about a cylinder immersed in its pool fifty feet away. I have my own ideas about these matters, but they are not relevant to the thesis I am presently defending. What I am arguing is that whatever view you take about what a creature can believe, you thereby commit yourself to a certain level of sophistication in the creature's capacity for picking up and processing information; if it can't pick up information about bugs, then it cannot hold beliefs about bugs (just as the altimeter that can't pick up information about the gross national product cannot represent the quantity). So if the frog does believe that there is a bug in front of it, then it is the sort of creature capable of picking up, processing, and responding to information that there is a bug in front of it. It is this conditional thesis for which I have been arguing. When we combine this conditional with what has been said about information, we reach the conclusion that anything the frog believes is the sort of thing it is (was[5]) capable of knowing.

3. LANGUAGE AND BELIEF

With appropriate modifications, the same can be said about our own conceptual situation: the conditions that must obtain for the acquisition of simple concepts are the same conditions that make possible the *knowledge* that these concepts apply. In our own case, though, the possibilities for confusion about this matter are much greater. For we not only believe things, we say things, and we sometimes say things we don't believe. That is, unlike the altimeter, frog, and dolphin, we have *dual* representational systems and they are not always synchronized. It is,

---

5 The temporal qualifier should always be understood. A creature may have acquired a concept *at a time* when he possessed a fully functional sensory system, one capable of picking up and processing information of a certain kind. Once the concept is acquired, though, the creature may have *lost* the information-processing capacity (e.g., have gone blind), hence losing the capacity to know what he can still believe.

therefore, easy enough to attribute to the one representational resources of the other – thus blurring the intimate relationship between belief and (the capacity for) knowledge.

Let me illustrate the problem in a simpleminded way. We will turn to a more interesting case in a moment. If I teach a child her colors and have her say "circular" whenever a blue object is presented, what will this show (assuming the child learns her lesson) about what the child believes or about what kinds of mistakes she is capable of making? Clearly, when the child looks at a blue cube and says "circular" she will be misrepresenting, linguistically misrepresenting, the properties of what she is talking about.[6] This, though, isn't very interesting. It certainly isn't a symptom of any *cognitive* or *conceptual* misrepresentation. The child *says*, "This is circular," but she *believes* it is blue. Through an unfortunate piece of education, she does not use the correct word to express what she believes. What she means by "circular" is *blue*. What we have done with this child is similar to what earlier we suggested doing with the altimeter: printing "Gross National Product in Dollars" on its face. In doing this we can make the instrument "say" that the gross national product is increasing, but we have given it a way of "saying" things it does not, indeed *cannot*, believe. And so it is with the child. The child's (linguistic) responses have a meaning that exceeds her (internal) powers of representation.

Something like this happens when children first learn to talk. The toddler who delights his mother by saying "Mommy" whenever she appears disappoints her when he says the *same* thing to his Aunt Mildred. When the child is corrected ("No, Jimmy, *I'm* Mommy, that's Aunt Mildred"), what is this a correction of? A false belief? But does Jimmy really believe that this other woman is his mother? Probably not. It seems more likely that the child simply believes Aunt Mildred is a woman, or a person, precisely what he believed of his mother when he called her "Mommy," and that he is using the word "Mommy" to express this less determinate notion. Correction here is not the weeding out of false beliefs, but the development of more discriminating set of

---

6 I earlier (circa second draft) thought that what the child *said* when it said "This is circular" was false. I thought this because it seemed to me that what the child was saying (with these words) was that the object was circular. Jon Barwise convinced me that this was not so. What the child is saying when it uses these words is that the object is blue. Hence, what the child is saying is true.

concepts and the correlative ability to express these more determinate concepts in linguistically appropriate ways.

Since, for most of us, the acquisition of our natural language goes hand in hand with the acquisition of the concepts to which this language gives expression, the ability to represent something verbally is developed in close association with the ability to represent something in the internal language of thought. Some philosophers prefer to say that these two abilities are not really distinct. That may or may not be so. I don't wish to take sides on this issue here. What is important for present purposes is the understanding that during learning our linguistic responses to stimuli have a meaning independent of whatever representational capacity the learner himself may have developed. Since this is so, the verbal mistakes that occur in classifying and identifying objects need not reflect a mismatch between the world and the respondent's inner representation of the world. The only mismatch may be between the world and the respondent's external (verbal) representation of the world.

This point is, I think, easy enough to accept when we are dealing with obvious examples like those described earlier. There are, however, profound implications for epistemology. Perhaps the best way to exhibit these implications is by another, less obvious, example.

Hilary Putnam has described a place, Twin Earth, in which there are two substances, H_2O and XYZ, chemically different but both having the superficial properties of water.[7] By "superficial" I mean the properties we (Earthlings) rely on (outside the laboratory) to identify something as water: taste, smell, feel, capacity for quenching thirst, and so on. Some of the lakes and rivers on Twin Earth are filled with H_2O; others are filled with XYZ (here I depart from Putnam's example). It rains H_2O in some parts of the country, XYZ in other parts. Twin Earthlings call both substances "water" since the liquids are (apart from elaborate chemical analysis, an analysis that they haven't yet perfected) indistinguishable.

Consider, now, a Twin Earthling (call him Tommy) being taught what water (or what the Twin Earthlings call "water") is on a part of Twin Earth in which there is both H_2O and XYZ. As it turns out, quite by accident, Tommy learns what water is by being exposed only to

---

7 "The Meaning of 'Meaning' " in *Language, Mind and Knowledge*, Minnesota Studies in the Philosophy of Science, 7, Minneapolis: University of Minnesota Press (1975); reprinted in *Mind, Language and Reality – Philosophical Papers*, Vol. 2, Cambridge, England (1975).

H_2O (it only happened to rain H_2O on the days he was outside, no XYZ ever happened to come out of his faucets at home, etc.). After learning what water is to the complete satisfaction of his parents, friends, and teachers, Tommy is miraculously transported to Earth where there is to be found *only* H_2O (XYZ cannot exist in the Earth's atmosphere). Since there are no other difference between Twin Earth and Earth, Tommy blends in without trouble. Everything Tommy says about water (using the word "water") will correspond to what his Earthling friends say and believe about water (also using the word "water").

As you may have expected, the question, once again, is not what Tommy says, but what Tommy believes. Tommy, I submit, does not have the same concept as his Earthling associates. Therefore, what Tommy *believes* when he says "This is water" is not what his Earthling friends believe when they say "This is water." What Tommy means by "water" is *either* H_2O *or* XYZ. This, of course, is how we (knowing all the facts of the case) would describe it, not Tommy. If asked, Tommy will say that he means *water* by "water" and he surely does mean this. But the point is that more things qualify as water for Tommy than for the Earthlings. If we should reverse the scenario and imagine an Earthling miraculously transported back to Twin Earth with Tommy, Tommy's belief of a puddle of XYZ that it was water (i.e., an instance of the concept he expresses with the word "water") would be true, while his Earthling friend's belief would be false. Since this is so, they must be expressing different beliefs with the words "This is water."

Putnam takes this result as showing that meanings are not in the head. Tommy and his Earthling friends can be identical in all relevant respects; yet, they have different concepts, different beliefs, different meanings. My intuitions (about this example) agree with Putnam's, but the moral I want to draw from this story goes beyond, and in some ways contrary to,[8] the moral Putnam draws from it. I think this example neatly illustrates a principle expressed earlier, the principle, namely, that a system's representational capabilities are determined by its information-handling resources. Or, to give a more restricted (not to mention cruder) expression of the principle, an individual can believe (and, in this sense,

---

8 "Contrary to" because the conclusion I draw from this example (as embellished) is that the extension of a concept (like "water") is *not* determined by causal factors. The same things (e.g., H_2O) *caused* Tommy to use the word "water" during learning as caused his Earthling associates to use this word during learning. What determines the extension (and, hence, the concept) are not facts about causal relations, but facts about the kind of information available during learning. Information and causation are related but only indirectly.

represent) only what he has the information-handling resources of knowing.

The difference between Tommy and his Earthling friends is to be found in the difference in the kind of information to which they were made responsive during the learning period when they acquired their respective concepts. Given the situation on Twin Earth, Tommy, although repeatedly exposed to H_2O (and never XYZ), was never exposed to the *information* that the liquid he saw was H_2O. All he ever received, processed, and responded to was a piece of disjunctive information, the information, namely, that the liquid was *either* H_2O or XYZ. This is all the information Tommy got because, on Twin Earth, this is all that one could learn about the character of the liquid from ordinary sensory transactions with it. Since it was this piece of information that was used to shape Tommy's discriminatory and identificatory responses, *this* is the concept he acquired and *this* is the kind of belief he subsequently has about the liquids he describes as water.

Since XYZ cannot be found on Earth (and this is no mere accident but a law of nature), Earthlings acquire a different concept because their discriminatory responses are shaped by a different piece of information: the information that the liquid is H_2O.[9] Since the lawful regularities prevailing in these two worlds are different, the kind of information to be found in physically indistinguishable signals is also different. Hence, the concepts developed in response to these physically indistinguishable signals are also different. This is why Tommy and his Earthling friends, although they *say* the same thing, although they were exposed to exactly *the same* liquids during learning (viz., H_2O), and although they developed their ideas in exactly the same way, have quite different beliefs about the liquid they see and describe.

The important point to notice about this example is how the concepts one develops, and hence the sorts of beliefs one is thereby capable of holding, neatly reflect one's epistemological strengths and limitations. There is, as it were, an epistemological preestablished harmony. We (Earthlings) have a more determinate concept than Tommy, a concept that, if he possessed it on Twin Earth, he would be incapable of knowing

9 I here assume that it is a law on Earth (but not, of course, on Twin Earth) that anything exhibiting the normal sensible properties of water *is* H_2O. If this is too strong, then I assume that on Earth (but not, of course, on Twin Earth) one can come to know that something is H_2O by looking, tasting, smelling, etc. It is this fact that supports my claim (in the text) that on Earth (but not on Twin Earth) the ordinary sensory stimulation associated with our perception of water carries the, information that it *is* water (H_2O).

(by ordinary sensory means) whether it ever, in fact, applied to the liquid running out of his faucet. Given the widespread prevalence of XYZ, Tommy would make frequent mistakes. He would, in other words, have a real epistemological problem *if he had our concept of water.*[10] But he doesn't have our concept of water and, given that he learns in roughly the way we learn what water is, there is no way for him to get it. The concept he does acquire (a concept the extension of which I am expressing as "either H_2O or XYZ") is a concept that he is cognitively prepared to apply to his surroundings. He *can know* that the liquid coming out of his faucet is what *he* means by "water."

To put the point in its most general form: if someone lives in a place where it is impossible to distinguish A-type things from B-type things, hence impossible to know that this particular thing is an A (or a B), then it is likewise impossible, under ordinary learning conditions, to develop a way of representing something as an A (or as a B). The most that will be developed is a way of representing something as A-or-B. And in this case we needn't worry about mistaking an A for a B (or vice versa) since we can never *take* anything as an A or as a B.

4. CONCLUSIONS AND QUALIFICATIONS

I have been arguing for a perfectly general thesis, and I am afraid that it cannot be defended in its most general form. There are exceptions that I have suppressed for expository purposes. So, before trying to state the upshot of this argument, let me briefly describe the qualification that is essential.

My thesis is meant to apply to simple or primitive concepts (representational structures), concepts that are not themselves composed of simpler conceptual elements (representational structures). In arguing that the possession of the concept X requires the possessor to have the resources for picking up, processing, and responding to the information that something is X, the argument works only for simple, ostensively learned concepts. I do not wish to argue that we cannot *manufacture* out of a corpus of simple concepts, and the appropriate syntactical machinery, complex concepts for the application of which we lack the requisite

---

10 As I understand the Causal Theory (of natural kind terms), Tommy would (according to this theory) have our concept of water since, by hypothesis, H_2O figured *causally* (just as it did for Earthlings) in his acquisition of this concept. This, I think, shows what is wrong with a causal theory.

information-processing capabilities. That is, there are obviously beliefs involving complex concepts (e.g., the belief that X is a miracle, that Y is a random sequence, or that there are no unicorns) that we lack the cognitive resources for knowing to be true. And it certainly seems that with linguistically sophisticated creatures such as ourselves, these complex concepts will be commonplace. But there can be no complex concepts without simple concepts, and it is to these latter primitive representational structures that the thesis of this essay is meant to apply.

The upshot, then, of this essay is that no matter how we choose to describe the conceptual sophistication of an agent, whether it be a frog, a dolphin, a computer, or a human being, we are committed to that agent's having the cognitive resources for *knowing* how things stand with respect to the situation being represented – at least with regard to the agent's primitive concepts. This, I think, completely turns the tables on the skeptic. The traditional arguments that we cannot know what we purport to know because we lack the appropriate cognitive endowments, because the information on which we rely is always equivocal or ambiguous in some fundamental respect, are arguments that, if successful in relation to simple concepts, show not that we cannot know what we believe, but that we do not believe what we think we believe.[11] If the information we receive about Xs is always too impoverished to specify an X as an X, then, admittedly, we have an epistemological problem about how we can ever know that there are Xs. But we also have a problem about how we can ever believe that there are Xs.

11 If the reader thinks it *could not* show this (viz., that we do not believe what we think we believe), so much the worse for the view that we could entertain (simple) beliefs that we could not know to be true.

5

Two Conceptions of Knowledge:
Rational vs. Reliable Belief

There are two ways to think about knowledge. One way is to start, so to speak, at the bottom. With animals. The idea is to isolate knowledge in a pure form, where its essential nature is not obscured by irrelevant details. Cats can see. Dogs know things. Fido remembers where he buried his bone. That is why he is digging near the bush. Kitty knows where the mouse ran. That is why she waits patiently in front of the hole. If animals are not conceptually sophisticated, do not posses language, do not understand what it takes to know, then this merely shows that such talents are not needed to know.

If, then, pursuing this strategy, you want to find out what knowledge is, look at what Fido has when he sees where his food bowl is or remembers where he buried his bone. Think about Kitty as she stalks a bird or pursues a mouse. And this, whatever it is, is exactly what we've got when we know that the universe is over ten billion years old and that water is the ash of hydrogen. It is true that in its grander manifestations (in science, for example) knowledge may appear to be totally beyond Fido's and Kitty's modest capacities, but this is simply a confusion of *what* is known (recondite and well beyond their grasp) with knowledge itself – something they have (albeit about more humble topics) in great profusion.

This, as I say, is one way of thinking about knowledge. Call it the *bottom-up* strategy. It appeals to those philosophers who seek some naturalistic basis for epistemological theory, some way of integrating philosophical questions about knowledge, perception, and memory with

Reprinted from *Grazer Philosophiche Studien* 4 (1991), 15–30, by permission of the publisher.

scientific concerns about the psychological and biological mechanisms for implementing our cognitive transactions with the world. From a bottom-up point of view, knowledge is an early arrival on the evolutionary scene. It is what animals need in order to coordinate their behavior with the environmental conditions on which their survival and well-being depend.

There is, however, another strategy, something I will call a *top-down* approach to understanding cognitive phenomena. It takes its point of departure from Descartes, from traditional worries about skepticism, from the normative considerations that dictate proper methods of inquiry and appropriate standards for belief. White-frocked scientists, not furry pets, are the exemplars, the models, the ideal. Patient and objective inquiry, supported by observation, testing, and experiment, leading (if one is lucky) to confirmation of one hypothesis over its rivals – *that*, and not brute perception, is the yardstick to be used in taking the measure of knowledge. Knowledge is what you get when you conduct inquiry, and fix belief, in *that* way. The rest is, at best, true opinion or an inferior grade of knowledge.

According to this second, top-down, strategy, knowledge is the result of an assessment and evaluation procedure in which conclusions are reached from premises in conformity with rules that are, if not justified, then rationally justifiable. The whole process need not, in every instance (perhaps not even in *most* instances), take place in a conscious, deliberate way. It may sometimes occur automatically (when the requisite inferences become habitual) or at a level where the evidential connections are used in some unconscious way in arriving at, say, perceptual judgments.[1] Nonetheless, whether conscious or not, it is the justificational relations embedded in this inferential structure that determine the epistemic merit of any judgment emerging from that structure. Conscious, critical, rational inference is the ideal; it sets the standard. A belief is justified, and it constitutes knowledge, only insofar as the process by means of which it is reached conforms to canons of scientific inference and rational theory choice.

I call this a top-down strategy for obvious reasons: Einstein, not Fido,

---

1 I am thinking here of "problem-solving" approaches to visual perception associated with Helmholtz and, more recently, Richard Gregory. According to Gregory, for instance, the visual system evaluates incoming data (generally impoverished) and arrives at the best "hypothesis" about distal conditions. Such inferences, of course, occur at an unconscious level. One sees the bowl, but seeing it consists in the visual system reaching a conclusion, via an inference, and generally from ambiguous data, that there is a bowl.

is the model. If animals and infants know anything, it is only because we charitably adopt toward them (as we do with some machines) a "cognitive stance": we *say* (with an indulgent wink) that they know, remember, and see things, yes, but we do so in a figurative way. In central cases – and it is with the central cases that epistemology has been (or should be) concerned – we reserve knowledge for those with the capacity to reason and evaluate their epistemic situation, for those who understand what it *takes* to know and have grounds for thinking they have what it takes.

The recent controversy between internalists and externalists (on the analysis of knowledge) is, I think, an instance of this more general strategic difference. Externalists, those who think knowledge is a matter of getting yourself connected to the facts in the right way (causally, informationally, etc.), whether or not you know or understand that you are so connected, tend to be bottom-uppers. Fido is (through normal eyesight) connected in the right way to his food bowl; hence, he can see (hence, knows) that the bowl is there, next to the table. Internalists, on the other hand, those who require for knowledge some justificatory structure in an agent's beliefs, tend to be top-downers. It isn't enough to be tracking (Nozick's term for being properly connected to) the facts. One must also know, be justified in believing, have reason to think, one *is* tracking the facts. We require not just information, but information that *that* is what we are getting. Fido may be tracking the location of his bowl, but if he has no internal understanding of this fact, no capacity for evaluating the quality of information on which he relies to find the bowl, then he does not know where his bowl is in any important or epistemologically relevant sense.

I am a bottom-upper. Keith Lehrer is a top-downer.[2] I don't know where he went wrong. It could have been his move, many years ago, from the North's bracing externalism (you don't need reasons to *know* it is cold in Minnesota) to the internalist smog of Providence, Rhode

2 Maybe *top-middler* would be a better word to describe some of Keith's more recent compromising efforts between externalism and internalism (if calling both views false can be called a compromise). See Lehrer 1988, pp. 329–330; 1990, p. 15; and 1989, pp. 131–132, 147, for his "doxastic reliabilism" and the "monster theory." Although Keith concedes the necessity of some "external" condition on knowledge (beyond that of truth, which, as he notes, 1989, p. 132, is an externalist requirement that almost everyone accepts), his insistence that there be an "internal" (i.e., subjective) rational acceptance of the satisfaction of this condition, his insistence that one needs the information that one is getting information, makes him a top-downer (an internalist) in my classification scheme. As he says (1989, p. 131), coherence remains, for him, the central notion in epistemology.

Island. But wherever it was he picked up the internalist virus, it has been with him for at least thirty years. He now exhibits unmistakable symptoms of terminal top-downism. I don't expect treatment – especially from a bottom-upper like myself – to help much now. He's probably got the bug for life. Nonetheless, I would like to try poking around with a sharp (or as sharp as I can make it) instrument. Even if I don't succeed in curing the patient (and, realistically, I do not even expect to penetrate the skin), maybe I can provoke some responsive groans.

To begin with, it won't do (on the part of either side) to say that there are different, or perhaps many, senses of the verb "to know" and that the bottom-uppers (or top-downers, take your pick) are preoccupied with an irrelevant, an unimportant, a not-epistemologically central, or a not very interesting (or not very interesting *to us*) notion of what it means to know. This may well be true, but one can't just *declare* it, pick up one's toys (the interesting-to-me sense of knowledge), and go home to play by oneself. Lehrer, at times, threatens to do this. In dismissing the kind of knowledge that animals, young children, and brain-damaged adults have – *exactly* the sort of cases that bottom-uppers think are of central importance for understanding knowledge – Lehrer, for instance, says (repeatedly) that this is not the sort of knowledge that concerns him. These senses of the word do not, he says, capture the sense of knowledge that is characteristically human, that distinguishes us from other beings. "I am concerned," he says, "with knowledge that a being could in principle and with training articulate" (1988, pp. 330–331).

The question, of course, is whether there *is* a sense of knowledge that distinguishes us from inarticulate beings. Is there a sense of "hunger" or "thirst" that distinguishes us from animals and young children, who cannot *say* they are hungry or *articulate* what it is like to be thirsty? If we are inclined to think (as I assume most of us do) that animals and infants, although quite unable to articulate it, can be thirsty in pretty much the same way we are thirsty, what is wrong with supposing that Fido's *got* exactly what we've got – knowledge – but he can't express it the way we can? Fido knows his food bowl is over there by the table and I know his food bowl is over there by the table, and we both know this in pretty much the same way – we both *see* that it's there. I, to be sure, differ from Fido in many interesting ways. I can *say* not only *what* I know (that the bowl is over there), but *that* I know. He can't. I have a reasonable grasp of what it takes to know; he doesn't. I have read Edmund Gettier; he can't. On demand, I might even be able to concoct a pretty good argument (starting from premises about how things *seem* to me) that the bowl *is* over there by the table – something that is quite beyond Fido's feeble abilities. But why is any of this relevant to whether Fido knows exactly what I know – that the bowl is by the table – and knows it, furthermore, in exactly the way I know it, by seeing? If Lehrer is, for whatever reasons, more interested in studying the cognitive exploits of articulate and reasonably intelligent human beings, more concerned with what constitutes "critical reasoning" (1990, p. 36), well and good. Let him do so. If he wants to study the talents and capacities that make possible our most cherished scientific achievements, the discovery of the double helix, for instance, and our most worthy practical attainments, the development of a system of justice, for example (1990, p. 5), he has every right to do so. But why suppose that what *distinguishes* us from Fido – including the great many things we know that Fido cannot know – is relevant to whether Fido knows anything at all and knows it, furthermore, in the same sense in which we know things? Superior intellectual accomplishments, our capacity to engage in critical discussion and rational confrontation (1990, p. 88), are certainly not relevant to whether Fido eats, sleeps, and defecates in exactly the same sense we do. Why, then, suppose it relevant to whether Fido can see, know, and remember in the same sense we do? One cannot simply *assume* that these are different senses without begging the key issue separating internalists and externalists.

One can, if one likes, study the way astrophysicists differ from ordinary mortals in their knowledge of processes occurring in distant stars, but it would be a great mistake to think that just because *what* they know, and their *ways* of knowing it, are beyond the intellectual capacities of ten-year-old children, the feeble-minded, and chimpanzees, that, therefore, astrophysicists know things in a sense of the word "knowledge" that is different from that applied to ten-year-old children, the feeble-minded, and chimpanzees.

Even if we should suppose, with Lehrer, that there is some special sense of knowledge that we have that Fido lacks, a sense that requires not just having received the relevant information (which Fido receives too), but an appreciation, understanding, or justification (that Fido presumably lacks) that one has received such information, an ability to "defend" a claim that one knows (which Fido obviously lacks), we can still ask whether this is an epistemologically interesting, useful, or common notion, one that we actually use in our everyday descriptions of epistemic phenomena. When I say that my neighbor recognized the bird as a Roufus hummingbird, am I crediting her with good old everyday knowledge or am I crediting her with *advanced* or *metaknowledge* (Lehrer's term for the kind of knowledge *he* is interested in, the kind that Fido can't have; 1988, p. 331)? If she knows it's a Roufus hummingbird but does not *metaknow* it, doesn't know it in Lehrer's *advanced* way, who cares? We could choose to talk about advanced thirst and metahunger (the sort of hunger and thirst that only very smart people can feel), but what would this show about whether Fido, children, and brain-damaged adults were ever hungry? Maybe the gourmand means something special when he speaks about being hungry for a good meal, a sense of "being hungry" that Fido never experiences, but this doesn't mean that Fido is never hungry in that more common sense of hunger that characterizes most of our talk about human hunger. Maybe Keith Lehrer is a cognitive gourmet. Maybe advanced knowledge and metaknowledge are cognitive delicacies, served exclusively in the academic classroom (the recipes for which appear exclusively in books on epistemology).[3] The real cognitive issues, the ones we all care about, though, concern good old meat-and-potatoes knowledge.[4]

So let us not *beg* the question by declaring, at the outset, that we are interested in a special sense of the verb "to know" or in a special kind of knowledge. Barring convincing grounds for thinking otherwise, we should begin by assuming that people intend to be attributing pretty much the same sort of thing to scientists, babies, chimpanzees, and spiders when they describe them as seeing, knowing, sensing, recognizing, distinguishing, hearing, and remembering things. Perhaps we can agree to draw the line before we reach instruments and machines. Although we often speak of artifacts in cognitive terms – as sensing, remembering, knowing, and recognizing things – there are (as there are not with many animals) reasons to treat such descriptions as figurative or metaphorical. After all, machines are inanimate objects; they don't have beliefs and thoughts, the sorts of internal, subjective attitudes that are

---

3 Which seems to be the opinion of my undergraduate students.
4 Likewise, it is, I think, too simple to dodge skepticism by multiplying senses of "know" – conceding "know for certain" to the skeptic and keeping "know" for our practical everyday selves (see Lehrer 1990, pp. 178–179). This, once again, seems to be the tactic of letting everyone have his own toy to play with: the skeptic gets *his* toy, certain knowledge, and we keep our toy, knowledge. Everybody is happy, and we get to keep talking the way we always talked.

typically taken to be part of what is involved in knowledge.[5] Perhaps spiders and bacteria – very primitive organisms – do not have beliefs either. If so, then they, too, should be classified with the artifacts – as knowing, seeing, and remembering only in a special, figurative sense of these words.[6] But unless someone has reasons to think that small children, mental defectives, and chimpanzees don't even have beliefs (or whatever subjective state we take to be constitutive of knowledge), we do not have the same reasons to treat our attributions of knowledge to them as in any way special or metaphorical.[7] I am willing to concede, in other words, that insofar as there are reasons to think that organism O does not (or cannot) have beliefs, or does not (or cannot) have beliefs of type T, then there are reasons for thinking that O does not (cannot) know, or does not (cannot) know, things of type T. This, in fact, is why I think machines do not have knowledge. They do not have beliefs. This, in fact, is why I think animals do not (indeed, cannot) know such things as that there are more real numbers than rational numbers or that Fido will be eight years old next Monday. They cannot have beliefs of this sort. Having certain beliefs requires having appropriate concepts, and it is hard to see how animals, lacking a language, could have the more technical ones. That is why Fido and Kitty cannot know *many* of the things we know; they do not even have the conceptual resources for understanding them. This, though, tells us something about the conceptual limits of animals. Unless, however, we are prepared to argue that animals (young children, brain-damaged adults, and so on) have no

5 Although this may be disputed in certain circles (e.g., artificial intelligence and cognitive science), I assume it here since it is common ground between top-downers and bottom-uppers: both externalists and internalists require, minimally, something like belief on the part of the knower. Lehrer requires more than this minimum, but more of this in a moment.

6 I leave aside the attribution of skills and talents (knowing how) since these, even for the most primitive organisms, are (I assume) quite literal. Minnows know how to swim and spiders know how to spin a web. We are here concerned with factual knowledge, knowledge in what Lehrer (1990, pp. 3–4) calls the informational sense (although, of course, I reject his claim that knowledge in this sense requires one to *recognize something as information* (p. 3).

7 Lehrer, of course, has a more demanding condition on knowledge than simple belief. He describes this as *acceptance*, and what he means by acceptance is pretty fancy, a mental state that Fido and Kitty (however able they might be to have beliefs) cannot have (1990, pp. 113ff). He may be right in imposing this stronger condition, of course, but we cannot, at *this* stage of the argument, accept this stronger condition. To do so would beg the question against the bottom-uppers since animals, infants, and the feeble-minded (brain-damaged) cannot (in Lehrer's sense) *accept* anything.

beliefs *at all*, it does not tell us anything about knowledge itself, about whether they know, or can know, the things they *do* have beliefs about. The question we are asking, or *should* be asking, is not whether Fido believes anything at all,[8] but whether, assuming there are things Fido believes, which (if any) of these beliefs qualify as knowledge. And why? If he can *think* his food bowl is over there by the table, why can't Fido know it and know it, moreover, in exactly the same sense in which I know it?

Lehrer has made it quite clear what it is he thinks animals (very young children, brain-damaged adults) lack that disqualify them as knowers. He does not challenge them as *believers*. A two-year-old child, a dog, and a mentally retarded adult can (for some suitable values of P) *think* P. What they cannot do, for any value of P, however, is *know* P. The reason they cannot is that although they can *get* the information needed to know, and although this information may cause them to believe P, they do not have the information that it is information (1990, pp. 162–164).[9] They are "... unable to discern the difference between correct information and misinformation or even understand the distinction between truth and deception" (1988, pp. 332–333). They lack the concept of veracity (1990, pp. 8–9). They lack resources that we possess, the capacity for knowing or telling that what they are receiving is genuine information (1990, pp. 162–164). For all these reasons they fail to know the things they believe.

If we accept these conditions on knowledge, it means that although poor Fido can get (and use) information – information he clearly needs to find his food bowl, to avoid obstacles as he moves about the house, and to get the stick he is told to fetch – he has no way of knowing any of this. Fido does not know where his food bowl is (although he always finds it when he is hungry), never knows where the sticks are he is told to fetch (although he always brings them back), and cannot know where the doorway is (although he always manages to walk *through* it and not

---

8 I assume here that the disagreement between the top-downers and the bottom-uppers, between internalists and externalists, is not over the question of whether animals can think. That strikes me as an issue in the philosophy of mind that is seldom, if ever, broached (or argued for) in the epistemological literature. Until we have convincing grounds for thinking otherwise, then, I will assume that animals have beliefs (although *what* beliefs they have may be difficult to say). If they do not know anything, it is for some *other* reason.

9 If the information (that P) is not good enough (without the information that it is information) to know P, one wonders what good the information that it is information is without the added (3rd level) information that this (2nd level) information (about the 1st level information) *is* information.

into the adjacent walls). Since he cannot know these things, it follows that, despite having good eyesight, he cannot (ever!) *see* where his bowl is, where the sticks (that he fetches) are, or where the doorway is.[10]

To my ear, as (I assume) to most ears, all of this sounds most implausible. In fact, it sounds downright false. Obviously Fido can see where his food bowl is. Of course these children, even very young children, can see where things are – their toys and dolls, for instance. Only a philosopher in the grip of theory would think to deny it. If a theory of knowledge has, as one of its consequences, that animals and children cannot see where *anything* is, then it is time to get a new theory.

It is, furthermore, too early to drag in a distinction to rescue the theory. Too early to insist that . . . well, yes, Fido can see (hence, know) where his bowl is, or a child can see where her toys are, in *some* sense of see (and know), but not in the sense of see (and know) that is philosophically important, relevant, or interesting (they don't have *advanced* knowledge or *metaknowledge* of such things). As I indicated earlier, if, at this stage of the proceedings, this is to be anything but a question-begging and ad hoc rescue of an internalist theory, we need an argument – not just a bald claim – that such distinctions (between senses of "know") actually exist. For the same reason it is also question-begging (if not blatantly false) to classify such examples as "borderline" and, hence, not to be used against internalist theories. There is nothing borderline about these examples – not unless one has *already* made up one's mind about what is to count as knowledge.[11]

Bottom-uppers like myself prefer examples like the ones just given, examples involving sense perception, because it is here that justification, inference, reasoning, and evidence (the sorts of things that top-downers think important) seem least relevant – seem, in fact, totally irrelevant. We know it, just as Fido knows it, because we can see it. We don't have to reason about it, think about it, have a justification for believing it. The justification – if, indeed, this kind of talk even makes sense in this context – lies in the seeing. As J. L. Austin was fond of pointing

10 It follows on two assumptions: (1) If one sees where X is, then one sees that X is *there* for some value of "there" (e.g., under the sofa, in the closet), and (2) if one sees that X is there, one knows that X is there. Both assumptions strike me as obvious.

11 Lehrer comes close to suggesting that he can classify anything he likes as borderline (and, hence, ineligible as a counterexample against him) because (1990, p. 32) the reasons for his classification are "theoretical." Unless I miss something, this is a way of saying that his theory will decide which examples are relevant to testing his theory. A nice arrangement.

out, when things are in front of your nose, you don't need evidence for thinking they are there.

Top-downers like Lehrer prefer, of course, to talk about different examples: Madame Curie discovering radium, Sherlock figuring out who poisoned Colonel Mustard, and so on. Everyone, for perfectly understandable reasons, wants to emphasize the cases that best fit their theory. But although top-downers and bottom-uppers (for obvious theoretical reasons) choose different examples to motivate their analysis, they should, when talking about the "same" example, at least agree about whether or not it is a genuine instance of knowledge – whether or not the person or animal sees, remembers, or knows in some intuitive, *preanalytic* sense. If philosophers cannot even agree about the data, about the classification of cases to be accounted for by a theory of knowledge, then bickering about the right analysis of knowledge is as silly as it is fruitless. They are not even talking about the same thing.

So I think it important to agree about cases *before* we start disagreeing about the best way to understand them, about the best way to analyze them. The question, then, is whether Fido can see where his food bowl is and see this, moreover, in the same sense in which we (adult human beings) can see where his food bowl is.[12] The way *we* find out (come to know) where bowls (and a great many other common objects) are located is (typically) by seeing where they are. That, I should suppose, is the way Fido finds out (comes to know) where they are. This, I submit, is the judgment of common sense and common language. It is the way everybody talks in their unguarded (unphilosophical) moments. In the absence of (non-question-begging) reasons for rejecting such intuitive judgments, then, what a theory of knowledge should supply is, among other things, an account of what it is that Fido has when he knows (by seeing) where his food bowl is. If Fido doesn't have the capacity to distinguish truth from deception, if he doesn't know that what he is getting from the optical input is correct information, then this shows as clearly as anything could show that such higher-level capacities are not needed to know.

Lehrer, obviously, disagrees. He will have a chance to tell us why he disagrees. Since he will have that opportunity, I will attempt to focus the discussion by considering an example that he (1988, p. 333) adapts

---

12 We are assuming, of course, that the bowl is in plain sight, that everyone (humans and Fido) has excellent vision, and so on. No tricks.

from me (Dretske 1981). We are, remember, engaged in preliminary skirmishing. We are not yet arguing about the right analysis of knowledge. We are trying to get clear about what an analysis of knowledge is supposed to be an analysis *of* – what cases are to *count* as genuine knowledge, as instances of what a theory of knowledge is a theory about.

A gauge on a control console registers pressure in a boiler. A nervous engineer, worried that the gauge might fail (allowing the pressure to reach critical and dangerous levels), installs a safety device whose function it is to monitor the gauge (and the mechanism connecting it to the boiler) and flash a warning light if it should happen to malfunction. Sometime later, after the installation is complete, the warning light-flashes. The gauge registers 190. The engineer (Lehrer, for obvious reasons, calls her Faith) ignores the warning light and, trusting the gauge, comes to the belief (on the basis of the reading on the gauge) that the pressure is 190. As things turn out, everything is working normally *except* the newly installed safety device; it *mistakenly* signals a malfunction in the pressure gauge. The pressure gauge is operating normally, delivering (as it has always delivered) information about the pressure. It *says* the pressure is 190 and the pressure is 190. Faith, therefore, not only comes to have a true belief (that the pressure is 190), but comes to have it on the basis of a reliably functioning gauge.

What is one to say about such a case? Faith has a true belief about the pressure, and this true belief is reached by trusting a gauge that delivers information that the pressure is 190. It turns out she is right (about the pressure), but being right isn't good enough for knowledge. Lehrer (I infer) thinks that common opinion will agree with him in saying that Faith does not know what the pressure is. This is not to be counted as an instance of knowledge. Since, by extension, Fido is in no better position than Faith – they both trust, in an unreflective and uncritical way, an old source of information – Fido doesn't know either. So, whether or not, in the first instance, common sense agrees with him about Fido, it (Lehrer might urge) *should* agree with him and, perhaps, *will* agree with him once the "stakes" are made clear in this way. And if common sense *does* agree with him, then, of course, externalists (like myself) are in trouble. For what such examples clearly suggest is that it isn't enough to be connected to the facts in the right way (the way Fido and Faith are). If one is irrational, stupid, uncritical, or simply too trusting about one's sources of information, if one doesn't know that one is getting genuine information, one is, by commonsense standards, judged not to know. But being rational, critical, and intelligent about

90

one's sources is just what internalism (of the sort favored by Lehrer) asserts.

Lehrer thinks (and says) that externalists like myself will classify this case differently, that we will say that Faith *knows* the pressure is 190. If this were so, then, of course, we would be disagreeing about cases once again, and the implication would be that externalists, operating with a strong theoretical bias, and contrary to commonsense intuitions, are judging the case so as to fit their theory. But Lehrer is wrong about this. At least he is wrong about me. The reason he thinks we disagree about this case is because he has changed the example. He has converted it into a case where Faith, the person whose knowledge (or lack of it) one is asked to judge, is being described as quite *unreasonable* in trusting the gauge. Why, for example, does she ignore the flashing warning light? She knows (we are told) that it signals a malfunctioning pressure gauge, and yet, she inexplicably ignores the light and trusts the gauge. What a remarkably stupid thing to do. Lehrer is certainly right: it is hard to credit her with knowledge. I join Keith (and, I assume, commonsense) in saying that in such circumstances Faith doesn't know.

But although we agree about how to classify the example, we disagree about why Faith doesn't know. Lehrer says it is because Faith doesn't know she is getting accurate information from the gauge. Externalists, bottom-uppers like myself, would say that she lacks knowledge because knowledge requires, among other things,[13] getting information (being properly connected to the facts) in something like *normal* circumstances, and Faith's circumstances are not at all normal. It is one thing to see (and thereby come to know) what time it is by glancing at a familiar clock situated in a familiar setting (on the wall of one's home, say). It is quite another to trust the same clock when it is sitting, partially disman-

---

13   Lehrer keeps saying that I think that if a person receives the information that P, then she knows that P (1990, p. 33; 1988, p. 332). This, of course, is not true. Human beings (not to mention animals, gauges, computers, etc.) receive enormous quantities of information every minute. Most of this information does not result in knowledge. Knowledge requires the receipt of information, yes, but it requires *more*. It requires that this information *cause belief*, and cause it, moreover, in something like normal conditions (see discussion in text).

   Lehrer also insists that externalists overlook the fact that knowledge requires not only receiving information (satisfaction of the externalist condition) but also *acceptance* of the fact that one is receiving information (acceptance of the fact that this externalist condition is satisfied). I never overlooked this fact. The fact that the information that P causes a belief that P evinces an acceptance (not, of course, in Lehrer's sense, but in a relevant ordinary sense) of the fact that one is getting such information. The information *doesn't* cause belief in those who do not (in the required sense) accept it *as* information.

tled but still running accurately, on a workbench at the local repair shop. There is no reason why externalists like myself have to treat these cases in the same way. Although information is still being transmitted, it is no longer clear that that, in fact, is what is causing belief.[14]

So externalists, bottom-uppers like myself, can agree with Lehrer that in *his* version of the example, Faith does not know. We disagree (not unexpectedly – given our different theories) about *why* she doesn't know, but at least we agree about the data – agree about the fact that, measured against a commonsense yardstick, she doesn't know. What remains to be settled, and this brings us back closer to Fido's situation, is whether there is agreement about the example in its original version, a version that more closely approximates (and was deliberately designed to approximate) ordinary cases of perceptual knowledge.

In my original version of the example, the attendant, the one who ignored the warning light and trusted the gauge, was not the same person as the engineer who installed the safety device. Although the engineer knows what the flashing light means (and would, were he behaving reasonably, mistrust the pressure gauge), the attendant, the one whose knowledge was being assessed, did not. She was, therefore, *not* being irrational in trusting the gauge. She was merely trusting a source of information that had, over the weeks, months, or years she had used it, proven reliable. She was, in this respect, just like Fido, young children, or a brain-damaged adult. She was just like you and me during most of our waking lives when we unthinkingly trust what our senses, our friends, and our books and newspapers tell us. So the question that it is important to get clear about, the question I want to put to Keith, the question the example (in its original version) was meant to pose, is this: assuming a reliable source of information (e.g., the pressure gauge) and perfectly normal circumstances from the point of view of the potential knower (i.e., *my* version of the example), does one know when caused to believe by the reliable source? Does Faith know in *my* version of the example?

The existence of a malfunctioning safety device, and the (misleading) counterevidence it supplies, is really an irrelevant detail. This was origi-

---

14 The discussion about "relevant conditions" in the recent literature is an attempt to specify the sorts of conditions in which reliable connections (that produce belief) yield knowledge. The counterfactual analysis of conclusive reasons (Dretske 1969) and information (Dretske 1981) are attempts to use the "logic" of counterfactuals to determine relevant circumstances.

nally included merely to make it hard for people like myself (externalists, bottom-uppers). It makes the case harder for externalists because (I have found) the presence of this counterevidence (misleading though it be) is enough to persuade some people to say that Faith does not know (even when she satisfies most externalist conditions for knowing). If we remove this small detail, though, we get something that is, in most people's opinion at least, a paradigm case of knowledge: Faith seeing (by the gauge) what the pressure is. If this isn't knowledge, the sort of thing a theory of knowledge is supposed to count as knowledge, I, for one, fail to understand the project anymore. If Faith cannot see what the pressure is (hence, *know* what the pressure is) by trusting a perfectly operating gauge in completely routine circumstances, then there isn't much left for a theory of knowledge to account for. For, as most people will recognize, the gauge is merely a sensory prosthetic – an extension of our biological information delivery (= perceptual) systems. It plays no essential role in the dialectic. If we cannot rely on *it* as a trusted provider of information, then it is hard to see why we should be able to rely on our eyes, ears, and nose. Or, indeed, anything at all.

But if, without checking or conducting special tests, Faith can come to know by trusting a reliable instrument, an instrument that is, in fact, delivering the right information, why can't Fido know when he trusts the deliverances of his equally reliable senses when they are delivering the required information?

REFERENCES

Dretske, F. 1969. *Seeing and Knowing*. Chicago, Ill.; University of Chicago Press.
Dretske, F. 1981. *Knowledge and the Flow of Information*. Boston, Mass.; MIT Press/A Bradford Book.
Lehrer, K. 1988. "Metaknowledge: Undefeated Justification," in: *Synthese* 74, 329–347.
Lehrer, K. 1989. "Knowledge Reconsidered," in: *Knowledge and Skepticism*, Marjorie Clay & Keith Lehrer (eds.). Boulder, Co.; Westview Press.
Lehrer, K. 1990. *Theory of Knowledge*. Boulder, Co.; Westview Press.

Part Two

Perception and Experience

6

Simple Seeing

I met Virgil Aldrich for the first time in the fall of 1969 when I arrived in Chapel Hill to attend a philosophy conference. My book, *Seeing and Knowing*,[1] had just appeared a few months earlier. Virgil greeted me with a copy of it under his arm, whisked me off to a quiet corner in a local coffee shop, and proceeded to cross-examine me on its contents.

I confess to remembering very little about this conversation. I was, of course, flattered by the attention, and delighted to see his copy of the book full of underlining and marginalia. He had obviously been *studying* it. This fact so overwhelmed me that I found it difficult to keep my mind on the conversation. What could I have written that he found so absorbing? Did he like it? Did he agree with me? It was hard to tell.

Since then I have discovered what provoked Virgil's interest. It seems we disagree about what *seeing* amounts to – what it means, or what is essential to, our seeing things. This, by itself, is not particularly noteworthy since (as I have also discovered) many, and sometimes it seems most, philosophers disagree with me on this topic. The significance of Virgil's and my disagreement about visual perception lies not in the fact that we disagree, but in *how* we disagree. For it turns out that we are more or less natural allies in this area. We are both trying to resist what we view as a mistaken conflation of perception with conception, both trying to preserve the distinction between sentience and sapience, both trying to isolate and describe a way of seeing, simple seeing as it has

Reprinted from D. F. Gustafson and B. L. Tapscott, eds., *Body, Mind*, and *Method*, pp. 1–15, copyright © 1979 by Kluwer Academic Publishers, with kind permission from Kluwer Academic Publishers.
1   Chicago (1969).

come to be called, that is distinct from, but nonetheless fundamental to, an organism's higher-level cognitive and conceptual activities. Our disagreement arises over the nature of this phenomenon.

Since our first meeting Virgil has lobbed a few shells into this embattled terrain.[2] Some of these missiles had my name on them. Others, although not directed at me, fell suspiciously close. I therefore welcome this opportunity to return his fire. And while I have my finger on the trigger, I intend to spray some shot in other directions.

The point may not need emphasis, but let me stress, nonetheless, that the issue over simple seeing concerns our seeing of *objects* and *things* – not *facts* about these things. The terms "object" and "thing" are dummy terms intended to cover such disparate items as tables, houses, cats, people, games, sunsets, signals, tracks, shadows, movements, flashes, and specks. We see all these things and more. Since the perception of events, states of affairs, conditions, and situations introduces special complications that do not concern us here, I will confine myself to such ordinary things as rocks, robins, mountains, and people.[3] Simple seeing is seeing *these* sorts of things. What is *not* at issue is our seeing *that* there are rocks in the road, *how many* people are in the room, *where* the cat is, *whether* the clock has stopped, *who* is at the door, or *what* is happening. When the verb "to see" has a factive nominal (that . . .) or a question word clause (who . . . , whether . . . , what . . .) as its complement, a description of what someone sees has epistemic implications.[4] It implies something about the conceptual resources of the perceiver. One cannot see *where* the cat is unless one sees *that* she is (say) under the sofa – without therefore knowing (hence believing) that she is under the sofa. This

2   I refer, in particular, to "Visual Noticing Without Believing," *Mind*, Vol. LXXXIII, No. 332, October 1974; "Sight and Light," *American Philosophical Quarterly*, Vol. 11, No. 4, October 1974; "On Seeing What Is Not There," *Rice University Studies*, Vol. 58, No. 3, Summer 1972; and his critical review of my book in *The Journal of Philosophy*, Vol. LXVII, No, 23, December 10, 1970.

3   The requisite distinctions get messy, but I want to talk about the verb "to see" insofar as it takes a direct object and, more specifically, a concrete noun phrase as its direct object. I will not be concerned with seeing, say, the pattern, the answer, the problem or the trouble.

4   There are a variety of noun phrases that, when used as direct objects of the verb "to see," give the resulting statement epistemic implications. Aside from those mentioned in the previous footnote, we have *the color, the shape., the size*, and so on. Psychologists' interest in the properties or dimensions of things (rather than in the things having these properties or dimensions) tends, I think, to mislead them into thinking that all statements about what we see have cognitive implications, that all seeing is knowing (or believing). There is, however, a significant difference between seeing the round X and seeing the roundness of X (its shape).

much is (or should be) uncontroversial. What is controversial, and what concerns us here, is whether one can see *the cat* under the sofa in a way that is free of such discursive implications.

Almost[5] everyone agrees that one can see an X (a star, a rock, a cat) without believing (and, therefore, without knowing) that it (what is seen) is an X. I have seen stars that I took to be airplane lights, rocks that I took to be small animals, and cats that I took to be squirrels. Disagreement exists over whether *some* belief is necessary to the seeing, whether one can seen an X without taking it to be anything whatsoever. This is not a question about whether one can see an X without any beliefs *at all*.[6] Nor is it a question about whether, *in fact*, people have beliefs about the things they see. It is a question about whether their having a belief *about the perceptual object* is *essential* to its being a perceptual object — essential, that is, to its *being seen*.

It is easy enough to ignore this question, or to miss its significance, by changing the subject — by talking not of seeing (say) a triangle, but of perceiving triangles. On the basis, then, of a technical stipulation (or simply on the basis of prevelant usage) one notes that the term "perception" is reserved for those sensory transactions that have some kind of cognitive upshot. The subject (infant, rat, pigeon) does not perceive the triangle (among the rectangles) unless it *identifies* it in some way, unless it displays some appropriate *discriminatory* response, unless it *recognizes* the triangle, if not *as* a triangle, then at least as the sort of thing to which a particular conditioned response is appropriate. According to this usage, perception requires some degree of conceptualization, some identification or categorization of the sensory input. What one perceives is limited by the stock of concepts (or, if "concepts" is too strong a word, by the battery of disciminatory responses) one has available for sorting and organizing the flux of stimulation. If one doesn't know what a triangle is, if one lacks the capacity to distinguish between triangles and other geometrical figures, then one does not perceive triangles. Geometrical figures, perhaps, but not triangles.

If this is the way perception is to be understood — and I think this *is* the way it is commonly understood in both psychology and philosophy

---

5 *Almost* everyone. I have met those who did not agree (and *still* don't agree) that one could see a pencil, say, without recognizing it as a pencil.

6 I put this point badly in *Seeing and Knowing*, p. 17, footnote. I said there that it may be necessary for the seer to have some beliefs, but that no *particular* belief was necessary. This is confused. What I should have said is that no belief *about the object being seen* is necessary to the seeing.

– then our question about simple seeing is a question not about visual perception, but about whatever it is that we use the ordinary verb "to see" (followed by a concrete noun phrase) to describe. What are we doing when we see something? Or, if this is not something we *do*, what conditions must obtain for us to see a robin, a sunset, or a star? In particular, can one see a robin without perceiving it? This question may sound a bit odd, but only because one is accustomed to conflating *seeing* with *visual perception*. But if perception is (either by stipulation or common understanding) cognitively loaded, if some degree of recognition or categorization is essential to our perception of things, it is by no means obvious that one must perceive something in order to see it. Quite the contrary. One *learns* to perceive (i.e., recognize, identify, classify) those things that, even before learning takes place, one can see. What else, one might ask, does one learn to identify?

A second way to muddle issues is by interpreting claims about simple seeing, not as claims about our ordinary (mature) way of seeing robins, trees, and people, but as claims about an underdeveloped stage of consciousness, a dim sort of visual awareness, that lower organisms (perhaps) experience but that human beings (if they experience it at all) quickly outgrow during infancy. This confusion, I suspect, is nourished by the failure to distinguish between quite different theses. We have, on the one hand, the claim that:

(1) Simply seeing X is compatible with no beliefs about X.

On the other hand we have such claims as:

(2a) Simply seeing X is incompatible with beliefs about X,

and

(2b) Simply seeing X occurs only if, as a matter of fact, the seer has no beliefs about X.

It is (1) that gives expression to the relevant view about simple seeing. At least it gives expression to the only view I have ever propounded and thought worthy of defense – despite persistent efforts to interpret me otherwise. To say (as I did in *Seeing and Knowing*) that seeing a robin (nonepistemically) is belief neutral is *not* to say that one cannot see a robin in this way with a belief to the effect that it is a robin, a bird, or a thing. It *is* to say that your seeing the robin is independent of, a relationship that *can* obtain without, such beliefs.

In my correspondence and discussions with Virgil I have often compared seeing X to stepping on X. This had led to some unfortunate misunderstandings, but the comparison was meant to illustrate the difference between (1) and such possible misinterpretations as (2a) and (2b). Just as one can step on X *with or without* a knowledge of (or belief about) what one is stepping on, one can see X *with or without* a knowledge of (or belief about) what one is seeing. Seeing X, just like stepping on X, is *compatible* with no beliefs about X.

Which is *not* to say that seeing X is incompatible with holding beliefs about X, that if you *do* recognize what you see, if you *do* take it to be something or other, that you no longer see it in the relevant sense. This interpretation of simple seeing (in accordance with (2a)) would make it into some mysterious kind of relation totally irrelevant to our ordinary perceptual experience. For we *do* recognize much of what we see. I seldom sit down at my typewriter in the morning without believing it to be my typewriter. This doesn't mean I don't see it. I doubt whether there is any sense of the verb "to see" that is inconsistent with the subject's believing something about the object seen – just as I doubt whether there is any sense of the verb "to step on" that is *incompatible* with the subject's believing something about that on which he steps.

There are passages in which, if I read him right, Virgil takes me to be defending something like (2b). He suggests, for example, that if one looks with good eyes at a billiard ball at arm's length in clear light, and (not realizing that it is a billiard ball) wonders what that red, shiny, round thing is, then one is not seeing it in my sense (nonepistemically) because one already knows too much about it.[7] One knows that it is red, shiny, and round. At other times he seems to suggest that if the *report* of what is seen conveys information about what is seen, then it cannot be a report of what is simply seen in my sense.[8] I plead innocent to both charges. They misrepresent me as defending (2b) or possibly (2a). The second charge commits the additional mistake of confusing the report of what is seen with the seeing. One could as well argue that stepping on X is an epistemic act because a report of what is stepped on will convey information about what is stepped on.

I make a fuss about this issue because I have repeatedly had it suggested to me that nonepistemic seeing, or simple seeing as we are now calling it, is something that occurs only rarely in adult human beings. Perhaps lower organisms (goldfish?) see things nonepistemically; perhaps

7 "Visual Noticing Without Believing," p. 525.
8 Review of *Seeing and Knowing* in *The Journal of Philosophy*, December 10, 1970, p. 1002.

infants see things nonepistemically (before they can focus on objects); and perhaps adults sometimes see things nonepistemically (in their peripheral vision while they are attending to other matters); but the vast majority of our perceptual encounters involve something more sophisticated than simple seeing. This, I submit, is a confusion of (1) with either (2a) or (2b). Once one is clear about this, it should also become clear that the sense in which an adult human being sees a familiar object in clear light with good eyes (and, as a result, recognizes it) is the *same* sense in which a six-month-old infant, a chimpanzee, or a pigeon sees something that is totally unfamiliar. Seeing *what* something is is compatible with, and in most instances requires, simply seeing it.[9]

There is, finally, one last source of confusion that has helped to blur whatever genuine differences may exist among philosophers about the nature of simple seeing. This is the mistake of supposing that the seer is in some special, privileged position for determining *what* is seen and, therefore, *whether* something is seen. This doctrine takes its most extreme, and least plausible, form in the view that if S does not believe she sees X, then S does not see X. A less extreme, but still implausible, version has it that if S believes she does not see X, then S does not see X. Transposition of the first yields the result that one cannot see X unless one believes one sees X – a flat-out denial of the thesis (expressed in (1)) that simple seeing is compatible with no beliefs about X. The second, less extreme, version is not a direct denial of (1), but it does have the implication that seeing X is incompatible with certain beliefs: viz., the belief that one does not see X.

The fact is, however, that people are not authorities about what they see – not, at least, in the way suggested by the preceding two principles. Whether or not you saw my grandmother is a question that in some situations I am in a better position to determine than you. If you, with a mistaken idea of who my grandmother is, smugly assert that you did not see my grandmother today, I can correct you by pointing out that you certainly did: she was the woman to whom you gave your seat on the bus. If you respond by saying that you did not realize that *that* little old lady was my grandmother, the lesson is clear. The question was a question not about who you identified today, but about who you saw today. You may be the authority about what you *believe* you see, but

---

9 That this was my intention is clear from the fact that my analysis of primary *epistemic* seeing (seeing *that* so-and-so is such-and-such) requires the subject to see (nonepistemically) so-and-so.

this does not make you an authority about what you see. In situations of this sort, one sees X without believing one sees X – while believing, in fact, that one does not see X.

Although this is perfectly obvious on one level, the illusion persists that if S does not believe she sees X, or (worse) believes she does not see X, then there are special problems associated with the claim that she does, nonetheless, see X. If, upon returning from the dresser drawer, a man sincerely asserts that he did not see the cuff link, if this is what he really believes, then he must not have seen it. This, though, is the evidential sense of "must," the sense in which we might say, "Since he does not believe he has ever been to Hawaii, he must not have been there." S's beliefs on such matters are (at best) only evidence for what she sees. If S does not believe she saw X, the quality of this belief as evidence that she did not see X depends on whether S knows what Xs look like, the conditions (normal or abnormal) in which she saw X, and a host of other cognitive factors that are independent of whether or not she saw X. What a person believes (about what she sees), and what she is consequently prepared to assert or deny about what she sees, is conditioned by the conceptual and cognitive resources she has available for picking out and identifying what she sees. If she does not know what a marsupial is, she isn't likely to believe that she sees one. And if she mistakenly believes that kangaroos are the only marsupials, she might well believe she sees no marsupials when, in fact, she sees them (opossums) all over the yard.

There are strong philosophical motivations for denying any belief-neutral form of seeing (simple seeing). The inspiration for such denials comes, I think, from positivistic and (more specifically) behavioristic sources. If S's seeing X is only *contingently* related to S's beliefs about X, if she *could* see X with no beliefs about X, then there is no secure basis in S's behavior (linguistic or otherwise) for determining whether or not she does see X. Seeing is deprived of its logical or conceptual links with the observational data base.

This epistemological consequence is alarming enough to goad some philosophers into interpreting good eyesight as a cognitive capacity so as to secure the requisite links with behavior. If seeing X can be interpreted as a form of believing (if not believing that it is X, at least believing that it is Y where "Y" is a description that applies to X), then, since believing has behavioral criteria, seeing does also. One of the currently fashionable ways of achieving this linkage is by identifying psychological states with functional states of the organism. Since a functional state is one that transforms certain inputs into certain outputs, since it is *defined* by its associated input – output matrix (Putnam's machine table), an organism is in a determinate mental state (e.g., seeing *X*) only if its input is being converted into appropriate output – only if it behaves, or tends to behave, in a certain kind of way. If seeing *X* is (in part at least) a psychological state, if psychological states are functional states, if functional states are defined by the output they produce, and if output is (aside from simple reflexes, tropisms, etc.) indicative of beliefs, then all seeing is believing.[10]

There is much to be said for functional theories. From an evolutionary standpoint it is hard to see how a perceptual system could develop unless it had a role to play in an organism's continuing adjustment to its surroundings, and this adjustment is obviously a matter of an organism's *responses* to its environment. But a mechanism (e.g., our sensory system) can *have* a function without the operations of this mechanism having functional criteria for their successful performance. Cam shafts also have a function. They lift valves.[11] But this doesn't mean that cam shafts cannot operate in the way they were designed to operate without lifting valves. If the valves are not being lifted, this does not mean that the cam shaft isn't rotating *so as* to lift the valves. For in order for a cam shaft to perform its function it must have the cooperation of a number of other auxiliary mechanisms (rocker arms, lifters, guides, etc.). If these other elements are not functioning properly, the cam shaft makes its appointed rounds, operating in the fashion it was designed to operate, without the usual consequences. The valves don't get lifted. And so it is with seeing. Unless the cognitive mechanisms are in proper working order (and *learning* is required to put them into proper working condition) the sensory systems (those responsible for our seeing, hearing, smelling, and tasting things) can perform their role in this total operation without the kind of cognitive effects associated with a fully mature, and properly functioning, organism.

10   This sort of functional analysis can be found in D. C. Dennett's *Content and Consciousness*, London, 1969. See also Hilary Putnam's "The Nature of Mental States," in *Materialism and the Mind – Body Problem*, edited by David Rosenthal, Englewood Cliffs, N.J.; 1971, and David Lewis's "An Argument for the Identity Theory" in the same volume, reprinted from *The Journal of Philosophy*, Vol. LXIII, 1, January 6, 1966.
11   This example is taken from Fodor, *Psychological Explanation*, New York, 1968. For my purposes it makes no difference whether we refer to the cam shaft *as a cam shaft* or *as a valve lifter* (i.e., in explicitly functional terms) as long as it is clear that we are referring *to* the cam shaft (and not some larger functional unit).

I do not expect these brief remarks to satisfy functional theorists.[12] What is needed is some positive account of the role simple seeing plays in the process of gathering and utilizing sensory information. To this positive account I now turn.

Some of our beliefs are about the things we see: I believe that *that* is my wife, that *this* is a bushing, that *those* are oaks. Such beliefs are called de re beliefs; what they are about (that, this, those) is *not* determined by whatever description (if any) the believer may happen to have available for describing or picking out what it is that his belief is about. The referent of the belief, what it is a belief about, is fixed by factors other than those descriptive elements we may possess for its specification. It is fixed by what you see, not by what you believe you see or believe about what you see.

Suppose that you see Marvin and believe that he is Michael. What makes this belief a false belief about Marvin rather than a true belief about Michael? If asked who it is that you believe to be Michael, you can point. Or you can try to describe what you see, and what you believe to be Michael, in terms sufficiently detailed to allow your listeners to identify the object of belief: that fellow standing in the field, the person talking to Hilda, and so on. The point to notice about these descriptions (and the gesture of pointing) is that they *may or may not* succeed in picking out whom (or what) you believe to be Michael. If you have mistaken a tree stump for Michael, your belief is about *the tree stump*, not (as you say) about a person standing in the field (there may be no person standing in the field). If you are (unwittingly) looking into a mirror, you will not be pointing at the person you believe to be Michael (which is not to say that your listeners couldn't discover whom you were talking about from your gesture and knowledge of the mirror). And there needn't be anyone talking to Hilda for you to believe *of* the person or thing (that you *believe* to be a person talking to Hilda) that it is Michael.

At the risk of incurring Virgil's displeasure, let me don my funster hat for the moment and describe a mildly unusual case.[13] I have just copied a letter on a high-quality machine. At arm's length in good light the

---

12 I have tried to do a little better in "The Role of the Percept in Visual Cognition," *Minnesota Studies in the Philosophy of Science*, Vol. IX, edited by Wade Savage, Minneapolis, 1978.

13 This example is an adaptation of one used by my colleague, Dennis Stampe, to illustrate a similar point.

copy is indistinguishable from the original. I place the copy (thought-lessly confusing it with the original) neatly on top of the original (so that only the copy is visible), gaze down at it (them?), and notice what I take to be a smudge on the top sheet. As it turns out, I am mistaken (it was only a shadow) but, as chance would have it, the original (which I cannot see) is smudged in just the way I thought the top sheet was. I obviously have a number of false beliefs: viz., that this sheet is smudged, that this sheet is the original letter. What makes these beliefs false is the fact that they are (contrary to what I believe) beliefs about the copy. What, then, makes these beliefs beliefs about the copy and not about the original?

It will come as no surprise to find that the answer to this question is that my beliefs are about the first sheet (the copy), not the second (the original), because I see the first sheet, not the second, and my belief is about what I see. This answer isn't very illuminating. For we are now trying to say what it is that constitutes one's seeing the first sheet, what makes the first (not the second) sheet the *perceptual object* and, therefore, the thing about which I have a belief. Since what I believe (that it is smudged, that it is the original letter) about the perceptual object is true of something (the second sheet) that is not the perceptual object, what I believe about what I see does not itself determine what I see. What does determine this?

It will not do to say that I am seeing the copy because I am *looking at* the copy (not the original) since any sense of "looking at" that does not beg the question (e.g., you can only look at things you see) is a sense in which I am also looking at the original.[14] If the copy was removed (revealing, thereby, the original letter) my experience would not change in any qualitative respect. Convergence, accommodation, and focus would remain the same since the original is (for all practical purposes) in the same place as the copy. Obviously, then, these factors, no more than belief, determine what it is that I see. What does?

---

14   Sometimes Virgil seems to suggest that looking at X is sufficient for seeing X. For example, he says that there is a weak sense of simply seeing something in which "to be looking at something is to see it." "Sight and Light," *American Philosophical Quarterly*, October 1974, note on p. 320. I doubt whether there is such a sense of the verb "to see." He goes on to say, however, that he distinguishes seven senses of "simply see." Since it isn't clear to me whether these are supposed to be distinct senses of the ordinary verb "to see" (or special senses of a technical term "simply see"), and since I am not sure I understand Virgil's sense of "looking at," I hesitate to pin this view on him.

It may be said that there is one belief I have that is true of, and *only* true of, the thing I see: namely, that I see it (assuming I see only one thing). This gets us nowhere. For what makes my belief (that I see it) true *of* the copy, not the original? What makes the copy, not the original, the referent of "it"? Answer: the fact that I see the copy (not the original) and what I refer to with "it" is what I see. Since this is so, we are back to where we started: what singles out the copy as the perceptual object, as the thing I see?

I have no doubt exhausted the patience of causal theorists by this time. Isn't it clear, they will tell us, that the perceptual object is determined by the causal antecedents of our visual experience? Light is being reflected from the copy, not the original, and since it is *this object* that is (causally) responsible for the experience I am having, it is *this* object that I see. The fact that removal of the copy (exposing, thereby, the original letter) would leave the experience qualitatively unchanged, would perhaps (if it was removed without my knowledge) leave all my beliefs unchanged, is immaterial. It would change what I see because it would change the *causal origin* of the resultant experience.

Whether a causal account is ultimately satisfactory or not (I shall have more to say about this in a moment), it does succeed in driving a wedge between perception and conception. It divorces questions about what we see from questions about what, if anything, we know or believe about what we see. It distinguishes questions about the *etiology* of our experience from questions about the *effects* of that experience. Insofar as it achieves this separation it succeeds in capturing the essence of simple seeing.

The causal theory gets this part of the story correct, and it is for this reason that it represents such an attractive candidate for the analysis of simple seeing. It explains, among other things, how it is possible to have all one's beliefs about *X false* while still being *about X*. What makes my beliefs *about* the copy is the fact that I stand to the copy in the appropriate causal relation, the relation that, according to this view of things, constitutes my *seeing* the copy. What makes all my beliefs false is the fact that nothing I believe (e.g., that it is smudged, that it is the original letter) is true of the thing to which I stand in this causal relation.

The difficulties in articulating a full-dress causal analysis are well known, and I do not intend to rehearse them here. I mention two problems only for the purpose of indicating why, despite its attractive features, I do not personally subscribe to such a view. There is, first, the problem of stating just how an object must figure in the generation of a person's experience to qualify as the object of that experience. Typically, of course, there are a great many causal factors that cooperate to determine the character of our sensory experience. Price's distinction between standing and differential conditions is a useful one in this regard, but, as Grice has made clear, we need more than this.[15] When you hear a doorbell ring, you hear the bell ring, not the button being depressed, even though both events (the bell's ringing and the button's being depressed) are causally involved in the production of your auditory experience. Both are differential conditions. What, then, singles out the bell's ringing (not the button's being pushed) as the perceptual object? The causal theory has little to say in answer to this question.

A second problem has to do with the nature of the causal relation itself. Just what do we mean when we say that A causes B, that A is causally responsible for B, or that B is one of A's effects? There is remarkably little agreement among philosophers about the answers to these questions. This intramural squabbling would not be particularly embarrassing to a causal analysis of perception *if* the disputed issues were not themselves germane to the questions we wanted answered about perception. But this is precisely what is not the case. The absorption of photons by the photosensitive pigment on the rods and cones, for example, is a quantum process with all that this implies about the indeterminacy of such events. This indeterminacy can be made to manifest itself under conditions of extremely low illumination: whether the subject will see a faint light is, in principle, unpredictable.[16] Is this to be called a causal process? It depends on which philosopher one asks.[17]

We get information about things by seeing, hearing, smelling, tasting, and touching them. To say that someone has *seen* X is to say that information about X has been delivered in a particular form, a form that differs, intrinsically, from the way information is coded when we hear,

15 H. H. Price, *Perception*, 1932, pp. 69ff; and H. P. Grice, "The Causal Theory of Perception," *Proceedings of the Aristotelian Society*, Vol. XXXV, 1961, reprinted in *Perceiving, Sensing and Knowing*, edited by Robert J. Swartz, Garden City, N.Y., 1965.

16 See, for example, "The Quantum Theory of Light and the Psycho-Physiology of Vision" in *Psychology: The Study of a Science*, edited by Sigmund Koch, New York, 1959.

17 One standard view of causality makes the cause part of some *nomically sufficient* condition for the effect (the so-called Reliability Analysis). Since (if we take contemporary physics seriously) there is no sufficient condition for a photon's absorption, nothing *causes* it to be absorbed on this analysis of causality. This, then, constitutes a break in the causal chain between subject and object.

smell, taste, or touch X.[18] If we do not press too hard on the idea of causality, we may say that this information is delivered by means of causal mechanisms and processes. When we see X, X (or some event associated with the presence of X) initiates a sequence of events that culminates in a distinctive sort of experience, the sort we call a *visual* experience. Typically, this experience embodies information about the color, shape, size, position, and movement of X. The role or function of the sensory systems in the total cognitive process is to get the message in so that a properly equipped receiver can modulate her responses to the things about which she is getting information. The sensory system is the postal system in this total cognitive enterprise. It is responsible for the *delivery* of information, and its responsibility ends there. What we *do* with this information, once received, whether we are even capable of interpreting the messages so received, are questions about the cognitive-conceptual resources of the perceiver. If you don't take the letters from the mailbox, or if you can't understand them once you do, don't blame the postal system. It has done its job. The trouble lies elsewhere.

This, in barest outline, is an information-theoretical account of simple seeing. It differs from a causal account not by denying that causal processes are at work in the delivery of information, but by denying that this is the *essence* of the matter. Seeing X is getting information (coded in a certain way) about X, and if information about X can be delivered by noncausal processes, so much the worse for causality. If the processes by means of which we see very faint stars are infected with the uncertainty, the inherent randomness, of quantum phenomena, and if such processes are not to be counted as causal in nature, then we see things to which we do not stand in the appropriate causal relation. But we still *see* them, and the reason we do is because the experience that is generated by the occurrence of these inherently random events embodies information about the distant stars (e.g., *where* they are).

I should want to say the same thing about the factors that Virgil finds so important to our seeing things: ocular focusing, binocular convergence, accommodation, illumination, and so on. Doubtless these things

18 The key to vision is not *what information* is delivered (information about the color, shape, and size of things) but *how* this information is delivered. We can, of course, *see* that something is hot, hard, or salty (by looking at the litmus paper). What makes these cases of *seeing* is that this information is delivered in characteristically visual form (roughly: in terms of the way things *look* rather than the way they feel or taste). Virgil. ("Sight and Light," p. 319) attributes to me the view that seeing is determined by *what we can tell* (about objects) rather than (as I believe) *how we tell it*.

are important. Ask an ophthalmologist. But, again, they don't touch the essence of simple seeing. They don't isolate what is essential to our seeing things. As things stand, I cannot see much if my eyeballs point in different directions. But a fish can. I cannot see the window frame very clearly if I focus on the trees I see *through* the window. But I do, sometimes, see the window frame *and* the trees. I may not be able to identify, or tell you much about, the other children playing in the schoolyard if I concentrate my attention on the little girl jumping rope. But it seems to me obvious that I see a great many children *besides* the one I watch. Look at a flag for a few moments. How many stars do you see? If the flag has fifty stars, and none of them are obscured by folds in the cloth or by other objects, it seems reasonable enough to say you saw them all. *All fifty.* Which one or ones did you *notice*? It sounds odd (at least to my ear) to say that you noticed every star on the flag, but not at all odd to say you saw them all.[19] What makes our visual experience the rich and profuse thing we know it to be is that we see *more* than we can ever notice or attend to. The sensory systems, and in particular the visual system, delivers more information than we can ever (cognitively) digest. The postal system deposits junk mail at a rate that exceeds our capacity to read it.

In speaking of sensory systems in the way that I have, as systems responsible for the delivery of information, it should be emphasized that the term "information" is being used here in the way we speak of light (from a star) as carrying information about the chemical constitution of the star or the way the height of a mercury column (in a thermometer) carries information about the temperature. These events or states of affairs carry or embody information about something else but, of course, no one may succeed in *extracting* that information. It is in this sense that our visual (auditory, tactual, etc.) experience embodies information about our surroundings. It can carry this information without the sub-ject's (undergoing the experience) ever extracting that information for

---

19 If I understand him correctly, Virgil would like to deny that peripherally seen objects are really seen or that we see the other stars on the flag if we notice, say, only the slightly off-color star on the upper right. "Acute full-fledged seeing, in the basic sense, requires undivided visual attention, and this involves full ocular concentration" ("Visual Noticing Without Believing," p. 521). Once again I am reluctant to attribute this view to him since I don't think I understand what he means by *noticing* something. Since he also distinguishes between "consummated" and "unconsummated" basic seeing, and takes some seeing *as more basic* than others, the issues are clouded by this fragmentation in senses of "seeing."

cognitive purposes. Once again, *learning* is required to crack the sensory codes.

In *Seeing and Knowing* I tried to distinguish this information-theoretical approach to simple seeing (or, as I then called it, "nonepistemic seeing") from a causal account by asking the reader to imagine someone able to tell what the objects on the far side of a massive wall were doing, what color they were, their shape and size, without any transmission of light between the objects and the subject. The point of this exercise was to illustrate that it was the delivery of information, not the causal connection, that was essential to our seeing things. As long as information about X is getting through, and as long as this information is being delivered in characteristically visual form, then X is being seen whether or not there is a causal process responsible for the delivery of this information. If it is found that the eyes played no essential role in this process, if light is unnecessary, then so much the worse for the standard scientific accounts of *how* we see. As a child I never found the visual exploits of Superman (seeing through buildings) incoherent or *logically* paradoxical. I still don't. This was just a fanciful ("fanciful" because, *as things stand*, no one can see things in this way) account of an extraordinary individual who could see things *in ways* that no one else could. Historians tell me that the ancients had even more bizarre conceptions of how we see things. They were wrong about *how* we see, but they weren't committing logical howlers.[20] They just didn't know, as we now know, how we obtain information about distant objects and events.

My earlier account of simple seeing as visual differentiation was (as I would now express it) a way of describing the subject's visual experience so as to ensure that it did carry information about the object seen. As long as X is differentiated from its background and surroundings in the relevant way, the experience embodies information about the relative size, shape, position, and movement of X. If light is being reflected from X in such a way that X is not visually differentiated from its background (e.g., a white sheet of paper fastened to a white wall at fifty paces), then, although light from X is being received, although the subject is *looking*

---

20 Virgil says ("Sight and Light," p. 319) that the suggestion that one might see the yellow of wax with cosmic rays is a logical howler. He goes on to explain that yellow already is another wave frequency, and cautions the reader to be careful about saying that this is a "contingent fact" I have tried to be careful, and I have the greatest respect for Virgil's conceptual acuity; but I confess to hearing only contingent falsehoods where he hears conceptual howlers.

at and *focussing on* X, no information about the size, shape, whereabouts, or movement of X is being received. Under such circumstances X cannot be seen.

My talk of experiences and their intrinsic qualities may sound quaint to contemporary ears. It sounds mentalistic – like an old ghost in a new machine.[21] Quite frankly, it is *intended* to sound mentalistic, but not in the way a dualist understands this. It is intended to sound mentalistic to precisely the degree that our talk of *seeing* things sounds mentalistic. We are, after all, trying to give an account of one important aspect of our conscious life. Why, in pursuit of that end, should one be forbidden to talk about our sensory experience? This needn't be a way of talking about images in the head, little pictures, muffled sounds, and diluted tastes monitored by an ethereal homunculus. To talk about our sensory experience is simply to talk about certain *internal* events and processes (internal in the sense of being distinct from either input or output) that are essential to one's seeing, hearing, and smelling things. What is important about these internal events, insofar as we are interested in the difference between seeing X and hearing X, is their intrinsic properties – *how* they code the information about X. This is mentalism, yes, but (as Fodor so nicely puts it[22]) a version of mentalism that contrasts not with materialism, but with behaviorism.

It seems to me, then, that one cannot formulate a satisfactory account of simple seeing by embellishing the Causal Theory with details about the way, in fact, we see things. All one gets is a bloated concept of seeing. Seeing objects is a way of getting information about them. What makes it seeing (rather than, say, hearing) is the intrinsic character of those events occurring in us that carry the information. What makes it X (rather than Y) that we see is that the information these internal events carry is information about X (rather than Y). Everything else, I submit, is empirical icing on the conceptual cake – something the scientist, not the philosopher, should provide.

---

21 My talk of experience in this connection is (I think) what prompts Virgil to charge me
    with mentalism and assorted other Cartesian sins.
22 *Psychological Explanation*, Chapter 2.

7

Conscious Experience[1]

There is a difference between hearing Clyde play the piano and seeing him play the piano. The difference consists in a difference in the kind of experience caused by Clyde's piano playing. Clyde's performance can also cause a belief – the belief that he is playing the piano. A perceptual belief that he is playing the piano must be distinguished from a perceptual experience of this same event. A person (or an animal, for that matter) can hear or see a piano being played without knowing, believing, or judging that a piano is being played. Conversely, a person (I do not know about animals) can come to believe that Clyde is playing the piano without seeing or hearing him do it – without experiencing the performance for herself.

This distinction between a perceptual experience of x and a perceptual belief about x is, I hope, obvious enough. I will spend some time enlarging upon it, but only for the sake of sorting out relevant interconnections (or lack thereof). My primary interest is not in this distinction but, rather, in what it reveals about the nature of conscious experience and, thus, consciousness itself. For unless one understands the difference between a consciousness of things (Clyde playing the piano) and a consciousness of facts (that he is playing the piano), and the way this difference depends, in turn, on a difference between a concept-free mental state (e.g., an experience) and a concept-charged mental state (e.g., a belief), one will fail to understand how one can have conscious experiences without being aware that one is having them. One will fail

1 I am grateful to Berent Enc, Güven Guzeldere, Lydia Sanchez, Ken Norman, David Robb, and Bill Lycan for critical feedback. I would also like to thank the Editor and anonymous referees of *Mind* for a number of very helpful suggestions.

to understand, therefore, how an experience can be conscious without anyone's – including the person having it – being conscious of having it. Failure to understand how this is possible constitutes a failure to understand what makes something conscious and, hence, what consciousness is.

The possibility of a person's having a conscious experience she is not conscious of having will certainly sound odd, perhaps even contradictory, to those philosophers who (consciously or not) embrace an inner spotlight view of consciousness according to which a mental state is conscious insofar as the light of consciousness shines *on* it – thus making one conscious *of* it.[2] It will also sound confused to those like Dennett (1991) who, although rejecting theater metaphors (and the spotlight images they encourage), espouse a kind of first-person operationalism about mental phenomena that links conscious mental states to those that can be reported and of which, therefore, the reporter is necessarily aware of having.

There is, however, nothing confused or contradictory about the idea of a conscious experience that one is not conscious of having. The first step in understanding the nature of conscious experience is understanding why this is so.

1. AWARENESS OF FACTS AND AWARENESS OF THINGS[3]

For purposes of this discussion I regard "conscious" and "aware" as synonyms. Being conscious of a thing (or fact) is being aware of it. Accordingly, "conscious awareness" and "consciously aware" are redundancies.

A. White (1964) describes interesting differences between the ordinary use of "aware" and "conscious." He also describes the different liaisons they have to noticing, attending, and realizing. Although my treatment of these expressions (for the purposes of this inquiry) as synonymous blurs some of these ordinary distinctions, even (occasionally) violating some of the strictures White records, nothing essential to my

---

2 I am thinking here of those who subscribe to what are called higher-order thought (HOT) theories of consciousness, theories that hold that what makes an experience conscious is its being an object of some higher-order thought or experience. See Rosenthal (1986, 1990, 1991), Armstrong (1968, 1980, especially Ch. 4, "What Is Consciousness?"), and Lycan (1987, 1992). I return to these theories in §4.

3 This section is a summary and minor extension of points I have made elsewhere; see especially Dretske (1969, 1978, 1979).

project is lost by ignoring the niceties. No useful theory of consciousness can hope (nor, I think, should it even aspire) to capture all the subtle nuances of ordinary usage.

By contrasting our awareness of things (x) with our awareness of facts (that P) I mean to be distinguishing particular (spatial) objects and (temporal) events[4] on the one hand from facts involving these things on the other. Clyde (a physical object), his piano (another object), and Clyde's playing his piano (an event) are all things as I am using the word "thing"; that he is playing his piano is a fact. Things are neither true nor false, although, in the case of events, states of affairs, and conditions, we sometimes speak of them as what makes a statement true. Facts are what we express in making true statements about things. We describe our awareness of facts by using a factive complement, a that-clause, after the verb; we describe our awareness of things by using a (concrete) noun or noun phrase as direct object of the verb. We are aware of Clyde, of his piano, and of Clyde's playing his piano (things); we are also aware that he is playing the piano (a fact).

Seeing, hearing, and smelling x are ways of being conscious of x.[5] Seeing a tree, smelling a rose, and feeling a wrinkle is to be (perceptually) aware (conscious) of the tree, the rose, and the wrinkle. There may be other ways of being conscious of objects and events. It may be that thinking or dreaming about Clyde is a way of being aware of Clyde without perceiving him.[6] I do not deny it (although I think it stretches usage). I affirm only the converse: that to see and feel a thing is to be (perceptually) conscious of it. And the same is true of facts: to see, smell, or feel that P is to be (or become) aware that P. Hence,

---

4   When I speak of events I should be understood to be including any of a large assortment of entities that occupy temporal positions (or duration): happenings, occurrences, states, states of affairs, processes, conditions, situations, and so on. In speaking of these as temporal entities, I do not mean to deny that they have spatial attributes – only that they do so in a way that is derived from the objects to which they happen. Games occur in stadiums because that is where the players are when they play the game. Movements (of a passenger, say) occur in a vehicle because that is where the person is when she moves.
5   White (1964, p. 42) calls "aware" a polymorphous concept (p. 6); it takes many forms. What it is to become or be aware of something depends on what one is aware of. To become aware of a perceptual object takes the form of seeing or hearing or smelling or tasting or feeling it.
6   One must distinguish Clyde from such things as Clyde's location, virtues, etc. One can be aware of Clyde's location and virtues without, at the time, perceiving them. But unlike Clyde, his virtues and location are not what I am calling things. See the later discussion of abstract objects.

(1) S sees (hears, etc.) x (or that P) $\Rightarrow$ S is conscious of x (that P).[7]

In this essay I shall be mainly concerned with *perceptual* forms of consciousness. So when I speak of S's being conscious (or aware) of something I will have in mind S's seeing, hearing, smelling, or in some way sensing a thing (or fact).

Consciousness of facts implies a deployment of concepts. If S is aware that x is F, then S has the concept F and uses (applies) it in his awareness of x.[8] If a person smells that the toast is burning, thus becoming aware that the toast is burning, this person applies the concept *burning* (perhaps also the concept *toast*) to what he smells. One cannot be conscious that the toast is burning unless one understands what toast is and what it means to burn – unless, that is, one has the concepts needed to classify objects and events in this way. I will follow the practice of supposing that our awareness of facts takes the form of a belief. Thus, to smell that the toast is burning is to be aware that the toast is burning is to believe that the toast is burning. It is conventional in epistemology to assume that when perceptual verbs take factive nominals as complements, what is being described is not just belief but knowledge. Seeing or smelling that the toast is burning is a way of coming to *know* (or, at least, verifying the knowledge) that the toast is burning. It will be enough for present purposes if we operate with a weaker claim: that perceptual awareness of facts is a mental state or attitude that involves the possession and use of concepts, the sort of cognitive or intellectual capacity involved in thought and belief. I will, for convenience, take belief (that P) as the normal realization of an awareness that P.

Perceptual awareness of facts has a close tie with behavior – with, in particular (for those who have language), an ability to *say* what one is aware of. This is not so with a consciousness of things. One can smell or see (hence, be conscious of) burning toast while having little or no

---

7 I will not try to distinguish direct from indirect forms of perception (and, thus, awareness). We speak of seeing Michael Jordan on TV. If this counts as seeing Michael Jordan, then (for purposes of this essay) it also counts as being aware or conscious of Michael Jordan (on TV). Likewise, if one has philosophical scruples about saying one smells a rose or hears a bell – thinking, perhaps, that it is really only scents and sounds (not the objects that give off those scents or make those sounds) that one smells and hears – then when I speak of being conscious of a flower (by smelling) or bell (by hearing), one can translate this as being indirectly conscious of the flower via its scent and the bell via the sound it makes.

8 Generally speaking, the concepts necessary for awareness of facts are those corresponding to terms occurring obliquely in the clause (the that-clause) describing the fact one is aware of.

understanding of what toast is or what it means to burn. "What is that strange smell?" might well be the remark of someone who smells burning toast but is ignorant of what toast is or what it means to burn something. The cat can smell, and thus be aware of, burning toast as well as the cook, but only the cook will be aware that the toast is burning (or that it is the toast that is burning).

The first time I became aware of an armadillo (I saw it on a Texas road), I did not know what it was. I did not even know what armadillos were, much less what they looked like. My ignorance did not impair my eyesight, of course. I saw the animal. I was aware of it ahead of me on the road. That is why I swerved. Ignorance of what armadillos are or of how they look can prevent someone from being conscious of certain facts (that the object crossing the road is an armadillo) without impairing in the slightest one's awareness of the things – the armadillos crossing roads – that (so to speak) constitute these facts. This suggests the following important result. For all things (as specified earlier) x and properties F,

(2) S is conscious of $x \Rightarrow$ S is conscious that x is F.

Although (2) strikes me as self-evident, I have discovered, over the years, that it does not strike everyone that way. The reason it does not (I have also found) is usually connected with a failure to appreciate or apply one or more of the following distinctions. The first two are, I hope, more or less obvious. I will be brief. The third will take a little longer.

(a) *Not Implying vs. Implying Not.* There is a big difference between denying that A implies B and affirming that A implies not-B (2) does not affirm, it denies, an implication. It does not say that one can be aware of a thing only by *not* being aware of what it is.

(b) *Implication vs. Implicature.* The implication (2) denies is a logical implication, not a Gricean (1989) implicature. *Saying* you are aware of an F (i.e., a thing, x, which is F) implies (as a conversational implication) that you are aware that x, is F. Anyone who said he was conscious of (e.g., saw or smelled) an armadillo would (normally) imply that he thought it was an armadillo. This is true but irrelevant.

(c) *Concrete Objects vs. Abstract Objects.* When perceptual verbs (including the generic "aware of" and "conscious of") are followed by abstract nouns (the difference, the number, the answer, the problem, the size, the color) and interrogative nominals (where the cat is, who he is talking to, when they left), what is being described is normally an awareness of some (unspecified) fact. The abstract noun phrase or interrogative nominal stands in for some factive clause. Thus, seeing (being conscious of) the difference between A and B is to see (be conscious) *that* they differ. If the problem is the clogged drain, then to be aware of the problem is to be aware that the drain is clogged. To be aware of the problem, it isn't enough to be aware of (e.g., to see) the thing that is the problem (the clogged drain). One has to see (the fact) *that* it is clogged. Until one becomes aware of this fact, one hasn't become aware of the problem. Likewise, to see where the cat is hiding is to see that it is hiding *there*, for some value of "there."

This can get tricky and is often the source of confusion in discussing what can be observed. This is not the place for gory details, but I must mention one instance of this problem since it will come up again when we discuss which aspects of experience are conscious when we are perceiving a complicated scene. To use a traditional philosophical example, suppose S sees a speckled hen on which there are (on the facing side) twenty-seven speckles. Each speckle is clearly visible. Not troubling to count, S does not realize that (hence, is not aware that) there are twenty-seven speckles. Nonetheless, we assume that S looked long enough, and carefully enough, to see each speckle. In such a case, although S is aware of all twenty-seven speckles (things), he is not aware of the number of speckles because being aware of the number of speckles requires being aware that there is that number of speckles (a fact), and S is not aware of this fact.[9] For epistemological purposes, abstract objects are disguised facts; you cannot be conscious of these objects without being conscious of a fact.

(2) is a thesis about concrete objects. The values of x are *things* as this was defined earlier. Abstract objects do not count as things for purposes of (2). Hence, even though one cannot see the difference between A and B without seeing that they differ, cannot be aware of the number of speckles on the hen without being aware that there are twenty-seven, and cannot be conscious of an object's irregular shape without being conscious that it has an irregular shape, this is irrelevant to the truth of (2).

As linguists (e.g., Lees, 1963, p. 14) observe, however, abstract nouns may appear in copula sentences opposite both factive (that) clauses and concrete nominals. We can say that the problem is *that his tonsils are inflamed* (a fact); but we can also say that the problem is, simply, *his*

---

9 I am here indebted to Perkins's (1983, pp. 295–305) insightful discussion.

(inflamed) *tonsils* (a thing). This can give rise to an ambiguity when the abstract noun is the object of a perceptual verb. Although it is, I think, normal to interpret the abstract noun as referring to a fact in perceptual contexts, there exists the possibility of interpreting it as referring to a thing. Thus, suppose that Tom at time t_1 differs (perceptibly) from Tom at t_2 only in having a moustache at t_2. S sees Tom at both times but does not notice the moustache – is not, therefore, aware that he has grown a moustache. Since, however, S spends twenty minutes talking to Tom in broad daylight, it is reasonable to say that although S did not notice the moustache, he (must) nonetheless have seen it.[10] If S did see Tom's moustache without (as we say) registering it at the time, can we describe S as seeing, and thus (in this sense) being aware of, a difference in Tom's appearance between t_1 and t_2? In the factive sense of awareness (the normal interpretation, I think), no; S was not aware that there was a difference. S was not aware at t_2 that Tom had a moustache. In the thing sense of awareness, however, the answer is yes. S was aware of the moustache at t_2, something he was not aware of at t_1, and the moustache is a difference in Tom's appearance.

If, as in this example, "the difference between *A* and *B*" is taken to refer not to the fact that *A* and *B* differ, but to a particular element or condition of *A* and *B* that constitutes their difference, then seeing the difference between *A* and *B* would be seeing this element or condition – a thing, not a fact. In this thing sense of "the difference" a person or animal who had not yet learned to discriminate (in any behaviorally relevant way) between (say) two forms might nonetheless be said to see (and in this sense be aware of) the difference between them if it saw the parts of one that distinguished it from the other. When two objects differ in this perceptible way, one can be conscious of the thing (speckle, line, star, stripe) that is the difference without being conscious of the difference (= conscious *that* they differ). In order to avoid confusion about this critical (for my purposes) point, I will, when speaking of our awareness or consciousness of something designated by an abstract noun or phrase (the color, the size, the difference, the number, etc.), always specify whether I mean thing-awareness or fact-awareness. To be thing-

---

10 If it helps, the reader may suppose that later, at t_3, S remembers having seen Tom's moustache at t_2 while being completely unaware at the time (i.e., at t_2) that Tom had a moustache. Such later memories are not essential (S may see the moustache and *never* realize he saw it), but they may, at this point in the discussion, help calm verificationists' anxieties about the example.

aware of a difference is to be aware of the thing (some object, event, or condition, x) that makes the difference. To be fact-aware of the difference is to be aware of the fact that there is a difference (not necessarily the fact that x is the difference). In the previous example, S was thing-aware, but not fact-aware, of the difference between Tom at t_1 and t_2. He was (at t_2) aware of the thing that made the difference, but not fact-aware (at t_2 or later) of this difference.

So much by way of clarifying (2). What can be said in its support? I have already given several examples of properties or kinds, F, that are such that one can be aware of a thing that is F without being aware that it is F (an armadillo, burning toast, a moustache). But (2) says something stronger. It says that there is no property F that is such that an awareness of a thing that is F requires an awareness of the fact that it is F. It may be felt that this is much too strong. One can, to be sure, see armadillos without seeing that they are armadillos, but perhaps one must, in order to see them, see that they are (say) animals of some sort. To see x (which is an animal) is to see that it is an animal. If this sounds implausible (one can surely mistake an animal for a rock or a bush) maybe one must, in seeing an object, at least see that it is an object of some sort. To be aware of a thing is at least be aware that it is . . . how shall we say it? . . . a thing. *Something or other.* Whether or not this is true depends, of course, on what is involved in being aware that a thing is a thing. Since we can certainly see a physical object without being aware that it is a physical object (we can think we are hallucinating), the required concept F (required to be aware that x is F) cannot be much of a concept. It seems most implausible to suppose that infants and animals (presumably, conscious of things) have concepts of this sort. If the concept one must have to be aware of something is a concept that applies to *everything* one can be aware of, what is the point of insisting that one must have it to be aware?

I therefore conclude that awareness of things (x) requires no fact-awareness (that x is F, for any F) of those things.[11] Those who feel that this conclusion has too little support are welcome to substitute a weaker version of (2): namely, there is no *reasonably specific property* F that is such that awareness of a thing that is F requires fact-awareness that it is F. This will not affect my use of (2).

---

11 For further arguments see Dretske (1969, Ch. 2; 1979; 1981, Ch. 6) and my reply to Heil in McLaughlin (1991, pp. 180–185).

2. CONSCIOUS BEINGS AND CONSCIOUS STATES

Agents are said to be conscious in an intransitive sense of this word (he regained consciousness) and in a transitive sense (he was conscious of her). I will follow Rosenthal (1990) and refer to both as *creature* consciousness. Creature consciousness (whether transitive or intransitive) is to be contrasted with what Rosenthal calls *state* consciousness – the (always intransitive) sense in which certain internal states, processes, events, and attitudes (typically in or of conscious beings) are said to be conscious.

For purposes of being explicit about my own (standard, I hope) way of using these words, I assume that for any x and P,

(3) S is conscious of x or that $P \Rightarrow$ S is conscious (a conscious being).

That is, transitive (creature) consciousness implies intransitive (creature) consciousness. You cannot see, hear, taste, or smell a thing without (thereby) being conscious.[12] You cannot be aware that your checkbook doesn't balance or conscious that you are late for an appointment (a fact) without being a conscious being.[13]

The converse of (3) is more problematic. Perhaps one can be conscious without being conscious of anything. Some philosophers think that during hallucination, for example, one might be fully conscious but (qua hallucinator) not conscious of anything. To suppose that hallucination (involving intransitive consciousness) is a consciousness of something would (or so it is feared) commit one to objectionable mental particulars – the sense data that one hallucinates. Whether or not this is so I will not try to say. I leave the issue open. (3) only endorses the innocent idea that beings who are conscious of something are conscious; it does not say that conscious beings must be conscious of something.

---

12 White (1964, p. 59): "Being conscious or unconscious *of* so and so is not the same as simply being conscious or unconscious. If there is anything of which a man is conscious, it follows that he is conscious; to lose consciousness is to cease to be conscious of anything."

13 One might mention dreams as a possible exception to (3): one is (in a dream) aware of certain things (images?) while being asleep and, therefore, unconscious in the intransitive sense. I think this is not a genuine exception to (3), but since I do not want to get sidetracked arguing about it, I let the possibility stand as a"possible" exception. Nothing will depend on how the matter is decided.

By way of interconnecting creature and state consciousness I also posit:

(4) S is conscious of x or that $P \Rightarrow$ S is in a conscious state of some sort.

Transitive creature consciousness requires state (of the creature) consciousness. S's consciousness of x or that P is a relational state of affairs; it involves both the agent, S, and the object (or fact) S is conscious of. The conscious state that (according to (4)) S must be in when he is conscious of x or that P, however, is not the sort of state the existence of which logically requires x or the condition described by P. Tokens of this state type may be caused by x or the condition described by "P" (and when they are, they may qualify as experiences of x or knowledge that P), but to qualify as a token of this type, x and the condition described by "P" are not necessary.

Thus, according to (4), when I see or hear Clyde playing the piano (or that he is playing the piano) and (thus) am conscious of him playing the piano (or that he is playing the piano), I am in a conscious state of some kind. When hallucinating (or simply when listening to a recording) I can be in the same kind of conscious state even if Clyde is not playing the piano (or I do not perceive him playing the piano). When Clyde is not playing the piano (or I am not perceiving him play the piano), we speak of the conscious state in question not as knowledge (that he is playing the piano) but as belief, not as perception (of Clyde playing the piano) but as hallucination (or perception of something *else*).[14]

I do not know how to argue for (4). I would like to say that it states the obvious and leave it at that. I know, however, that nothing is obvious in this area. Not even the obvious. (4) says that our perceptual awareness of both things (smelling the burning toast) and facts (becoming aware that it is burning) involves, in some essential way, conscious subjective (i.e., nonrelational and, in this sense, internal or subjective) states of the perceiver – beliefs (in the case of awareness of facts) and experiences (in the awareness of things). Not everything that happens in or to us when we become conscious of some external object or fact is conscious, of course. Certain events, processes, and states involved in the processing of sensory information are presumably not conscious. But

---

14 For purposes of illustrating distinctions I use a simple causal theory of knowledge (to know that P is to be caused to believe that P by the fact that P) and perception (to perceive x is to be caused to have an experience by x). Although sympathetic to certain versions of these theories, I wish to remain neutral here.

something, some state or other of S, either an experience or a belief, has to be conscious in order for S to be made conscious of the things and facts around him. If the state of S caused by x is not a conscious state, then the causation will not make S conscious of x. This is why one can *contract* poison ivy without ever becoming aware of the plant that poisons one. The plant causes one to occupy an internal state of some sort, yes, but this internal state is not a conscious state. Hence, one is not (at least not in contracting poison ivy) conscious of the plant.

David Armstrong (1980, p. 59) has a favorite example that he uses to illustrate differences in consciousness. Some may think it tells against (4). I think it does not. Armstrong asks one to imagine a long-distance truck driver:

After driving for long periods of time, particularly at night, it is possible to "come to" and realize that for some time past one has been driving without being aware of what one has been doing. The coming-to is an alarming experience. It is natural to describe what went on before one came to by saying that during that time one lacked consciousness. Yet it seems clear that, in the two senses of the word that we have so far isolated, consciousness was present. There was mental activity, and as part of that mental activity, there was perception. That is to say, there was minimal consciousness and perceptual consciousness. If there is an inclination to doubt this, then consider the extraordinary sophistication of the activities successfully undertaken during the period of "unconsciousness." (p. 59)

Armstrong thinks it plausible to say that the driver is conscious (perceptually) of the road, the curves, the stop signs, and so on. He *sees* the road. I agree. There is transitive creature consciousness of both things (the roads, the stop signs) and facts (that the road curves left, that the stop sign is red, etc.). How else explain the extraordinary performance?

But does the driver thereby have, in accordance with (4), conscious experiences of the road? Armstrong thinks there is a form of consciousness that the driver lacks. I agree. He thinks that what the driver lacks is an introspective awareness, a perception-like awareness, of the current states and activities of his own mind. Once again, I agree. The driver is neither thing-aware nor fact-aware of his own mental states (including whatever experiences he is having of the road). I am not sure that normal people have this in normal circumstances, but I'm certainly willing to agree that the truck driver lacks it. But where does this leave us? Armstrong says (p. 61) that if one is not introspectively aware of a mental state (e.g., an experience), then it (the experience) is "in one good sense of the word" unconscious. I disagree. The only sense in which it is unconscious is that the person whose state it is is not conscious of having it. But from this it does not follow that the state itself is unconscious. Not unless one accepts a higher-order theory according to which state consciousness is analyzed in terms of creature consciousness of the state. Such a theory may be true, but it is by no means obvious. I shall, in fact, argue that it is false. At any rate, such a theory cannot be invoked at this stage of the proceedings as an objection to (4). (4) is, as it should be, neutral about what makes the state of a person (who is transitively conscious of x or that P) a conscious state.

I therefore accept Armstrong's example, his description of what forms of consciousness the driver has, and the fact that the driver lacks an important type of higher-level (introspective) consciousness of his own mental states. What we disagree about is whether any of this implies that the driver's experiences of the road (whatever it is *in* the driver that is required to make him conscious *of* the road) are themselves unconscious. We will return to that question in the final section.

Many investigators take perceptual experience and belief to be para-digmatic conscious phenomena.[15] *If* one chooses to talk about state consciousness (in addition to creature consciousness) at all, the clearest and most compelling instance of it is in the domain of sensory experi-ence and belief. My present visual experience of the screen in front of me and my present perceptual beliefs about what is on that screen are internal states that deserve classification as conscious if anything does. (4) merely records a decision to regard such perceptual phenomena as cen-tral (but by no means the only) instances of conscious mental states.

Such is my justification for accepting (4). I will continue to refer to the conscious states associated with our consciousness of things (hearing Clyde playing the piano) as experiences and our consciousness of facts (that he is playing the piano) as beliefs. This is, I think, fairly standard usage. I have not, of course, said what an experience or a belief is. I won't try. That is not my project. I am trying to say what makes (or doesn't make) an experience conscious, not what makes it an experience.

Consciousness of things – for example, seeing a stoplight turn green – requires a conscious experience of that thing. Consciousness of a fact – that the stoplight is turning green – requires a conscious belief that this is a fact. And we can have the first without the second – awareness of

---

15   E.g., Baars (1988), Velmans (1991), Humphrey (1992).

124

the stoplight's turning green without an awareness that it is turning green – hence a conscious experience (of the light's turning green) without a conscious belief (that it is turning green). Likewise, we can have the second without the first – a conscious belief about the stoplight, that it is turning green, without an experience of it. Someone I trust tells me (and I believe her) that the stoplight is turning green. So much by way of summary of the relationships between the forms of consciousness codified in (1) through (4).

We are, I think, now in a position to answer some preliminary questions. First: can one have conscious experiences without being conscious that one is having them? Can there, in other words, be conscious states without the person in whom they occur being fact-aware of their occurrence? Second: can there be conscious states in a person who is not thing-aware of them? These are important preliminary questions because important theories of what makes a mental state conscious, including what passes as orthodox theory today, depend on negative answers to one (or, in some cases, both) of these questions. If, as I believe, the answers to both questions are affirmative, then these theories are simply wrong.

3. EXPERIENCED DIFFERENCES REQUIRE DIFFERENT EXPERIENCES

Glance at Figure 1 enough to assure yourself that you have seen all the elements composing constellation Alpha (on the left) and constellation Beta (on the right). It may be necessary to change fixation points in order to foveate (focus on the sensitive part of the retina) all parts of

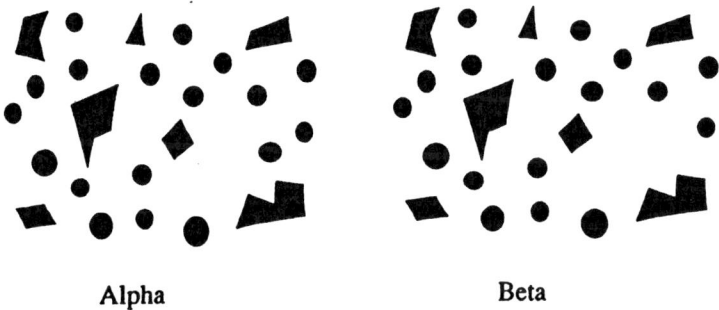

Alpha   Beta

Figure 1

SPOT

Figure 2

Alpha and Beta. If the figure is being held at arm's length, though, this should not be necessary, although it may occur anyway via the frequent involuntary saccades the eyes make. A second or two should suffice.

During this brief interval some readers may have noticed the difference between Alpha and Beta. For expository purposes, I will assume no one did. The difference is indicated in Figure 2. Call the spot, the one that occurs in Alpha but not Beta, Spot.

According to my assumptions, then, everyone (when looking at Figure 1) saw Spot. Hence, according to (1), everyone was aware of the thing that constitutes the difference between Alpha and Beta. According to (4), then, everyone consciously experienced (i.e., had a conscious experience of) the thing that distinguishes Alpha from Beta. Everyone, therefore, was thing-aware, but not fact-aware, of the difference between Alpha and Beta. Spot, if you like, is Alpha's moustache.

Let E(Alpha) and E(Beta) stand for one's experience of Alpha and one's experience of Beta, respectively. Alpha and Beta differ; Alpha has Spot as a part; Beta does not. E(Alpha) and E(Beta) must also differ. E(Alpha) has an element corresponding to (caused by) Spot. E(Beta) does not. E(Alpha) contains or embodies, as a part, an E(Spot), an experience of Spot, while E(Beta) does not. If it did not, then one's experience of Alpha would have been the same as one's experience of Beta and, hence, contrary to (4), one would not have seen Spot when looking at Alpha.[16]

One can, of course, be conscious of things that differ without one's experience of them differing in any intrinsic way. Think of seeing

16 I do not think it necessary to speculate about how E(Spot) is realized or about its exact relation to E(Alpha). I certainly do not think E(Spot) must literally be a *spatial* part of E(Alpha) in the way Spot is a spatial part of Alpha. The argument is that there is an intrinsic *difference* between E(Alpha) and E(Beta). E(Spot) is just a convenient way of referring to this difference.

visually indistinguishable objects – similar-looking thumb tacks, say. One sees (experiences) numerically different things, but one's experience of them is the same. Both experiences are conscious, and they are experiences of different things, but the differences in the experiences are not conscious differences. The differences are extrinsic to the experience itself. It is like having an experience in Chicago and another one in New York. The numerically different experiences may be qualitatively identical even though they have different (relational) properties – one occurs in Chicago, the other in New York. The perception of (visually) indistinguishable thumb tacks is like that.

The experiences of Alpha and Beta, however, are not like that. They are qualitatively different. They differ in their relational properties, yes, as all numerically different objects do, but they also differ in their intrinsic properties. These two experiences are not only experiences of qualitatively different objects (Alpha and Beta), they are experiences of the qualitative differences. The respects in which Alpha and Beta differ are not only visible, they are (by hypothesis) seen. One is, after all, thing-aware of Spot, the difference between Alpha and Beta. The experiences are not distinguished in terms of their intrinsic qualities by the person who has the experiences, of course, but that is merely to say that there is, on the part of this person, no fact-awareness of any differences in her experience of Alpha and her experience of Beta. That, though, is not the issue. The question is one about differences in a person's conscious experiences, not a question about a person's awareness of differences in her experiences. It is a question about *state* consciousness, not a question about *creature* consciousness.

Once one makes the distinction between state and creature consciousness and embraces the distinction between fact- and thing-awareness, there is no reason to suppose that a person must be able to distinguish (i.e., tell the difference between) her conscious experiences. Qualitative differences in conscious experiences are *state* differences; distinguishing these differences, on the other hand, is a fact about the *creature* consciousness of the person in whom these experiences occur.

The argument assumes, of course, that if one is thing-aware of the difference between Alpha and Beta (i.e., thing-aware of Spot), then E(Alpha) and E(Beta) must differ. It assumes, that is, that *experienced* differences require different experiences. What else could experienced differences be? The difference between E(Alpha) and E(Beta), then, is being taken to be the same as the difference between seeing, in broad daylight, directly in front of your eyes, one finger raised and two fingers raised. Seeing the two fingers is not like seeing a flock of geese (from a distance) where individual geese are "fused" into a whole and not seen. In the case of the fingers, one sees both the finger on the left and the finger on the right. Quite a different experience from seeing only the finger on the left. When the numbers get larger, as they do with Alpha and Beta, the experiences are no longer discernibly different to the person having them. Given that each spot is seen, however, the experiences *are*, nonetheless, different. Large numbers merely make it harder to achieve fact-awareness of the differences on the part of the person experiencing the differences. E(Spot) is really no different than the difference between experiencing one finger and two fingers in broad daylight. The only difference is that in the case of Alpha and Beta there is no fact-awareness of the thing that makes the difference.[17]

Since the point is critical to my argument, let me emphasize the last point. In speaking of conscious differences in experience it is important to remember that one need not be conscious of the difference (= conscious that such a difference exists) in order for such differences to exist. Readers who noticed a difference between Alpha and Beta were, thereby, fact-aware of the difference between Alpha and Beta. Such readers may also have become fact-aware (by inference?) of the difference between their experience of Alpha and their experience of Beta – that is, the difference between E(Alpha) and E(Beta). But readers who were only thing-aware of the difference between Alpha and Beta were not fact-conscious of the difference between Alpha and Beta. They were not, therefore, fact-conscious of any difference between E(Alpha) and E(Beta) – their conscious experience of Alpha and Beta. These are conscious differences of which no one is conscious.

In saying that the reader was conscious of Spot – and, hence, in this

17 Speaking of large numbers, Elizabeth, a remarkable eidetiker (a person who can maintain visual images for a long time) studied by Stromeyer and Psotka (1970), was tested with computer-generated random-dot stereograms. She looked at a 10,000-dot pattern for one minute with one eye. Then she looked at another 10,000-dot pattern with the other eye. Some of the individual dots in the second pattern were systematically offset so that a figure in depth would emerge (as in using a stereoscope) if the patterns from the two eyes were fused. Elizabeth succeeded in superimposing the eidetic image that she retained from the first pattern over the second pattern. She saw the figure that normal subjects can see only by viewing the two patterns (one with each eye) simultaneously.

I note here that to fuse the two patterns, the *individual dots* seen with one eye must somehow be paired with those retained by the brain (*not* the eye; this is not an after-image) from the other eye.

sense, the difference between Alpha and Beta – without being conscious of the fact that they differed, we commit ourselves to the possibility of differences in conscious experience that are not reflected in conscious belief. Consciousness of Spot requires a conscious experience of Spot, a conscious E(Spot); yet, there is nothing in one's conscious beliefs – either about Spot, about the difference between Alpha and Beta, or about the difference between E(Alpha) and E(Beta) – that registers this difference. What we have in such cases is internal *state* consciousness with no corresponding (transitive) *creature* consciousness of the conscious state.[18] With no creature consciousness we lack any way of discovering, *even in our own case*, that there exists this difference in conscious state. To regard this as a contradiction is merely to confuse the way an internal state like an experience can be conscious with the way the person who is in that state can be, or fail to be, conscious of it.

It may be supposed that my conclusion rests on the special character of my example. Alpha contains a numerically distinct element, Spot, and our intuitions about what is required to see a (distinct) thing, are, perhaps, shaping our intuitions about the character of the experience needed to see it. Let me, therefore, borrow an example from Irvin Rock (1983). Once again, the reader is asked to view Figure 3 (after Rock 1983, p. 54) for a second and then say which, Alpha or Beta at the bottom, is the same as the figure shown at the top.

As closer inspection reveals, the upper left part of Alpha contains a few wiggles found in the original but not in Beta. Experimental subjects asked to identify which form it was they had seen did no better than chance. Many of them did not notice that there were wiggles on the figure they were shown. At least they could not remember having seen them. As Rock (1983, p. 55) observes:

Taken together, these results imply that when a given region of a figure is a nonconsequential part of the whole, something is lacking in the perception of it, with the result that no adequate memory of it seems to be established.

No adequate *memory* of it is established because, I submit, at the time the figure is seen there is no fact-awareness of the wiggles. You cannot remember *that* there are wiggles on the left if you were never aware that

---

18 I return, in the next section, to the question of whether we might not have thing-awareness of E(Spot) – that is, the same kind of awareness of the difference between E(Alpha) and E(Beta) as we have of the difference between Alpha and Beta.

Alpha   Beta

Figure 3

there were wiggles on the left.[19] Subjects were (or may well have been) aware (thing-aware) of the wiggles are (they saw them), but never became aware that they were there. The wiggles are what Spot (or Tom's moustache) is: a thing one is thing-aware of but never notices. What is lacking in the subject's perception of the figure, then, is an awareness of certain facts (that there are wiggles on the upper left), not (at least not necessarily) an awareness of the things (the wiggles) on the left.

In some minds the second example may suffer from the same defects as the first: it exploits subtle (at least not easily noticeable) differences in detail of the object being perceived. The differences are out there in the objects, yes, but who can say whether these differences are registered in here, in our experience of the objects? Perhaps our conviction (or *my* conviction) that we do see (and, hence, consciously experience) these points of detail, *despite* not noticing them, is simply a result of the fact that we see figures (Alpha and Beta, for instance) between which there are visible differences, differences that *could* be identified (noticed) by an appropriate shift of attention. But just because the details are visible does not mean that we see them or, if we do, that there must be some intrinsic (conscious) difference in the experience of the figures that differ in these points of detail.

---

19 Although there may be other ways of remembering the wiggles. To use an earlier example, one might remember seeing Tom's moustache without (at the time) noticing it (being fact-aware of it). Even if one cannot remember *that* Tom had a moustache (since one never knew this), one can, I think, remember *seeing* Tom's moustache. This is the kind of memory (episodic vs. declarative) involved in a well-known example: remembering how many windows there are in a familiar house (e.g., the house one grew up in) by imagining oneself walking through the house and counting the windows. One does not, in this case, remember that there were twenty-three windows, although one comes to know that there were twenty-three windows by using one's memory.

This is a way of saying that conscious experiences, the sorts of experiences you have when looking around the room, cannot differ unless one is consciously aware that they differ. Nothing mental is to count as conscious (no state consciousness) unless one is conscious of it (without creature consciousness). This objection smacks of verificationism, but calling it names does nothing to blunt its appeal. So I offer one final example. It will, of necessity, come at the same point in a more indirect way. I turn to perceptually salient conditions, conditions it is hard to believe are not consciously experienced. In order to break the connection between experience and belief, between thing-awareness and fact-awareness, then, I turn to creatures with a diminished capacity for fact-awareness.[20]

Eleanor Gibson (1969, p. 284), in reporting Kluver's studies with monkeys, describes a case in which the animals are trained to the larger of two rectangles. When the rectangles are altered in size, the monkeys continue to respond to the larger of the two – whatever their absolute size happens to be. In Kluver's words, they "abstract" the LARGER THAN relation. After they succeed in abstracting this relation, and when responding appropriately to the larger (A) of two presented rectangles (A and B), we can say that they are aware of A, aware of B (thing-awareness), and aware that A is larger than B (fact-awareness). Some philosophers may be a little uncomfortable about assigning beliefs to monkeys in these situations, uncomfortable about saying that the monkey is aware *that* A is larger than B, but let that pass. The monkeys at least exhibit a differential response, and that is enough. How shall we describe the monkeys' perceptual situation *before* they learned to abstract this relation? Did the rectangles *look* different to the monkeys? Was there any difference in their experience of A and B *before* they became aware that A was larger than B? We can imagine the difference in size to be as great as we please. They were not fact-aware of the difference, not aware that A is larger than B, to be sure. But that isn't the question. The question is: were they conscious of the condition of A and B that, so to speak, makes it true that A is larger than B?[21] Does their experience of

---

20   The following is an adaptation of the discussion in Dretske (1981, pp. 151–152).

21   *Conditions*, recall, are things in my sense of this word. One can be aware of an object's condition (its movement, for instance) without being aware that it is moving. This is what happens when one sees an adjacent vehicle's movement *as* one's own movement or an object's movement as an expansion or contraction. It is also what occurs in infants and, perhaps, animals who do not have the concept of movement: they are aware of O's movement, but not aware that O is moving.

objects change when, presented with two objects, the same size, one of these objects expands, making it much larger than the other? If not, how could these animals ever learn to do what they are being trained to do – distinguish between A's being larger than B and A's not being larger than B?

It seems reasonable to suppose that, prior to learning, the monkeys were thing-aware of a difference that they became fact-aware of only after learning was complete. Their experience of A and B was different, consciously so, before they were capable of exhibiting this difference in behavior. Learning of this sort is simply the development of fact-awareness from thing-awareness.

The situation becomes even more compelling if we present the monkeys with three rectangles and try to get them to abstract the INTER-MEDIATE IN SIZE relation. This more difficult problem proves capable of solution by chimpanzees, but monkeys find it extremely difficult. Suppose monkey M cannot solve it. What shall we say about M's perceptual condition when he sees three rectangles, A, B, and C, of descending size. If we use behavioral criteria for what kind of facts M is conscious of and assume that M has already mastered the first abstraction (the LARGER THAN relation), M is aware of the three rectangles, A, B, and C. M is also aware that A is larger than B, that B is larger than C, and that A is larger than C. M is not, however, aware that B is INTERMEDIATE IN SIZE even though this is logically implied by the facts he is aware of. Clearly, although M is not (and, apparently, cannot be made) aware of the fact that B is intermediate in size, he is nonetheless aware of the differences (A's being larger than B. B's being larger than C) that logically constitute the fact that he is not aware of. B's being intermediate in size is a condition the monkey is thing-aware of but cannot be made fact-aware of. There are conscious features of the animal's experiences that are not registered in the animal's fact-awareness and, hence, not evinced in the animal's deliberate behavior.

4. WHAT, THEN, MAKES EXPERIENCES CONSCIOUS?

We have just concluded that there can be conscious differences in a person's experience of the world – and, in this sense, conscious features of her experience – of which that person is not conscious. If this is true, then it cannot be a person's awareness of a mental state that makes that state conscious. E(Spot) is conscious, and it constitutes a conscious difference between E(Alpha) and E(Beta) even though no one, including the person in whom it occurs, is conscious of it. It follows, therefore, that what *makes* a mental state conscious cannot be our consciousness of it. If we have conscious experiences, beliefs, desires, and fears, it cannot be our introspective awareness of them that makes them conscious.

This conclusion is a bit premature. The argument mounted in §3 was primarily directed at higher-order-thought (HOT) theories that take an experience or a belief (mental states) to be conscious in virtue of their being the object of some HOT-like entity, a higher-order mental state that (like a thought) involves the deployment of concepts. My concern in §3, therefore, was to show that conscious experience required no fact-awareness – either of facts related to what one experiences (e.g., Spot) or of facts related to the experience itself (e.g., E(Spot). One does not have to be fact-aware of E(Spot) in order for E(Spot) to be conscious.

This leaves the possibility, however, that in order for one's experience of Spot to be conscious, one must be thing-aware of it. Perhaps, that is, E(Spot) is conscious, not because there is some higher-order *thought* (involving concepts) about E(Spot), but rather because there is a higher-order *experience* (a nonconceptual mental state) of E(Spot), something that makes one thing-aware of E(Spot) in the same way one is thing-aware (perceptually) of Spot. This is a form of the HOT theory that Lycan (1992, p. 216) describes as Locke's "inner sense" account of state consciousness. What makes an experience conscious is not one's (fact) awareness that one is having it, but one's (thing) awareness of it.

To my mind, Rosenthal (1990, pp. 34ff.) makes a convincing case against this "inner sense" version of state consciousness. He points out, for example, that one of the respects in which experiences are unlike thoughts is in having a sensory quality to them. E(Alpha), for instance, has visual, not auditory or tactile, qualities. If what made E(Alpha) into a conscious experience was some higher-order experience of E(Alpha), one would expect some distinctive qualia of this higher-order experience to intrude. But all one finds are the qualia associated with E(Alpha), the lower-order experience. For this reason (among others) Rosenthal himself prefers a version of the inner spotlight theory of consciousness in which the spotlight is something in the nature of a fact-awareness, not thing-awareness, of the lower-order mental state or activity.

Aside, though, from the merits of such specific objections, I think the inner sense approach loses all its attraction once the distinction between thing-awareness and fact-awareness is firmly in place. Notice, first, that if it is thing-awareness of a mental state that is supposed to make that mental state conscious, then the inner sense theory has no grounds for saying that E(Spot) is not conscious. For a person might well be thing-aware of E(Spot) – thus making E(Spot) conscious – just as he is thing-aware of Spot, without ever being fact-aware of it. So on this version of the spotlight theory, a failure to realize, a total unawareness of the fact *that* there is a difference between E(Alpha) and E(Beta), is irrelevant to whether there is a conscious difference between these two experiences. This being so, the inner sense theory of what makes a mental state conscious does nothing to *improve* one's epistemic access to one's own conscious states. *As far as one can tell*, E(Spot) (just like Spot) may as well not exist. What good is an inner spotlight, an introspective awareness of mental events, if it doesn't give one epistemic access to the events on which it shines? The inner sense theory does nothing to solve the problem of what makes E(Spot) conscious. On the contrary, it multiplies the problems by multiplying the facts of which we are not aware. We started with E(Spot) and gave arguments in support of the view that E(Spot) was conscious even though the person in whom it occurred was not fact-aware of it. We are now being asked to explain this fact by another fact of which we are not fact-aware: namely, the fact that we are thing-aware of E(Spot). Neither E(Spot) nor the thing-awareness of E(Spot) makes any *discernible* difference to the person in whom they occur. This, surely, is a job for Occam's razor.

If we do not have to be conscious of a mental state (like an experience) for the mental state to be conscious, then, it seems, consciousness of something cannot be what it is that makes a thing conscious. Creature consciousness (of either the factive or thing form) is not necessary for state consciousness.[22] What, then, makes a mental state conscious? When S smells, and thereby becomes aware of, the burning toast, what makes his experience of the burning toast a conscious experience? When S becomes aware that the light has turned green, what makes his belief that the light has turned green a conscious belief?

This is the big question, of course, and I am not confronting it in this essay. I am concerned only with a preliminary issue – a question about the relationship (or lack thereof) between creature consciousness and state consciousness. For it is the absence of this relation (in the right form) that undermines the orthodox view that what makes certain men-

---

22 Neither is it sufficient. We are conscious of a great many internal states and activities that are not themselves conscious (heartbeats, a loose tooth, hiccoughs of a fetus, a cinder in the eye).

tal states conscious is one's awareness of them. Nonetheless, although I lack the space (and, at this stage, the theory) to answer the big question, I would like to indicate, if only briefly, the direction in which these considerations lead.

What makes an internal state or process conscious is the role it plays in making one (intransitively) conscious – normally, the role it plays in making one (transitively) conscious of some thing or fact. An experience of x is conscious not because one is aware of the experience, or aware that one is having it, but because, being a certain sort of representation, it makes one aware of the properties (of x) and objects (x itself) of which it is a (sensory) representation. My visual experience of a barn is conscious not because I am introspectively aware of it (or introspectively aware that I am having it), but because it (when brought about in the right way) makes me aware of the barn. It enables me to perceive the barn. For the same reason, a certain belief is conscious not because the believer is conscious of *it* (or conscious of having it[23]), but because it is a representation that makes one conscious of the fact (that *P*) that it is a belief about. Experiences and beliefs are conscious not because you are conscious of them, but because, so to speak, you are conscious *with* them.

This is not to deny that one may, in fact, be conscious of one's own experiences in the way one is, in ordinary perception, conscious of barns and other people. Perhaps we are equipped with an introspective faculty, some special internal scanner, that takes as its objects (the *xs* it is an awareness of), one's experiences of barns and people. Perhaps this is so. Perhaps introspection is a form of metaspectation – a sensing of one's own sensing of the world. I doubt this. I think introspection is best understood not as thing-awareness, but as fact-awareness – an awareness that one has certain beliefs, thoughts, desires, and experiences *without* a corresponding awareness of the things (the beliefs, thoughts, desires, and experiences) themselves. Introspection is more like coming to know (be aware) that one has a virus than it is like coming to see, hear, or feel (i.e., be aware of) the virus (the thing) itself.

Whether these speculations on the nature of introspection are true or not, however, is independent of the present thesis about consciousness.

---

23 If fact-awareness was what made a belief conscious, it would be very hard for young children (those under the age of three or four years, say) to have conscious beliefs. They don't yet have a firm grasp of the concept of a belief and are, therefore, unaware of the fact that they have beliefs. See Flavell (1988) and Wellman (1990).

The claim is not that we are unaware of our own conscious beliefs and experiences (or unaware that we have them). It is, instead, that our being aware of them, or that we have them, is not what makes them conscious. What makes them conscious is the way they make us conscious of something else – the world we live in and (in proprioception) the condition of our own bodies.

Saying just what the special status is that makes certain internal representations conscious while other internal states (lacking this status) remain unconscious is, of course, the job for a fully developed theory of consciousness. I haven't supplied that. All I have tried to do is to indicate where not to look for it.

REFERENCES

Armstrong, D. M. 1968: *A Materialist Theory of the Mind*. London: Routledge and Kegan Paul.
  1980: *The Nature of Mind and Other Essays*. Ithaca, New York: Cornell University Press.
Astington, J., P. Harris, and D. Olson, eds. 1988: *Developing Theories of the Mind*. New York: Cambridge University Press.
Baars, B. 1988: *A Cognitive Theory of Consciousness*. Cambridge: Cambridge University Press.
Dennett, D. C. 1991: *Consciousness Explained*. Boston: Little, Brown and Company.
Dretske, F. 1969: *Seeing and Knowing*. Chicago: University of Chicago Press.
  1978: "The role of the percept in visual cognition," in Savage 1978, pp. 107–127.
  1979: "Simple seeing," in Gustafson and Tapscott 1979, pp. 1–15.
  1981: *Knowledge and the Flow of Information*. Cambridge, Massachusetts: MIT Press/ A Bradford Book.
  1990: "Seeing, believing and knowing," in Osherson, Kosslyn, and Hollerback 1990.
Flavell, J. H. 1988: "The development of children's knowledge about the mind: From cognitive connections to mental representations," in Astington, Harris, and Olson 1988.
Gibson, E. 1969: *Principles of Perceptual Learning and Development*. New York: Appleton-Century-Crofts.
Grice, P. 1989: *Studies in the Way of Words*. Cambridge, Massachusetts: Harvard University Press.
Gustafson, D. F., and B. L. Tapscott, eds. 1979: *Body, Mind and Method: Essays in Honor of Virgil Aldrich*. Dordrecht, Holland: D. Reidel Publishing Company.
Humphrey, N. 1992: *A History of the Mind: Evolution and the Birth of Consciousness*. New York: Simon and Schuster.
Lees, R. B. 1963: *The Grammar of English Nominalizations*. Bloomington, Indiana: Indiana University Press.

Lycan, W. 1987: *Consciousness*. Cambridge, Massachusetts: MIT Press/A Bradford Book.

    1992: "Uncertain materialism and Lockean introspection." *Behavioral and Brain Sciences* 15.2, pp. 216–217.

McLaughlin, B., ed. 1991: *Critical Essays on the Philosophy of Fred Dretske*. Oxford: Basil Blackwell.

Milner, A. D., & M. D. Rugg, eds. 1992: *The Neuropsychology of Consciousness*. London: Academic Press.

Osherson, D., S. Kosslyn, and J. Hollerback, eds. 1990: *An Invitation to Cognitive Science, Volume 2, Visual Cognition and Action*. Cambridge, Massachusetts: MIT Press/A Bradford Book.

Perkins, M. 1983: *Sensing the World*. Indianapolis, Indiana: Hackett Publishing Company.

Rock, I. 1983: *The Logic of Perception*. Cambridge, Massachusetts: MIT Press/A Bradford Book.

Rosenthal, D. 1986: "Two concepts of consciousness." *Philosophical Studies* 94.3, pp. 329–359.

    1990: "A theory of consciousness." Report No. 40, Research Group on Mind and Brain, ZiF, University of Bielefeld.

Rosenthal, D. 1991: "The independence of consciousness and sensory quality," in Villanueva 1991, pp. 15–36.

Savage, W., ed. 1978: *Minnesota Studies in the Philosophy of Science: Perception and Cognition*, Vol. IX. Minneapolis, Minnesota: University of Minnesota Press.

Stromeyer, C. F., & J. Psotka 1970: "The detailed texture of eidetic images." *Nature* 225, pp. 346–349.

Velmans, M. 1991: "Is human information processing conscious?" *Behavioral and Brain Sciences* 14.4, pp. 651–668.

Villanueva, E., ed. 1991: *Consciousness*. Atascadero, California: Ridgeview Publishing Company.

Wellman, H. M. 1990: *The Child's Theory of the Mind*. Cambridge, Massachusetts; MIT Press/A Bradford Book.

White, A. R. 1964: *Attention*, Oxford: Basil Blackwell.

8

Differences That Make No Difference[1]

Never mind differences that make no difference. There are none. I want to talk, instead, about differences that do not make a difference *to anyone*, differences of which no one is aware. There are lots of these.

According to Daniel Dennett, though, there are fewer than you might have thought. There are, to be sure, physical differences – even some that exist in you – of which you are not aware. There are also conscious events in me, and differences among them, that you don't know about. But there are no conscious events in *you* that escape your attention. If you do not believe yourself to be having conscious experience φ, then φ is not a conscious experience at all. Dennett calls this view, a view that denies the possibility in principle of consciousness in the absence of a subject's belief in that consciousness, first-person operationalism.[2] Dennett is a first-person operationalist. For him there are no facts about one's own conscious life – no, as it were, conscious facts – of which one is not conscious.

Philosophers like to call each other names. I'm no exception. The preferred term of abuse these days, especially among materialists, seems to be "Cartesian." So I will use it. First-person operationalism sounds like warmed-over Cartesianism to me. For Descartes, the mind is an open book. Everything that happens there is known to be happening there by the person in whom it is happening. No mental secrets. For Dennett, too, there are no secrets, no facts about our conscious lives

Reprinted from *Philosophical Topics* 22 (1 and 2) (Spring and Fall 1994), 41–57, by permission of the publisher.
1 I am grateful to Güven Güzeldere for many helpful suggestions.
2 D. Dennett, *Consciousness Explained* (Boston: Little, Brown & Co., 1991), 132.

that are not available for external publication. Differences that make no difference to the publicity department, to what a person knows or believes and can thus exhibit in overt behavior, are not conscious differences.

The mind is like everything else: There is more to it than we are aware. If making a difference to someone is understood, as Dennett understands it, as a matter of making a difference to what that person believes or judges, then conscious differences need make no difference to anyone – not even to the person in whom they occur.

1. HIDE THE THIMBLE

From *Content and Consciousness*[3] to *Consciousness Explained*, a span of over twenty years, Dennett has been resolute in his conviction that awareness of something – an apple or a thimble – requires some kind of cognitive upshot. In the 1969 book (chapter six, "Awareness and Consciousness"), this is expressed as the idea that awareness of an apple on a table is awareness that there is an apple on a table. Awareness that there is an apple on a table, in turn, gets cashed out[4] as a content-bearing internal state like a judgment or a belief that controls behavior and (for those who can speak) speech. In 1991, the same view is expressed by saying that Betsy, who is looking for a thimble in the children's game "Hide the Thimble," does not see the thimble until she "zeros in on" it and identifies it as a thimble. Only when an appropriate judgment is made – "Aha, the thimble" – will she see it. Only then will she become aware of it. Only then will the thimble be "in" Betsy's conscious experience.

As a historical note, the same year *Content and Consciousness* appeared, I published *Seeing and Knowing*.[5] Although I was concerned primarily with epistemological issues, how seeing gives rise to knowing, I made a great fuss about what I called nonepistemic perception, perception that does not require (although in adult human beings it is normally accompanied by) belief or knowledge. In contrast to seeing facts (*that* they are apples and thimbles), seeing *objects* (apples and thimbles) is a case of nonepistemic perception. I made a fuss about nonepistemic perception because so many bad arguments in epistemology (and, at that time, in

---

3 Dennett, *Content and Consciousness* (London: Routledge and Kegan Paul, 1969).
4 Ibid., 118.
5 F. Dretske, *Seeing and Knowing* (Chicago: University of Chicago Press, 1969).

the philosophy of science) were pivoting on a confusion between the perception of objects and events (like oscilloscopes and eclipses), on the one hand, and the perception of facts (that they are oscilloscopes and eclipses), on the other. The perception of objects and events, I argued, could, and often did (especially in the case of children, animals, and theoretically untutored adults), occur in the absence of conceptual uptake – without such propositional attitudes as knowledge, identification, belief, and recognition. When it comes to objects and events, seeing is not knowing, and it isn't believing either.

At the same time, therefore, that I was arguing that awareness of apples was quite distinct from awareness that they are apples or, indeed, awareness of any fact about the apples, Dennett was assuming that these were essentially the same thing, that awareness of things is awareness of facts about those things.[6]

Although Dennett's book was, in many ways, an absolute eye-opener for me (awakening my interest in the philosophy of mind), we were obviously in disagreement about a fundamental point concerning perceptual consciousness and, therefore, the nature of perceptual experience. Since the perception of objects and events was, for me, a relation between a perceiver and a thing that could exist without the perceiver's understanding what was being perceived – or even *that* something was being perceived – perception could not be understood in terms of judgment, belief, or knowledge. Cognitively speaking, seeing is like touching, a relationship between a person (or animal) and an object that can exist (although it normally does not exist) without identification or recognition. One does not need the concept of a thimble – does not need to understand what a thimble is – to touch it. Neither does one need the concept of a thimble to see a thimble. This, by the way, is why

---

6 Since I have just introduced the term "awareness" and will shortly be talking about consciousness, I should perhaps take this opportunity to register a point about usage. I take seeing, hearing, tasting, etc., an object or event, X, to be ways of being (perceptually) aware of X. I assume the same with factive clauses: To see or smell that P – that the toast is burning, for example – is to be (perceptually) aware that P. I also follow what I take to be standard usage and take perceptual awareness of X (or that P) to be a form – in fact, a paradigmatic form – of consciousness (of either X or that P). This is what T. Natsoulas ("Consciousness," *American Psychologist* 33 [1978]: 904–914) calls "consciousness 3," and he describes this as our most basic concept of consciousness. It should also be evident that I use the verbs "aware" and "conscious" interchangeably. There are some subtle differences between these verbs (see A. R. White's *Attention* [Oxford: Basil Blackwell, 1964]), but I don't think any of these nuances bear on the disagreement between Dennett and me. So I ignore them.

the context "S sees . . ." is referentially transparent.[7] If S sees X, and X = Y, then S sees Y. Compare: If S touches X, and X = Y, then S touches Y. Of course, many of the objects we see every day are objects we identify in some way or another. But this is also true of the objects we touch. I don't always, but I often know what I'm touching. I do not normally touch thimbles and apples without knowing what I'm touching. The same is true of perception. I do not always, but I often know what I'm seeing – especially so when I see familiar objects at close range in good light. But that isn't the point. The point is not what is usually true of the objects one sees and touches, but what must be true to see and touch them, what it is that constitutes the seeing and touching. Knowledge, belief, recognition, judgment, identification – none of this is necessary.[8]

In view of Paul Grice's work on conversational implicatures,[9] I hope it is not necessary to mention (I'll do it anyway) the irrelevance of what we would say (or deny) we saw or touched. I would not normally say I saw, touched, or stepped on a thimble unless I thought I saw, touched, or stepped on a thimble – unless I recognized or identified (as a thimble) what I saw, touched, or stepped on. None of this is relevant to what it takes to see, touch, or step on a thimble. And I would be quick to deny that I saw a thimble if I returned empty-handed from a search for a thimble through a cluttered drawer. The denial is conversationally appropriate and perfectly reasonable, not to mention informative to my impatient wife, even when it is false. I *did* see it; I just failed to recognize it – at least as a thimble. What I imply, and therefore, the information I succeed in communicating with this false statement is, of course, that I did not find (identify, recognize) the thimble. As so often happens in communication, listeners are more interested in the implied truths than in the false statements that imply them.

---

7 In calling this a referentially transparent context, I mean to restrict the values of "X" and "Y" to noun phrases referring to specific objects and events (e.g., "the apple on the table," "the thimble on the mantle"). When interrogative nominals (what X is, who X is, where X is), factive clauses (that it is X), and abstract nouns (the difference, the pattern, the problem, the answer) follow the perceptual verb, the context is no longer transparent.

8 As certain forms of agnosia testify: "Associative agnosia is also often taken to be a more specific syndrome, in which patients have a selective impairment in the recognition of visually presented objects, despite apparently adequate visual perception of them" (M. J. Farah, *Visual Agnosia* [Cambridge, Mass.: MIT Press, 1990], 57).

9 P. Grice, "Logic and Conversation," in P. Cole and J. Morgan, eds., *Syntax and Semantics* (New York: Academic Press, 1975).

In a footnote in *Consciousness Explained*,[10] Dennett asks whether identification of a thimble comes after or before becoming conscious of it. He tells us that his Multiple Drafts model of consciousness "teaches us" not to ask this question. One can understand why he wouldn't want to ask this question and, therefore, why he would favor a theory that did not let one ask it. He doesn't want to hear the answer. Are we really being told that it makes no sense to ask whether one can see, thus be aware of, thus be conscious of, objects before being told what they are? Does it make no sense to ask, Macbeth style, "What is this I see before me?"

That it does make sense seemed obvious to me in 1969. It still does. Frankly, I thought when Dennett read my book it would seem obvious to him. Apparently it didn't. Maybe he didn't read the book. Whatever the explanation, he is still convinced that seeing is a form of knowing (or believing or taking – see later), that being conscious of a ϕ is being conscious that it is a ϕ.[11]

I remain convinced that as long as these perceptual attitudes – seeing objects and seeing facts, being aware *of* apples and being aware *that* they are apples – are conflated, it is hard (to be honest, I think it is impossible) to give a plausible theory of consciousness. One has already suppressed one of the most distinctive elements of our conscious life – the difference between experience and belief.

2. ANIMALS AND INFANTS

Cats and birds can see thimbles as well as (probably better than) little girls. They have better eyesight. The department in which little girls surpass birds and cats is in the conceptual department: They know, while

---

10   *Consciousness Explained*, 335.
11   Given his commitment to the view that all seeing is seeing-that, I do not understand Dennett's reaction to the work of Anne Treisman. In "Time and the Observer: The Where and When of Consciousness in the Brain" (*The Behavioral and Brain Sciences* 15 [1992]: 335, n. 8), Dennett and (coauthor) M. Kinsbourne say that Treisman has conducted important experiments to support her claim that seeing should be distinguished from identifying. I didn't think experiments were needed to establish this. Are experiments also needed to establish that *touching* X should be distinguished from identifying X? Aside from the issue of whether experiments are needed, though, I am puzzled as to why Dennett, who thinks seeing thimbles *is* identifying thimbles, believes Treisman's experiments *support* the view that seeing should be distinguished from identifying. Are we to conclude that he thinks Treisman's important experiments are a failure? Has he told her about this?

cats and birds do not, what thimbles are. They know that, other things being equal, things that look like *that* are thimbles. When they see things that look like *that*, then they can judge them to be, identify them as, take them to be, thimbles. They can, as a result, not only see thimbles, but, when they are attentive and the thimbles are not too far away, see that they are thimbles – something quite beyond the capacity of birds and cats. This, though, is no reason to deny that animals can see thimbles. That would be to confuse ignorance with blindness.

In replying to criticisms by Lockwood and Fellows and O'Hear, Dennett questions the "methodological assumption" that animals and infants are conscious.[12] Whether or not infants and animals are conscious, he declares, has no clear pretheoretical meaning. What Dennett is doing here, of course, is recapitulating Descartes's answer to Arnauld. Holding that all conscious phenomena are thoughtlike in character, Descartes concluded that animals, lacking the power of thought, could not be perceptually conscious of anything. If sheep seem to see the wolves from whom they run, the appearances are deceptive. Such flight is an unconscious reflex to retinal stimulation.

Dennett is no Cartesian, but he does, like Descartes, have a theory of consciousness to which conceptually impoverished animals (and infants) are an embarrassment.[13] How can a bird who cannot take a thimble to be a thimble, cannot judge, believe, think (let alone say) that something is a thimble, see a thimble? How can sheep be aware of wolves if they cannot judge them to be wolves? Descartes's bold way out of this problem was to deny that animals were conscious of anything. Dennett's way out – not quite so bold – is to insist that it *isn't clear* that animals (not to mention infants) are conscious of anything. For dialectical purposes, though, the result is the same: Embarrassing counterexamples are neutralized. One cannot use the fact – obvious to most of us – that animals can see to argue that seeing is not believing.

For the sake of joining issues, I am willing to defer to Dennett's judgments about what is, and what isn't, *clear* in this area, but I have my suspicions about what is shaping his convenient intuitions on this matter. It wasn't so long ago, after all, that this, or something very like this, *was*

12 Dennett, "Living on the Edge," *Inquiry* 36 (1993): 144–145.
13 Other theories of consciousness – in particular the so-called Higher-Order Thought (HOT) theory according to which an experience is not conscious unless one *thinks* (judges, knows) one is having it – also seem driven to deny consciousness to animals. See, e.g., Peter Carruthers, "Brute Experience," *The Journal of Philosophy* 86 (1989): 258–269.

clear to Dennett. In *Consciousness Explained* he said that "birds and fish and reptiles and insects clearly [!] have color vision, rather like our 'trichromatic' (red–green–blue) system."[14] If Dennett still believes this, one is left to conclude that he thinks color vision doesn't enable an animal to see colors. Either that or seeing colors is not a way of being aware of colors. Or, perhaps, that being aware of colors does not require consciousness.

There is the further fact, as Dennett himself points out in *Consciousness Explained*,[15] that according to his own theory,[16] lower animals (including frogs) have beliefs and wants (he adds that there is no good reason for putting these words in quotation marks). Since perceptions are also part of the intentional stance, lower animals presumably have perceptions too. Is one to infer, then, that the intentional stance entitles one to attribute perceptual beliefs about X to animals but not perceptual awareness of X? Why? Why go skittish about this part of the intentional stance?

It isn't only pet owners (and new parents) who will strenuously disagree with Dennett's treatment of animals and infants. I think scientists who make it their business to study animals will too. Horn is typical:

The evidence available, mainly from studies of the visual abilities of vertebrates, including macaques, rats, chickens and pigeons . . . gives no support to the view that the visual capacities of these animals resemble those of humans with blindsight, and no reason, therefore, to infer that these animals are unaware of the stimuli to which they respond.[17]

3. COGNITIVISM

Cognitivists (as I call them) are people who interpret perception, including the perception of thimbles and wolves, as some form of cognitive or conceptual achievement, as a species of identifying, knowing, judging, recognizing, taking, or believing. All awareness-of is awareness-that, all seeing is seeing-as. Sensations are minithoughts. Hence, following Descartes, if one cannot think, one cannot feel or experience. The ignorant, the ones who cannot think the appropriate thoughts, are thereby ren-

---

14 *Consciousness Explained*, 377.
15 Ibid., 194.
16 At least the theory set forth in *The Intentional Stance* (Cambridge, Mass.: MIT Press, 1987).
17 G. Horn, "What Can the Bird Brain Tell Us about Thought without Language?" in L. Weiskrantz, ed., *Thought without Language* (Oxford: The Clarendon Press, 1988).

dered unconscious. Confronted with examples of perception that do not involve recognition, cognitivists typically give ground by diluting the cognitive requirements of perception. Quantifiers are shuffled. Although there is nothing in particular you must see something as in order to see it, you must, in order to see it, see it as something or other. Although you can see a thimble without seeing that it is a thimble, without taking it to be a thimble, you must, in order to see it, at least take it to be something in Granny's sewing basket or, maybe, just a shiny thing up there on the mantle. This maneuver has the welcome result of allowing people who are ignorant of thimbles to see them, but it still requires too much. It has the unwelcome result of making *noticing* – forming beliefs about – a thimble necessary for *seeing* a thimble. Even if one doesn't balk at this (some people, I know, don't), there is the fact that people can see objects without believing they are seeing anything. People have seen things when they thought they were hallucinating or imagining – when they took themselves to be seeing nothing at all.[18] If some hallucinations are similar enough to veridical perception to convince the hallucinator that he is really seeing something, then, by parity of reasoning, they are similar enough to convince some perceivers that they are hallucinating. Hence, perceiving physical objects, including thimbles, must be possible without believing one is perceiving anything – while, in fact, believing one is perceiving nothing. If seeing really is believing, it is hard to see what the beliefs are supposed to be.[19]

This debate has a long and undistinguished history. I will not try to summarize it here. I merely intend to locate Dennett within a certain tradition, a tradition that seeks to understand sensory phenomena in cognitive or conceptual terms. The motives for this assimilation in current philosophy of mind are usually functional (*Consciousness Explained* defends "a version of functionalism").[20] Beliefs, as behavior-dedicated mental states, are, in principle, detectable in the behavior of the organism in which they occur. Given the game she is playing, Betsy's belief that the object she sees is a thimble will result in her sitting down. From a

---

18 A well-known experimental demonstration of this is C. W. Perky, "An Experimental Study of Imagination," in D. C. Beardslee and M. Wertheimer, eds., *Readings in Perception* (Princeton, N.J.: Princeton University Press, 1958).

19 One could insist that in order to see a thimble one must at least believe that it is *something or other*, where that is meant to include figments of one's own imagination. Philosophers are capable of defending almost anything, I know, but this doesn't sound like a move that Daniel Dennett would be happy to make. So I ignore it.

20 *Consciousness Explained*, 31.

functionalist's point of view, then, it would be convenient if Betsy's thimble-sightings were Betsy's thimble-beliefs. For then Betsy's thimble-sightings would (together with her desires) have behavioral relevance. We could tell, from the outside, that she saw the thimble. If, on the other hand, there could be thimble-sightings without thimble-beliefs, if Betsy could experience a thimble without realizing it, then – good grief! – how could we ever find out she saw a thimble? How could Betsy ever find out she saw a thimble?[21] What possible functional role would thimble-sightings have? If the difference between seeing a thimble and not seeing a thimble is going to make a difference to anyone, the cognitivist concludes, it had better be identified with a difference between taking and not taking – between judging and not judging – an object to be a thimble.

David Armstrong is a cognitivist who has long appreciated the problems inherent in telling this kind of story about sense experience, the problem of analyzing how things seem in terms of belief and judgment. The problem, as he put it in his 1968 book,[22] is that there is, quite simply, perception without either belief or the acquiring of belief. After citing some examples he concludes:

> All these cases seem to show that we ought to make a distinction between the beliefs that we acquire in perception, and the perceptual experience on which these beliefs are based.[23]

Armstrong makes the distinction, but he prefers to do so by assimilating perceptual experience to perceptual belief. Experiences are inclinations to believe or what Armstrong calls potential beliefs – beliefs we would have if we did not have certain other beliefs. Adapting Armstrong's analysis to the thimble example, we get something like this: Betsy's seeing a thimble is Betsy's acquiring a potential belief, a physical event in her brain that would be a belief if certain other beliefs didn't interfere.

This does not seem like much progress. Armstrong's potential beliefs are as elusive as are the experiences they are meant to replace. How

---

21 The answer to this question, an answer that cognitivists tend to overlook, is: Ask someone! Other people may be able to supply information that, together with what you already know, helps you to discover what (or who) you saw. The way I tell I saw Harold's cousin last night is to ask Harold whether his cousin was at the party I attended last night. What does he look like, where was he standing, when did he arrive? Was he in that crowd of people I was watching? If so, I must have seen him.

22 D. Armstrong, *A Materialist Theory of the Mind* (New York: Humanities Press, 1968).

23 From an excerpt in J. Dancy, ed., *Perceptual Knowledge* (Oxford: Oxford University Press, 1988), 134.

146

does one tell that Betsy had a potential belief that some object was a thimble (or whatever potential belief an experience of the thimble is supposed to be)? How does Betsy tell she has one? In observing a crowd of people or a shelf full of books, does one have a potential belief for *each* (visible) person and book? The difference between having a potential belief and having no belief at all sounds like a difference that doesn't make a difference. Potential beliefs about thimbles seem to be "cognitions" one can have without knowing one has them. Why trade experiences one can have without knowing it for cognitions one can have without knowing it?

George Pitcher is another cognitivist who understands the problems in accounting for sense experience.[24] Realizing that X can look red to S without S's consciously believing that X is red, Pitcher identifies X's looking red with an unconscious belief state.[25] In order to account for the "richness" of perceptual consciousness – seeing a red ball among a cluster of other colored objects – the belief state with which the "look" of things is identified is said to be a large set of such unconscious beliefs.[26] Finally, for the person who mistakenly thinks he is experiencing an illusion, a person who sees an oasis before him when he consciously believes that there is no oasis before him and that nothing there in the desert even looks like an oasis,[27] Pitcher resorts[28] to suppressed, or "partially" or "mostly" suppressed, inclinations to believe. According to this way of talking, Betsy's thimble-sightings turn out to be her thimble-caused-suppressed-inclinations-to-believe.

Once again, it is hard to see what is gained by these verbal maneuvers. The difference between a visual experience and a belief about what you experience seems reasonably clear pretheoretically. Why must the distinction be rendered in quasi-cognitive terms – especially when this results in the awkward identification of conscious experience with unconscious beliefs and inclinations? After all the huffing and puffing, we are left with a difference that doesn't make a difference to anyone. So why bother?

Dennett, working within this tradition, has his own philosophically "correct" way of talking about perceptual experiences. In "Time and

---

24   G. Pitcher, *A Theory of Perception* (Princeton, N.J.: Princeton University Press, 1971).
25   Ibid., 29.
26   Ibid., 72.
27   Ibid., 83.
28   Ibid., 93.

the Observer: The Where and When of Consciousness in the Brain,"[29] Dennett and Kinsbourne talk about microjudgments and microtakings. Microjudgments are "sort of like" judgments or decisions.[30] They are contentful states or discriminations[31] that are the multiple drafts and narrative fragments of *Consciousness Explained*. These judgments, decisions, drafts, narrative fragments, contentful states, registrations, interpretations, and discriminations (all these terms are used) are sort of like judgments in much the same way that Armstrong's potential beliefs were sort of like real beliefs and Pitcher's suppressed inclinations were sort of like real inclinations. The persons in whom they occur need never know, need never be aware, that they are taking place. This, presumably, is why these contentful states, these decisions and discriminations, are labeled "micro" – a prefix that does exactly the work of "unconscious." There can be microjudgments in S that X is so-and-so without S ever judging that X is so-and-so. There can be contentful discriminations in S of X from Y without S consciously discriminating X from Y. That, apparently, is why Dennett speaks of cells and circuits *in* people, not people themselves, as making microjudgments.[32] The job of Dennett's micro "cognitions" and multiple "drafts" is to do precisely what potential or suppressed "beliefs" do for Armstrong and Pitcher: provide a cognitive rug under which to sweep conscious experience.[33]

Philosophers are free to use words as they please. As long as one is clear about *what* microjudgments are, there is, I suppose, no harm in describing Betsy's nervous system, when she sees a thimble, as swarming with microjudgments about all manner of topics. But if we choose to talk this way, then we must also be prepared to say that, in the same sense, automobile fuel gauges are making "contentful discriminations" when they distinguish an empty from a full tank of gasoline. Ringing

29 Dennett and Kinsbourne, "Time and the Observer," 183–247.
30 Ibid., 238.
31 Ibid., 184, 185.
32 We are told (ibid., 190) that even the ganglion cells in the rabbit's retina have the content "from left to right." Also see *Consciousness Explained*, 134–135, where the cortex is described as making discriminations, decisions, and judgments.
33 The resemblance between Dennett and Pitcher is really quite remarkable at times. To account for the richness of sense experience, Pitcher postulated *many* unconscious beliefs. Dennett is more economical. He needs to posit only one microjudgment because he is much more liberal with the content he is prepared to give that judgment: "*There is no upper bound* on the 'amount of content' in a *single* proposition, so a single, swift, rich 'propositional episode' might (for all philosophical theory tells us) have so much content, in its brainish, non-sentential way, that an army of Prousts might fail to express it exhaustively in a library of volumes" ("Living on the Edge," 150).

doorbells are "deciding" that someone is at the door. And a thermometer is "interpreting" the increased agitation of the molecules as a room
temperature of 78°. We can talk this way, yes,[34] but one must be careful
not to conclude from this way of talking that anything significant is
being said about the nature of perceptual experience. One has certainly
not shown that seeing an object, being perceptually aware of a thimble,
consists in a *judgment* that it is a thimble (or anything else) in anything
like the ordinary sense of the word "judgment." One is certainly not
entitled to conclude that "there is no such phenomenon as really seeming over and above the phenomenon of judging that something is the
case." Once the bloated terminology is eliminated, all one can really
conclude is that perception is a complex causal process in which there
are, in the nervous system, different responses to different stimuli. Causal
theorists have been saying that sort of thing for years. No one took *them*
to be propounding a theory of consciousness. Perhaps they could have
improved their case by calling the products of such causal processes
"narrative fragments" or "microtakings." It sounds so much more . . .
uh . . . mental.

4. CONSCIOUS EXPERIENCE

Despite his reputation as an instrumentalist, Dennett is a rugged (not just
a "sort of")[35] realist about conscious experience: "Conscious experiences
are real events occurring in the real time and space of the brain, and
hence they are clockable and locatable within the appropriate limits of
precision for real phenomena of their type."[36] He is, however, also a
cognitivist: "There is no such phenomenon as really seeming – over and
above the phenomenon of judging in one way or another that some-

---

34 I like to talk this way myself, but to avoid confusion I prefer to use the word "informa-
    tion" for these (largely) causal relationships – see my *Knowledge and the Flow of Information*
    (Cambridge, Mass.: MIT Press, 1981). Information can be described in propositional
    terms, and in this sense it (like judgment and belief) has propositional content. But lest
    we start ascribing judgments, decisions, and takings to doorbells, fuel gauges, and ther-
    mometers, I think it useful to distinguish information from such conceptual phenomena
    as belief and judgment. Dennett did too in *Content and Consciousness*; see his distinction
    between intelligent and nonintelligent storage of information (pp. 45ff.).
35 The reference to "sort of" realism comes from Dennett's own description of his position
    in "Postscript: Reflections: Instrumentalism Reconsidered," in D. Rosenthal, ed., *The
    Nature of Mind* (Oxford: Oxford University Press, 1991), 627.
36 Dennett and Kinsbourne, "Time and the Observer," 235.

thing is the case."[37] Perceptual awareness is real enough, yes, but it consists of judgments all the way down – or out (to the retina).

I have no quarrel with Dennett's realism. I am taking issue only with his cognitivism, the idea that seeing or hearing X – being perceptually aware or conscious of X – is a species of judgment. I reject the idea that conception of objects is necessary to, let alone identical with, their perception.

It is important to understand that the disagreement is not about the existence of qualia – at least not if qualia are conceived in the way Dennett conceives of them when he quines qualia.[38] I'll return to the issue of qualia in the next section. Here I only mean to point out that the dispute about qualia – what they are and whether they exist – merely muddies *these* waters. What Dennett is rejecting in his well-known essay against qualia is the existence of mental particulars that are (1) ineffable, (2) intrinsic, (3) private, and (4) directly or immediately apprehensible. I, too, have serious doubts about whether anything can have all these properties. Thus, I am happy, for the sake of argument, and because I agree with so much of what he says about qualia, to grant that our experience of the world has none of these qualities. That, though, is not the point. The point is not whether perceptual experience is ineffable. It isn't. It is not whether the properties external objects seem to have are intrinsic properties of our experience. I agree that they are not. Neither is the quarrel about our direct apprehension of experience. The issue, rather, is whether our experience is constituted by thoughtlike entities, entities that, like beliefs and judgments, require some conceptual understanding on the part of the agent of that which the judgment is about.

If perceptual experience of a ϕ is not a judgment, a belief, a taking (macro, mini, or micro) of ϕ to be a ϕ (or whatever), what is it? I have elsewhere answered this question in terms of the way sensory information is coded.[39] There is more information in our experience of the world than can normally be processed in a way appropriate to belief and judgment. The transition from an experience of X to a belief about X is a conversion of sensory information from analog to digital form. I have

37 *Consciousness Explained*, 364.
38 Dennett, "Quining Qualia," in A. J. Marcel and E. Bisiach, eds., *Consciousness in Contemporary Science* (Oxford: The Clarendon Press, 1988).
39 See my "The Role of the Percept in Visual Cognition," in W. Savage, ed., *Minnesota Studies in the Philosophy of Science: Perception and Cognition*, vol. 9 (Minneapolis, Minn.: University of Minnesota Press, 1978) and *Knowledge and the Flow of Information*.

sometimes illustrated this process with examples involving our perception of complex scenes: crowds of people, shelves full of books, a sky full of stars, arrays of numbers, and so on. Since Dennett has used similar examples to reach an opposite conclusion, let me sharpen our points of disagreement by considering such an example.

Consider a two-year-old child – I will call her Sarah – who knows what fingers are but has not yet learned to count, does not yet know what it means to say there are five fingers on her hand, five cookies in the jar, and so on. Sarah can, I claim, see all five fingers on her hand – not one at a time, but all five at once.[40] This is, I know, an empirical claim, but it is an empirical claim for which there is, for normal two-year-olds, an enormous amount of evidence. Whether or not Sarah sees all five fingers depends, of course, on Sarah, the lighting, the angle at which she sees the fingers, and so on. Let us suppose, though, that Sarah is a child of average eyesight (intelligence has nothing to do with it), that she is looking at the fingers in good light, and that each finger is in plain view. Part of what it means to say that Sarah sees all five fingers is that if you conceal one of the fingers, things will look different to Sarah. There will then be only four fingers she sees. There will not only be one less (visible) finger in the world, but one less finger in Sarah's experience of the world. This difference in the world makes a difference in Sarah's experience of the world, and it makes a difference even when Sarah is unable to judge *what* difference it makes or even that it makes a difference. I would like to say that the same is true of birds and cats, but, out of deference to Dennett's unstable intuitions, I promised not to mention animals again.

I have heard cognitivists insist that one can see five objects, even without judging there to be five, by executing five judgments, one for each object seen. Although Sarah cannot count to five – thus cannot take there to be five objects – she can, simultaneously as it were, take there to be *a* finger five different times. Cognitivists are a stubborn bunch, but this strikes me as a fairly desperate move, not one that Dennett would happily make. Cognitivists want to define what is seen in terms of *what* one judges, the content of a judgment, not in terms of

---

40 There is a sense in which one can see *n* objects without seeing any of the *n* objects. One might, for example, see a flock of eighty-four birds or a herd of thirty-six cows without seeing any individual bird or cow. The flock or herd, seen from a great distance, might look like a spot in the distance. This is not the sense in which I say Sarah sees five fingers. Sarah sees *each* of the five fingers, not (just) a heap (flock, herd, pile) of five fingers.

properties of the judgment itself. An object is supposed to look blue, according to orthodox cognitivism, if and only if one takes it to be (or look?) blue, not if the taking is itself blue. Likewise, one would suppose, seeing five fingers is a matter of taking there to be five fingers, not of there being five finger-takings.

I know this is tedious. Nonetheless, these facts, although painfully obvious, appear to need repetition. For it follows from these facts that there is a sense in which objects can look φ to a person without that person judging or believing that anything is or looks φ. If Sarah had the concept FIVE and knew the difference between FIVE and FOUR, she would have a way of describing what she sees and a way of describing the way things look. But the fact that she is not able to describe the way things look does not mean that things do not look that way to her. Although *she* cannot describe the way five fingers look to her, *we* can:

Dennett denies that the multiplicity, the richness, the fiveness, is in Sarah's experience of the world. A child who does not judge there to be five fingers is not conscious of five fingers:

> When we marvel, in those moments of heightened self-consciousness, at the glorious richness of our conscious experience, the richness we marvel at is actually the richness of the world outside, in all its ravishing detail. It does not "enter" our conscious minds, but is simply available.[41]

This is false. It is false not on philosophical grounds, but (for anyone willing to admit that *one* object can "enter" a conscious mind) false on straightforward empirical grounds. The ravishing detail of the world does not cease to exist when we close our eyes. Our experience of this ravishing detail does cease to exist when we close our eyes. So the ravishing detail is not *only* "in" the world.[42]

I take such situations to be critically important, and I harp about them at wearisome length in order to bring out the basic difference between perceptual experience and perceptual belief. A person's experience of the world can exhibit[43] the property φ even if the person in whom that experience occurs does not have the concept φ, does not understand what it means to be φ, is unable (therefore) to make judgments or have

---

41 *Conscious Explained*, 408.
42 M. J. Farah (*Visual Agnosia*, 18) points out that counting requires seeing more than one object at a time and, I would add (since otherwise why would you be counting?), seeing more than you know or judge yourself to be seeing.
43 I choose this word carefully. I explain why later.

beliefs to the effect that something is φ. In terms of descriptive detail, Sarah's experience of five fingers exceeds her powers of judgment. She experiences more than she can know, more than she can believe or judge. This, indeed, is what the adjective "phenomenal" is meant to signify. Phenomenal properties are, in exactly this sense, independent of belief. Your experience can exhibit φ even though you may not be able to judge that something is φ. It is in this sense that fiveness is a phenomenal property of Sarah's experience of her own hand.[44]

Although the point is especially obvious with regard to numbers, the same holds true for color, shape, orientation, movement, and many other properties. Although they would not describe it that way, something can look blue and hexagonal to persons who have neither the concept *blue* nor the concept *hexagonal* – to anyone, therefore, who is unable to judge or describe it as looking this way.

Dennett is rightfully skeptical of the more extravagant feats of "filling in" alleged for perceptual experience. Does one really see hundreds of Marilyn Monroe pictures spread across the wall? There may be a hundred "out there" on the wall, but how many are "in here," in one's experience of the wall? I don't know. Given what we know about diminished acuity outside the fovea, probably not as many as it seems, certainly not as many as are actually out there. But, often enough, there are a lot more "in here" than I bother to discover by counting. Personally, I think it fairly easy to see, in a brief glance, dozens, sometimes hundreds, of objects. I do it all the time.[45] But we needn't quarrel about big numbers. The argument for phenomenal experience is made as well with five objects as it is with a hundred. If one can see five objects without judging or taking there to be five, and seeing five involves a different experience from seeing four, then experience of the world exhibits properties that are not exhibited in judgment.

---

44 This way of putting the case for phenomenal properties is, I think, quite close to Ned Block's insightful suggestions about the need to distinguish what he calls phenomenal consciousness from access consciousness. See Block's "Inverted Earth," in J. Tomberlin, ed., *Philosophical Perspectives, 4: Action Theory and Philosophy of Mind* (Atascadero, Calif.: Ridgeview Publishing Co., 1990); "Consciousness and Accessibility," *The Behavioral and Brain Sciences* 13 (1990): 596–598; "Evidence against Epiphenomenalism," *The Behavioral and Brain Sciences*, 14 (1991): 670–672; and his review of Dennett's *Consciousness Explained* in *The Journal of Philosophy* 90 (1993): 181–192.

45 I argue this point in greater detail in "Conscious Experience," *Mind* 102 (1993): 263–283.

5. QUALIA

In "Quining Qualia" Dennett tells us that qualia are the way things look or appear.[46] As long as one understands the look to be what I just called the phenomenal appearances (= the way things look that is logically – although surely not causally – independent of what a person believes or judges), this is a workable definition. It captures what most philosophers mean to be arguing about when they argue about qualia. I'm willing to work with it.

According to this definition, then, a person who sees a blue hexagon in normal circumstances will have an experience that exhibits the qualia *blueness* and *hexagonality*. These are among the person's visual qualia whether or not that person is able to judge or say that there is, or appears to be, a blue hexagon in front of her. Although I promised not to mention animals again, I cannot forbear saying that it will also be the qualia of normally sighted chimpanzees and a great variety of other mammals. If there are genuine doubts about this, the evidence lies in discrimination and matching tests plus a little neurophysiology.[47]

I said earlier that I agreed with much that Dennett has said about qualia. If qualia are supposed to be ineffable, intrinsic, privileged, and so on, then, I agree, there are no qualia. But there is no reason to throw a clean baby out with dirty bathwater. We can, as Flanagan argues, keep the qualia and renounce the philosophical accretions.[48] I do not believe in sense data, but I don't renounce sense perception because philosophers have said confused things about it.

Consider ineffability. If S's qualia are identified with the way things look to S, then, since something can look ϕ to a person unable to judge that it is ϕ, a person's qualia may be quite ineffable by that person at the time she has them. Sarah, at two years old, cannot express the fiveness that she experiences. But we can. I did. Those of us who know what properties objects have – and, thus, the ways that objects will appear in normal conditions – can describe our own and other people's qualia. I did this for Sarah and I can do it for chimps. If chimps and children can see blue hexagons, and if they are not color-blind, then, whether or not they know it, their visual qualia are *hexagonality* and *blueness*. In normal

---

46   "Quining Qualia," 42.

47   See, for example, S. Walker, *Animal Thought* (London: Routledge and Kegan Paul, 1983), ch. 7; D. R. Griffin, *Animal Minds* (Chicago: University of Chicago Press, 1992).

48   O. Flanagan, *Consciousness Reconsidered* (Cambridge, Mass.: MIT Press, 1992).

viewing conditions, that is the way blue hexagons look to normally sighted children and chimps. There is nothing ineffable about their qualia.

In fact, according to Dennett's own characterization, it is difficult to see how qualia could fail to be effable. If a phenomenal property, a quale, is simply one of the ways things can appear to be, and we assume that things sometimes *are* the way they appear to be, then a catalog of qualia is, presumably, a list of the way things are: blue, hexagonal, bigger than a bread box, moving, loud, far away, bright, salty, circular, angry, upset, and so on. Qualia, in fact, are just our old, familiar properties. If qualia are the properties of phenomenal consciousness, there is nothing "sublimely inaccessible" about them.[49] The problem is not with qualia but with the way experiences "exhibit" qualia. More of this in a moment.

Also, if we remember that in the definition of qualia the sense of "looks" or "appears" is the phenomenal sense, the sense in which something can look ϕ to a person unable to make ϕ-judgments, then qualia, quite clearly, do not enjoy privileged epistemological status. Most of a two-year-old's qualia are completely inaccessible to the two-year-old. This is not to say that the two-year-old doesn't *have* qualia. It is only to say that she does not know, perhaps cannot know, *what* qualia it is she has. Introspection isn't going to help Sarah figure out that there appear to be five fingers on her hand. Others, those who have the relevant concepts and are in a position to make informed judgments about how things look to Sarah, have better access (epistemologically speaking) to some of Sarah's qualia than she does. That is why we, or at least informed ethologists, know more about a chimp's qualia than the chimp does. Sarah and the chimp "enjoy" the qualia, yes. They are, after all, *their* qualia. But we know better than they what it is they are enjoying. In that sense there is no privileged access.

Up to this point I have been careful to say that experiences "exhibited" phenomenal properties (qualia). Sarah's experience of five fingers exhibits *fiveness*. Her experience of blue hexagons exhibits *blueness* and *hexagonality*. I avoided saying that one's experiences *had* the properties they exhibited. I avoided saying it because frankly, it sounds silly. This

49 Dennett and Kinsbourne, "Time and the Observer," 240. I may appear to be skating rather cavalierly over the inverted-spectrum problem here. I admit the appearances but deny the reality. I do not, however, have the time to justify this claim. So the appearances will have to stand.

is an instance of the old Sense-Datum Fallacy – the fallacy of inferring that if an object, *X*, looks φ, then something (the look of *X*?, an *X*-ish sense-datum?) must be φ.[50] An experience of five fingers is different from an experience of four, and different in a way that depends on the number of fingers being viewed, but the experience of five need not itself be five nor need it differ *numerically* from the experience of four. An experience of blue exhibits the property blue, but need not itself be blue nor need it be a different color (if it is colored at all) than the experience of red. Qualia, if these are the way things seem, are not to be understood as properties of the seeming. If this is what it means to deny that qualia are intrinsic properties of experiences, then, once again, I agree with Dennett that qualia are not intrinsic properties of experience.

But if qualia are not intrinsic properties of experience, if my experience of blue need not itself be blue, what is the relation between an experience and the qualia it exhibits? How can an experience exhibit the qualia *blueness* (during hallucination, for instance) if there is nothing either inside or outside the head that is blue?

It is the search for an answer to this question, a question about the relationship between an experience of blue and the blue that is experienced, that drove many philosophers into sense-data wonderland. If something looks blue and there is no available object either inside or outside the head that is blue, then some object has to be invented, a sense datum, to bear or have the property blue. Dennett rightly rejects this nonsense. Along with other card-carrying cognitivists, he avoids the fallacy by replacing sense data with their modern equivalent: minijudgments or microtakings. When an object looks blue, there need be nothing in the head that is blue. Why? Because looking blue is, you see, a form of judgment, a microjudgment, that something is blue, and just as a judgment that something is edible need not itself be edible, a judgment that something is blue need not itself be blue. Blue sense data are thereby banished. Replacing them are, let us say, soggy gray judgments (microtakings, potential beliefs, suppressed cognitions) that something is blue – something one might actually hope to find in the brain if one knows what to look for.

---

50 Dennett and Kinsbourne ("Time and the Observer") do an excellent job of exposing this fallacious pattern of inference when it occurs in our thinking about representations – especially those having to do with temporal properties. The properties represented are not, or need not be, properties of the representation.

The trouble with this answer, as I have been at pains to argue, is that the microjudgments, the potential beliefs, the suppressed inclinations, have to occur in persons and animals incapable of making the corresponding judgments or having the relevant beliefs. Why, then, call them judgments or beliefs? If Sarah's visual system can "take" there to be five fingers on her hand without Sarah's taking there to be five fingers on her hand, what sorts of inventions are these microtakings, these narrative fragments, these partial drafts? Until we know, we won't know what conscious experience is.

9

The Mind's Awareness of Itself

The hard problem of consciousness, the place where the explanatory gap is widest – viz., the nature of phenomenal experience – is especially vexing for people who believe that:

(1) Conscious perceptual experiences exist inside a person (probably somewhere in the brain)[1]
(2) Nothing existing inside a person has (or needs to have[2]) the properties one is aware of in having these experiences.

Reprinted from *Philosophical Studies* (1999), 1–22, copyright © 1999 by Kluwer Academic Publishers, with kind permission from Kluwer Academic Publishers. My thanks to Bill Lycan, Tom Nagel, and Ned Block for helpful criticisms.

1 Locating the mind (thoughts, experiences, etc.) inside the head is not a denial of externalism about the mind. Externalism is the view that what makes a mental state the mental state it is are factors existing outside the person. Externalism is consistent with (indeed, I think it implies) the claim that mental states are inside the person. What is external (according to externalism) are not the thoughts and experiences themselves, but (some of) the factors that make them thoughts and experiences. Money is no less *in* my pocket by having the factors that make it money existing outside my pocket.

2 The parenthetical qualification is necessary because, of course, there are exceptions. Sometimes there is something existing in the head of a person having an experience that has the properties that person is aware of in having that experience. Think, for example, of seeing your own teeth (in a mirror) or a human brain. In seeing someone else's brain, something in your head (viz., your brain) has the properties (gray, brain-shaped, etc.) that you are aware of. This, of course, is the exception. Typically, we do not see things that look like things in our heads. I will here be concerned with visual experiences (e.g., that of seeing or – in hallucination – seeming to see, a pumpkin) the phenomenal qualities of which (color, shape, movement, texture, distance) are not properties of anything in the brain of the experiencer. For this reason I will generally omit the qualification "or needs to have" and simply assume that nothing in the head has the properties that one is aware of in having the experience.

I later (§3) return to other exceptions to (2), proprioception – e.g., headaches, itches, cramps, and thirst, bodily sensations that (according to some) are internal and have the

The experience I have when I see (dream of, hallucinate) a large orange pumpkin has to be inside me. Why else would it cease to exist when I close my eyes, awaken, or sober up? Yet, nothing inside me – certainly nothing in my brain – has the properties I am aware of when I have this experience. There is nothing orange and pumpkin-shaped in my head. How, then, can I be aware of what my perceptual experiences are like – presumably a matter of knowing what qualities they have – if none of the properties I am aware of when I have these experiences are properties of the experience?

Surely, though, we are, in some sense, aware of our own conscious experiences. We have, if not infallible, then privileged, access to their phenomenal character. I may not know what it is like to be a bat, but I certainly know what it is like to be me, and what it is like to be me is primarily – some would say it is exclusively – a matter of the phenomenal qualities of my perceptual (including proprioceptive) experience. I am aware – directly aware – of what it is like to see (dream of, hallucinate) orange pumpkins. If such awareness is incompatible with (1) and (2), so much the worse for (1) and (2).

This is a problem that some philosophers have given up trying to solve. Others spend time tinkering with (2). The problem is real enough, but (2) is not the culprit. The solution lies in distinguishing between the fundamentally different sorts of things we are aware of and, as a result, the different forms that awareness (or consciousness[3]) of things can take. Once these distinctions are in place, we can see why (1) and (2) are compatible with privileged awareness of one's own experience. We can have our cake and eat it too.

By way of previewing the argument for this conclusion, let *o* be an object (or event, condition, state – i.e., a spatiotemporal particular), *P* a property of *o*. We speak of being aware of *o*, of *P*, and of the fact that *o* is *P*. These differences in the ontological kinds of which we are aware are reflected in corresponding differences in the acts of awareness. Awareness of *P* is a much different mental state from awareness of the *o* that is *P*, and both differ from an awareness of the fact that *o* is *P*.

In thinking about the mind's awareness of itself, these differences are

properties of which one is aware in having these sensations. For the present I mean to focus exclusively on perceptual modalities – hearing, seeing, smelling, tasting, and feeling – that are of (or purport to be of) external objects and conditions.

3   I use these terms interchangeably when they are followed by a word or phrase specifying *what* we are aware (conscious) of.

important. For if $\mathfrak{e}$ is some mental particular and $\mathfrak{P}$ a property of $\mathfrak{e}$[4] we must not confuse awareness that $\mathfrak{e}$ is $\mathfrak{P}$ with awareness of either $\mathfrak{e}$ or $\mathfrak{P}$. For one can be aware of the former – aware, that is, that one's experience is $\mathfrak{P}$ – without being aware of either the experience ($\mathfrak{e}$) itself or the quality ($\mathfrak{P}$) that helps make it that kind of experience.

Therein lies an answer to the puzzle generated by (1) and (2), the puzzle of how one can be aware of internal affairs – aware of what one's experiences are like – without being aware of these experiences themselves or of the properties that give them their phenomenal character. The mind's awareness of itself is an awareness of *facts* about itself, an awareness that internal experience, $\mathfrak{e}$, is $\mathfrak{P}$. It is not an awareness of the internal object $\mathfrak{e}$ or the property $\mathfrak{P}$ out of which such facts are composed. The facts we are aware of in knowing what it is like to experience orange pumpkins are, to be sure, facts about internal affairs – thus the truth of (1) – but the properties we are aware of in achieving this awareness (being universals[5]) exist nowhere. *They* aren't in the head. Thus the truth of (2).

1. OBJECTS, PROPERTIES, AND FACTS

When an object is moving, I can be aware of (A) the moving object; (B) the fact that it is moving; (C) the movement; (D) all of these; (E) none of these. Consider:

Case A: I study the minute hand of a clock. The hand is moving, so the object I see, the object I am aware of, is a moving object. I do not, however, sense, I am not aware of, its movement. Nor (thinking the clock is broken) am I aware of the fact that it is moving. I am aware (I see) the moving hand, *o*, but I am aware of neither its movement, *M*, nor the fact that it is moving: that *o* is *M*.

Case B: I observe the minute hand on the clock for several minutes. I see that the hand is in a different position now than it was a moment

---

4　Throughout this essay I will use *o* to designate an external physical object (e.g., a pumpkin) $\mathfrak{e}$ a mental particular (e.g., a visual experience of *o*); *P*, *M*, and *C* properties of *o*; and $\mathfrak{P}$, $\mathfrak{M}$, and $\mathfrak{C}$ (Old English font) properties of $\mathfrak{e}$.

5　I assume that universals (and, a fortiori, the universals one is aware of) are neither inside nor outside the head. Awareness of colors, shapes, and movements, when there is no external object that has the property one is aware of, is not, therefore, a violation of (2). A measuring instrument (a speedometer, for example) can (when malfunctioning) be "aware of" (i.e., represent) a speed of 45 mph without any object's (inside or outside the instrument) having this magnitude.

ago. I thus become aware that it is moving. Nonetheless, I still do not perceive the movement. The minute hand moves too slowly for that. I know it is moving, but I cannot see it move. I am aware of o and that o is M but not M.

Case C: I observe the movement of a nearby vehicle and mistakenly take it to be my own movement. I stomp on the brakes. Nothing happens. In this case I was aware of both the neighboring vehicle and its movement without at the time being aware that it (the adjacent vehicle) was moving. I thought I was moving. Awareness of o and M, but not of the fact that o is M.

Case D: I observe the second hand of another clock. Unlike the minute hand of the first clock, the movement of this object is plainly visible. I am aware of the moving hand, its movement, and also the fact that it is moving. When one becomes aware of the fact that o is M by awareness of both o and the M of o, I call it *direct* fact-awareness. I am directly aware that the second hand is moving but indirectly aware that the minute hand is moving.

Case E: I am aware of neither the object, nor its properties, nor the fact that it has those properties. There are unobservable objects (e.g., electrons) that have properties (e.g., spin) I am not conscious of. I am, to be sure, aware of the fact that electrons have this property (I read about it in a book), but there was a time when I was not aware. There was a time, in other words, when I was unaware of o, the property S, and the fact that o was S (not to mention the fact that there were os).

I will call these three forms of awareness o-awareness (for *object-awareness*[6]), f-awareness (for *fact*-awareness), and p-awareness (for *property*-awareness). When the kind of awareness is clear from the context – when, for example, I am talking about an awareness (and, thus, a p-awareness) of properties – I will generally drop the distracting prefixes. There are times, though, when it is important to specify exactly which

---

6 I count token events (e.g., particular battles, deaths), states of affairs (my lamp being on, your key being lost), conditions (the mess in his room), situations (= conditions), and processes (my tooth decaying, the maple tree shedding its leaves) as objects. They are, to be sure, peculiar objects about which a great deal more could (and probably should) be said (especially about our awareness of them), but I do not have the time to discuss these complications. For my purposes it is enough to note that token events, states, and conditions are spatiotemporal particulars that are (like apples and stars) distinct from both the facts and properties from which I distinguish objects. Events and conditions have a (temporal) beginning and an end. Properties do not. Neither do facts. As Dostoyevsky put it, a person's suffering (an event or condition) ends, but the fact that the person suffers endures forever.

form of awareness is at issue, and on these occasions the prefixes will appear. Although I use movement (a relational property) to illustrate these distinctions, I could just as well have used any other property. I can, for instance, be *f*-aware that the wine is sweet (someone told me it was or I read the label) without being aware of the wine or its sweetness (I do not taste the wine for myself). One sees a fabric in normal light – thus experiencing (becoming *p*-aware of) its color (blue, say) – without realizing, without being *f*-aware, that it is blue. One thinks, mistakenly, that the illumination is abnormal and the fabric only *looks* blue. And one can be aware of the color of Tim's tie – that particular shade of blue – without being *o*-aware of his tie or the fact that it is blue. One sees another object of exactly the same color. If it sounds odd to speak of being aware of an object's color without actually seeing the object, imagine someone pointing at another object (a color sample perhaps) and saying, "*That* is the color of his tie."[7] What you are made *p*-aware of when you see the color sample *is* the color of his tie. One might also be *p*-aware of the color of his tie while being aware of no object at all. Imagine hallucinating about a homogeneous expanse of color that exactly matches the blue of his tie.

This last claim may sound false – at least controversial. When a person hallucinates about pink rats, isn't the person aware of colored, rat-shaped images? Isn't awareness of properties (colors, shapes, sizes, orientations, etc.) always (and necessarily) awareness of objects having these properties? To insist on this point is a way of denying (2). It is a way of saying that, at least in hallucination, there *is* something (an image, a sense

---

7 Depending on the property in question, it will sometimes sound odd to say that one is aware of *o*'s *P*-ness without being aware of *o*. For example, can one become aware of the second hand's movement without being aware of (seeing, feeling, or somehow sensing) the second hand itself? Can one be aware of *my* movement (executing a dance step, say) by observing another person execute the same movement?

We are sometimes, of course, interested not in universal properties but in particular instancings of these universal properties – what philosophers call *tropes*. Although two objects, *a* and *b*, are the same color or execute the same movement (i.e., instantiate the same universal property *P*), *a*'s color (trope) is not the same as *b*'s color (trope), nor is the movement (trope) of *a* the same as the movement (trope) of *b*. As a fact about ordinary usage, I think we generally mean to refer to something like a trope when we speak of *a*'s movement or the movement of *a* – a universal property, movement, *as realized in a particular individual*. We perhaps come closer to the universal property in speaking of the movement that an individual executes.

My claim that property-awareness is independent of object-awareness, then, is a claim about our awareness of universal properties, the properties objects can share with other objects, and not an object's particular "value" (trope) of this shareable property.

datum) in one's head that has the properties one is aware of in having the experience. Since I am here exploring the possibility of understanding conscious experience given the truth of both (1) and (2), I assume, to the contrary, that hallucinations are experiences in which one is aware of properties (shapes, colors, movements, etc.) without being *o*-conscious of objects having these properties. To suppose that awareness of property *P* must always be an awareness of an object having property *P* is what Roderick Chisholm (1957) called the Sense-Datum Fallacy. Following Chisholm, and in accordance with (2), I will take this to *be* a genuine fallacy. Hallucinating about pumpkins is not to be understood as an awareness of orange pumpkin-shaped objects. It is rather to be understood as *p*-awareness of the kind of properties that *o*-awareness of pumpkins is usually accompanied by.

Awareness (i.e., *p*-awareness) of properties without awareness (*o*-awareness) of objects having these properties may still strike some readers as bizarre. Can we really be aware of (uninstantiated) universals? Yes, we can, and, yes, we sometimes are. It is well documented that the brain processes visual information in segregated cortical areas (see Hardcastle 1994 for references and discussion). One region computes the orientation of lines and edges, another responds to color, still another to movement.[8] As a result of this specialization it is possible, by suitable manipulation, to experience one property without experiencing others with which it normally co-occurs. In the aftereffect called the *waterfall phenomenon*, for instance, one becomes aware of movement without the movement's being *of* any thing. There is apparent motion without the appearance of anything moving. To obtain this effect one stares for several minutes at something (e.g., a waterfall) that moves steadily in one direction. In transferring one's gaze to a stationary scene one then experiences movement in the opposite direction. Remarkably, though, this movement does not "attach" itself to objects. None of the objects one sees appear to be moving. Yet, one experiences movement. As a psychologist (Frisby 1980, p. 101) puts it, "although the after-effect gives a very clear illusion of movement, the apparently moving features nevertheless seem to stay still!" One becomes, he says, "aware of features

---

8 This gives rise to what psychologists call the *binding problem*: how does the nervous system "pull together," so to speak, all the information about different properties into a unified experience of a single object – an object that has all those properties? How does the brain put this shape together with this color and that movement to get (the appearance of) an orange pumpkin moving to the left?

remaining in their 'proper' locations even though they are seen as moving." Frisby describes this as "contradictory," but it is nothing more than p-awareness of one property (movement) without this movement's being instantiated (as it normally is) in or by some object. One's movement detectors are active, but they are not *made* active by any object possessing the normal constellation of visual properties (shape, color, texture, etc.).

Everyday perception is generally a mixture of object-, property-, and fact-awareness. Usually we become aware of facts by becoming aware of the objects and properties that constitute these facts. I become aware that his tie is blue by seeing his tie and its color. I become aware that gas is escaping by smelling the escaping gas. Perceptual modalities being what they are, though, we are often made aware of facts by being made aware of properties altogether different from those involved in these facts. We become f-aware that the metal is hot by seeing it change *color*, not by seeing or feeling its temperature. Instruments, gauges, and natural signs (tree rings, tracks in the snow, cloud formations, etc.) have familiarized us with the various ways awareness of facts is mediated by awareness of objects and properties quite different from those involved in the facts. I see that the water is 92°F by an awareness not of the water, but of a thermometer and the height of its mercury column. Use of language in communication is another source of f-awareness in which there is little or no connection between the objects (sounds and marks) and properties (spatial and temporal arrangement of symbols) we perceive and the facts (reported on) that communication makes one f-aware of. When f-awareness is mediated by awareness of properties and/or objects other than those involved in the fact, the f-awareness is *indirect*. Thus, awareness that your daughter has a fever is indirect when you use a thermometer, direct when you feel her forehead.

The phenomenology of perceptual experience is determined by the totality of qualities one is p-aware of. Object and fact awareness contribute nothing. Phenomenally speaking, one can be aware of different objects (e.g., twins) while having exactly the same (type of) experience. Likewise, different people (or the same person at different times) can be having the same experience while being aware of quite different facts: one person is aware that the flower he sees is a geranium; the other is aware of the same flower – it looks the same to him – but he is not aware that it is a geranium. Same object and property awareness, different fact-awareness. Object-awareness has to do not with the qualities of one's experience, but with the causal relations of the experience to objects in the world. Fact-awareness has to do not with the qualities of one's experience, but with the kind of knowledge these experiences give rise to.

There is, then, a virtual[9] independence (conceptual, not causal; the facts one is aware of may affect, causally, the properties one is aware of, the way an object looks) between f-awareness, o-awareness, and p-awareness when the awareness is perceptual. We can, and we often do, have one without the others. If this is also true – and why shouldn't it be? – of awareness of mental affairs, this tells us something important about awareness of our own conscious states. I begin by describing what it tells us about a special class of conscious experiences – *perceptual* experiences.

2. PERCEPTUAL EXPERIENCE

Perceptual experiences are phenomenally rich in a way that beliefs are not. Unlike a belief or judgment (an f-awareness) that a pumpkin is moving toward you (something you can have without awareness of either the pumpkin or its movement), seeing a pumpkin move involves an experience that is phenomenally quite different from experiencing a green bean move toward you, a red tomato moving to the left, a ripe banana rotating in place, and so on. The experience of a moving pumpkin, although it is caused by a pumpkin (and, according to causal theorists, must be so caused in order to be rightly classified as an experience *of* a pumpkin), is detachable from external causes in the sense that the very same kind of experience – an experience having the same phenomenal character – could occur (and in pumpkin hallucinations does occur) without a pumpkin.

This much, I hope, is philosophical (not to mention psychological) common sense. Disagreement arises when we turn to questions about

9 "Virtual" because there are relations other than these forms of awareness that I must (given my limited purposes here) ignore. For instance, it might be argued (plausibly, I think) that o-awareness requires p-awareness of some properties – if not the properties the object actually has, then the properties it appears to have. You can't perceive (thus be aware of) an object unless it appears some way to you, and if appearing ϕ to S is a way of S being p-aware of the property ϕ, then o-awareness requires p-awareness of ϕ for *some* property ϕ. This, I think, is one possible (and for my money, the only plausible) way of construing the doctrine that all seeing is seeing as.

I am willing to concede some degree of dependence. It will not be important for the use to which I will put these distinctions. I will exploit only the *degree* of independence my examples have already established.

our awareness not of pumpkins, their properties,[10] and facts about them, but of our experience (e) of a pumpkin, *its* properties, and facts about *it*. Letting $\mathfrak{P}$ stand for a property of a pumpkin experience, a property that helps makes this experience the kind of experience it is, how does one become aware that e is $\mathfrak{P}$? Is this achieved by an awareness of e and $\mathfrak{P}$ or is it, instead, indirect – mediated by an awareness of some other object and (or) property?

John Locke (1959) thought that the mind's awareness of itself was quasi-perceptual and, thus, direct. We become aware that a visual experience is $\mathfrak{P}$ in the same way we can (if we trust common sense) become aware that a pumpkin is P – by means of o-awareness of the experience and p-awareness of $\mathfrak{P}$ According to some philosophers, all fact-awareness begins here.[11] Thus, awareness of facts about a pumpkin, that it is P, are reached via inference from o-awareness of e and p-awareness of one or more of *its* properties. We become fact-aware of what is going on outside the mind in something like the way we become f-aware of what is happening outside a room in which we watch TV. The only objects we are aware of are in the room (e.g., the television set); the only properties we are aware of are properties of those objects (patterns on the screen). *Only f-awareness* – awareness of what is happening on the playing field, concert hall, or broadcast studio – is capable of taking us outside the room.

I will not discuss such theories (basically sense-data theories). I set them aside, without argument, because they all deny thesis (2), and my

---

10 I will typically use movement and shape as my examples of properties that we can (and do) become aware of in visual perception. I could as well use (I sometimes do use) color, but for obvious reasons (relating to the thesis I am proposing) I prefer to avoid the "secondary" properties and concentrate on the "primary" ones since some people will surely insist that it is not the pumpkin that is (phenomenally) orange, but our experience (or some proper part of our experience) of the pumpkin. The only relevant property that the pumpkin has is a disposition to produce orange es (pumpkin experiences) in properly situated perceivers.

   I do not share this view of color (and the other so-called secondary properties). I do not see how any materialist can (see (1) and (2) and the following discussion). I take color, the surface property of things that we experience in experiencing objects, to be an objective property of the objects we experience. For this reason I sometimes use color, smell, sounds, etc. in my examples. For those who find this realism objectionable (or question-begging), please substitute an appropriate primary property – e.g., movement shape, orientation, extension – whenever I use an objectionable secondary property. I don't think anything important hangs on my choice of examples.

11 For skeptics it often *ends* here. If f-awareness is a form of knowledge, the *only f-awareness* is of mental affairs – i.e., facts of the form: that e is $\mathfrak{P}$.

purpose here is to understand the mind's awareness of itself in a way compatible with (1) and (2). Contrary to (2), sense-data theories affirm that there is something in a person's head that has the properties the person is aware of when he sees or hallucinates about an orange pumpkin. Sense data are inside, and sense data actually have the properties one is aware of when one sees or hallucinates about a pumpkin. The sense datum is orange. It is bulgy and shaped like a pumpkin. It moves – at least it does so relative to other sense data. In having a visual experience of a pumpkin it is the bulgy orange sense datum, an internal object, one is o-aware of, and it is the properties of this internal object one is p-aware of. Awareness of pumpkins is, at best, indirect. It is the same type of awareness (i.e., f-awareness) that one has of Boris Yeltsin when one "sees" him on TV.

Armed as we now are with the distinction between object-, property-, and fact-awareness, though, we are in a position to understand what goes wrong in traditional arguments for indirect realism. We are in a position to understand – and, thus, resist – arguments against (2). The mistake in traditional arguments lies in failing to distinguish between f-awareness of experience, that it has phenomenal character $\mathfrak{P}$, on the one hand, and, on the other, p-awareness of the qualities (e.g., $\mathfrak{P}$) that give it this character. Failing to distinguish these forms of awareness, one concludes, mistakenly, that awareness of what it is like to see (experience) pumpkins must be awareness of the properties (i.e., $\mathfrak{P}$) of these experiences. *That* is the first mistake – the mistake of inferring p-awareness of the properties of experience from f-awareness of the fact that experience has those properties. The second mistake (this is optional; the major damage has already been done) is inferring o-awareness from p-awareness – that is, inferring that one must be o-aware of e in order to be p-aware of e's properties. The conclusion? To be aware of what it is like to experience pumpkins, one must be aware of one's own pumpkin experiences in something like the way one is aware of pumpkins.

The fact that we don't have to be p-aware of an object's properties to be f-aware that it has those properties does not mean that we are *not* aware of our own experiences and their properties. It only shows that an awareness – even a privileged awareness – of what it is like to have an experience is not, by itself, a good reason to think we are aware of either the experience or its properties. Once the distinctions between kinds of awareness are in place, privileged awareness of what it is like to have an experience *may* simply be a form of fact-awareness, an indirect awareness of a fact about an experience that is both psychologically immediate and epistemically privileged.

But how is this possible? How is it possible to be aware in both a privileged and (or so it often seems) a direct way of facts about one's experiences without being aware of either the experiences themselves or their properties? If one's f-awareness of one's own experience is supposed to be indirect, like becoming aware, by looking at X-ray photographs, that one's arm is broken, what objects and properties is it an awareness *of* that is supposed to give one this awareness? I can become (indirectly) aware that my arm is broken by having the doctor tell me it is or by looking at the photographs for myself, but what could possibly bring about an indirect fact-awareness of the quality of one's own experience that would preserve the immediacy and privileged character of this awareness? No one tells us – indeed, no one can tell us – what our own experiences are like the way a doctor can tell us about our broken bones. X-rays are not of much help in telling what it is like to be a bat or what it is like to see orange pumpkins. What, then, is supposed to tell us what qualities our experiences have if we are not, in having them, p-aware of them? There must be something (other than the experience) that tells us this since, in accordance with (1) and (2), we are now assuming that the properties we are aware of in having the experience are not properties of the experience. If we are to be made f-aware of what our experiences are like – that they are $\mathfrak{P}$ for some value of "$\mathfrak{P}$" – then we must be made f-aware of this fact by an awareness of properties and objects other than those of the experience itself. What are these other objects and properties?

They are – what else? – the objects and properties these experiences make us aware of. One is made aware of what a pumpkin experience is like (that it is $\mathfrak{P}$) not by an awareness of the experience, but by an awareness of the pumpkin and an awareness of its (the pumpkin's) properties. When the perception is veridical, the qualities one becomes p-aware of in having a perceptual experience are qualities of external objects (the pumpkins) that one experiences, not qualities of the pumpkin experience. One becomes f-aware of experience – that it is $\mathfrak{P}$ – by p-awareness of P – the pumpkin's properties. The reason p-awareness of P can make one f-aware that one's experience is $\mathfrak{P}$ is that $\mathfrak{P}$ *is* the property of being an experience, in fact a p-awareness, of P. P, the property one is aware of in having the experience, tells one what specific kind of experience e is: it is an e of the $\mathfrak{P}$ kind – that is an awareness-of-P-kind. Even when there are no pumpkins, even when hallucinating, it is nonetheless true that *what* (properties) one is *p*-aware *of* in having the pumpkin experience are color, shape, texture, distance, and movement – properties that pumpkins normally have.

Consider the following analogy. One does not have to see (be aware of) pictures of *o* (a photograph of a pumpkin, say) in order to be made aware of what these pictures are like. It is sometimes enough to look at what these pictures are pictures *of* (viz., the pumpkins) in order to tell what the picture is like. The same is true of a visual experience of pumpkins. Visual experiences of pumpkins are not pictures of pumpkins, of course, but the analogy holds. To know what the experience is like, what properties it has, it is enough for the experiencer to "look at" what the experience is an experience *of* (something that, as the expenencer, she cannot help but be doing). *That* will tell her what the (relevant) properties of the experience are.[12]

The key to this account is the relation between P, the property we are *p*-aware of in having experience e, and the property of the experience ($\mathfrak{P}$) that we thereby become *f*-aware that e has. If P is the pumpkin's movement, a property one becomes aware of in observing a moving pumpkin, then $\mathfrak{P}$ is the property of being a *p-awareness-of-P*. $\mathfrak{P}$ is the property a possibly stationary experience has that makes it an experience of movement.[13] Although $\mathfrak{P}$ is not a property one is *p*-aware of,

---

12 The analogy may mislead in one respect. It may be thought, for instance, that looking at what a photograph is a photograph of does *not* tell me what the photograph is like. I also have to know something about the camera and film that produced the photo. Was the camera in focus, for instance? Wide angle or telephoto? Was it color film or black and white? Unless I know these things, looking at what the photo is a photo of tells me next to nothing about what the photo is like.

All this is true, and it is an important disanalogy. It is, in fact, the reason why one cannot tell what it is like to be a bat by looking at what the bat "looks" at (perceives) – a moth, say. We don't know enough about the bat's "camera" and "film" to tell much about what the bat's internal "pictures" of the moth are like. But this point, although important, does not upset the usefulness of the analogy. For in the case of experience, the person having the experience, the experiencer, looks at objects *with* the "camera" and "film" whose characteristics are (or may be) unknown to third parties. The person sees objects, as it were, *through* the lens and *with* the preloaded film – hence, *as* these objects are represented in his experience of them.

13 If one is a reductive materialist (like me), one will take $\mathfrak{P}$ to be some physical property of the brain, a property the having of which makes an internal state into an experience, a *p*-awareness, a representation, of movement. I try to give an account of this property (in Dretske 1995). For present purposes, though, reductive accounts of $\mathfrak{P}$ are beside the point. All that is needed to achieve compatibility with (1) and (2) is that $\mathfrak{P} \neq P$ – i.e., the property (i.e., $\mathfrak{P}$) of an experience that makes it an experience (a *p*-awareness) of P (i.e. movement) is not (or need not) itself be P (the property we are aware of in having the experience).

it is a property that (helps) make an experience the kind of experience it is – an experience of a *moving* pumpkin.

What this means is that *if* we follow philosophical convention and take qualia to be properties of one's experiences (and not the properties one experiences), then it is 𝔅, not *P*, that is the quale. Nonetheless, it is *P* (i.e., movement), not 𝔅 (an awareness of movement), that one is *p*-aware of. One is (or can be – see §4) aware of the quale 𝔅, to be sure, but this is *fact*-, not *property*-awareness. One's experiences of movement do not (or need not) have the properties one is *p*-aware of in having these experiences. The experiences of movement don't (needn't) move. Nonetheless, when experiencing movement, the property the experience has is 𝔅, a *p*-awareness of movement.

This account of the mind's awareness of itself gives a neat and, I think, satisfying account of both the psychological immediacy (i.e., the seeming directness) of introspective knowledge and the epistemically privileged character of self awareness. *F*-awareness of the fact that one's experience (of *P*) is 𝔅 is psychologically immediate because, although it is indirect (one is not *p*-aware of 𝔅), one cannot have an experience of this sort without thereby being aware of a property – viz., *P* – of external objects that reveals to the person having the experience exactly what property – viz., an awareness of *P* (= 𝔅) – it is that his or her experience has. Technically speaking (given my earlier definitions), this is indirect fact-awareness, yes, but the fact one is indirectly aware of is so directly given by the properties (of external objects) one is aware of that the process (from *p*-awareness of *P* to *f*-awareness that one's experience is 𝔅), when it occurs, *seems* direct and immediate. It can be made to seem even more direct, of course, if one confuses the properties one is aware of in having the experience with the properties of the experience. *F*-awareness that ℯ is 𝔅 is also privileged because *only* the person having the experience is necessarily (in virtue of having it) aware of a property (i.e., *P*) that reveals what kind of experience (viz., 𝔅) he is having. Other people might also be experiencing *P*, of course, but unless they know you are, they can only guess about the character of your experience.

Before leaving this discussion of perceptual experience, it may be useful to see how a familiar (to philosophers) scenario plays out on this account. What Jackson's (1986) Mary does not have before she emerges from her colorless room is an awareness of red (or of any other color). Assuming that colors are objective properties (if they aren't, we don't need Jackson's argument to refute materialism; (1) and (2) will do the

170

job), Mary knows all about tomatoes – that they are red (P) – and she knows all about what goes on in other people's heads when they see red objects (there is something in their brain that has the property $\mathfrak{P}$), but she does not herself have internal states of this sort. If she did, she would, contrary to hypothesis, be p-aware of (she would actually experience) the color red. Once she walks outside the room, objects ($\mathfrak{e}$s) in her head acquire $\mathfrak{P}$ – she becomes p-aware of red. She is now aware of things (i.e., p-aware of colors) she was not previously aware of. Using our present distinctions to express Jackson's point, the question posed is not whether Mary is now aware of something she was not previously aware of (of course she is; she is now p-aware of colors), but whether Mary is now f-aware of things that she was not previously f-aware of. The answer, on the present account of things, is No.[14] Mary always knew that ripe tomatoes were red (P) and that ripe tomato experiences were $\mathfrak{P}$ – viz., awarenesses of red. There are no other relevant *facts* for her to become aware of (although there are now ways of expressing these facts that were not previously available to her[15]). Emerging from the color-free room gives her an awareness of properties (P) that figure in the facts (that o is P) she was already aware of, but it doesn't give her an awareness of any new facts.

We have now taken the first step in this account of the mind's awareness of itself. In a way that is consistent with both (1) and (2) and in a way that preserves the essential features of the mind's awareness of itself (the psychological immediacy and epistemically privileged character of this awareness) we have an account – at least the broad outlines of one – of how we are aware of our own experiences of the world. What remains to be done is to see whether this account can be generalized to *all* mental states. My efforts at generalization (§3) will be feeble. I can, at this point, do little more than gesture in what I take to be the appropriate directions. I close (in §4) with a mildly interesting implication of this account of self-awareness.

---

14   There is the fact that she now occupies states having $\mathfrak{P}$, but this doesn't count since this fact wasn't a fact until she recovered her color vision. What Mary doesn't know is supposed to be a fact about the world as it existed *before* she recovered her color vision.

15   The fact she was formerly aware of that she expressed as "Experience $\mathfrak{e}$ is a p-awareness of red" can now (now that she is p-aware of red) be expressed as "Experience $\mathfrak{e}$ is a p-awareness of *this*."

Up to this point I have focused exclusively on conscious perceptual experiences, mental episodes that are *of* things – whatever objects and properties we are, in having the experience, made aware of. Perceptual experiences are being identified with internal states having properties (e.g., $\mathfrak{P}$) that make them *p*-awarenesses, experiences, of the properties (e.g., *P*) that external objects have. Something, e, in my head having the property $\mathfrak{P}$ (a property that is not movement) constitutes my awareness of movement (*P*). I can become *f*-aware that something in me has $\mathfrak{P}$ by an awareness of *P*. If e's having $\mathfrak{P}$ is caused by a pumpkin having *P* (i.e., by the movement of a pumpkin), then I am aware of a pumpkin's movement. I see it move. If there is no such object, I am aware of movement without being aware of any moving object and, thus, without being aware of any object's movement. I hallucinate about or visualize movement.

This account works nicely enough for phenomenal experiences that are, in some ordinary sense, *of* or *about* things (mental states the having of which makes us perceptually aware of things). For this reason it is tempting to try extending the account to mental states that are, in some related (but, perhaps, different) sense, also *of* or *about* things: beliefs, desires, intentions, hopes, and, in general, the propositional attitudes. Just as my experience of movement has a property that makes it a *p*-awareness of movement, perhaps my belief (i.e., my *f*-awareness) that some object, *o*, is moving is, likewise, an internal state having a property, $\mathfrak{P}$ (not itself movement), a property the having of which makes an internal state into a conceptual representation or depiction (i.e., an *f*-awareness) of movement. Just as the English word "movement" need not itself be moving in order to figure in a representation (a sentence, for example) of something as moving, so too, perhaps, there are symbols (concepts?) in the head that do not (or need not) have the properties they represent objects as having. If this were so, then thoughts, just like experiences, would be mental states that would not (or need not) have the properties we become *f*-aware of in having these thoughts.

If this were so, then we could tell the same story about awareness of these states that we told about our *f*-awareness of perceptual experiences. We become *f*-aware that we are having thoughts about movement (internal states with $\mathfrak{P}$) by actually thinking about movement. It is the movement we think *about* – the content of our thought – that (when

172

we introspect) "tells us" *what* we are thinking about and, hence, if we understand what thinking amounts to, *that* we are thinking about movement (not color or shape). Just as I reach the f-awareness that I am experiencing movement from a p-awareness of movement, so too I reach an f-awareness that I am thinking that o moves from an f-awareness that o is moving.[16]

I will not pursue this line of thought any further here since it seems like a more or less obvious extension of the present theory, and there are much more difficult problems to face. Unlike the propositional attitudes there are a great many mental states (emotions, moods, and so forth) that, unlike experiences and thoughts (both of which seem representational at some level), do not, at least not on the surface, make us aware of anything (either of objects, properties, or facts). And it is these states that pose the real problem for the present account. When I am hungry, have a splitting headache, or am depressed, for instance, I seem to be aware of mental objects (the hunger, the ache, the depression) and their properties (the headache is *splitting*, the hunger *gnawing*, the depression *constant*). Surely in such cases I am aware not only of the fact that I have certain feelings or am in a certain mood, but also of the feelings and moods themselves – the pain, the hunger, the depression.

This, I concede, is a natural way to talk about feelings, emotions, and moods. What I think worth questioning, though, is whether this way of talking doesn't embody a confusion between *awareness* of something (an act) and the *something* of which we are aware (the object of that act) – a confusion that is fostered by a failure to distinguish between the different things we can be aware of. Why suppose, for instance, that feelings of hunger are internal mental objects (i.e., conditions, states) we are o-aware of and not awarenesses (i.e., experiences) of certain internal (non-mental) objects – a chemical state of the blood, say? Just as we conceived of visual experiences as internal states having the property of being awarenesses of P (for some P of an external o), why can't hunger be similarly conceived of as an internal experience (a p-awareness) of the properties of an *internal o*? Why can't an itch in one's arm be thought of *not* as something in the arm (brain?) one is o-aware of, but an o-awareness (in the head) of a physical state of the arm? Why can't we,

---

16 Of course, if o isn't in fact moving, then I can't be f-aware that it is moving. It merely *seems*(in some doxastic sense of "seems" that is distinct from the phenomenal) that o is moving.

173

following Damasio (1994), conceive of emotions, feelings, and moods as perception of chemical, hormonal, visceral, and musculoskeletal states of the body?

This way of thinking about pains, itches, tickles, and other bodily sensations puts them in exactly the same category as the experiences we have when we are made perceptually aware of our environment. The only difference is that bodily sensations are the experiences we have of objects in the body (the stomach, the head, the joints, etc.), not objects outside the body. What gives these sensations their phenomenal character, the qualities we use, subjectively, to individuate them, are the properties these experiences are experiences of, the properties (of various parts of the body) that these experiences make us p-aware of (irritation, inflammation, time of onset, injury, strain, distention, intensity, chemical imbalance, and so on). What gives a (veridical) visual experience of an orange pumpkin *its* particular quality ($\mathfrak{P}$) are the qualities of the pumpkin (viz., P) that this experience (in virtue of being $\mathfrak{P}$) is an experience of. Likewise, what gives headaches their particular quality (what distinguishes them from pains in the back, itches, thirst, anger, or fear) are the properties (and these include *locational* properties) that these experiences are p-awarenesses of. Just as one becomes aware of external objects in having visual and olfactory experiences, so one becomes aware of various parts of the body (and the properties of these parts) in having bodily sensations – for example, pain. Having a headache is not an awareness – certainly not an o-awareness – of a mental entity: a pain in the head. The only awareness one has of pain is an f-awareness that one has it. In saying that one feels pain, what one is really saying is not that one is o-aware of something mental (viz., a pain), but that one feels (is aware of) a part of the body the feeling (awareness) of which *is* painful (is pain). Once again, the phenomenal qualities (= qualia) of these mental states are not the properties of those parts of the body one becomes p-aware of in occupying these states. They are, instead, *awarenesses* (= $\mathfrak{S}$) of these properties (P). We do not have to be aware of the state (e) itself (or *its* properties $\mathfrak{S}$) to be aware – authoritatively aware – that we occupy a state of that phenomenal kind. P gives our conscious awareness its phenomenal character and tells us what kind of experience we are having.

But can such an account possibly work for *all* experiences – for love and hatred, joy and depression, ennui and anxiety? Even if such feelings are not all properly classified as "experiences," they all seem to have an associated phenomenology that calls out for explanation. Can what-it-is-

174

like to have these feelings or experiences always be interpreted (using the model of perceptual experiences) not as internal objects we are o-aware of, but as awarenesses of the properties of internal objects? Can the entire phenomenology of the conscious mind be boiled down to the properties (of bodily parts and external objects) that we are p-aware of in having these experiences?

Whether it can or not, this is clearly the direction suggested by our analysis of perceptual experience. It may turn out, of course, that even if our account of perceptual experience is on target, perceptual experiences are unique. Other feelings, moods, and emotions – itches, pains, hunger, anger, jealousy, pleasure, and anxiety – may have a phenomenal character that they get from other sources. If the story I have told about perceptual experience is plausible, though, it is tempting to try extending it to other qualia-laden mental states along similar lines. I leave the argument that it can be so extended to another time.

4. PREREQUISITES OF SELF-AWARENESS

F-awareness, unlike p-awareness and o-awareness, requires an understanding of what one is aware of.[17] One cannot be f-aware that o is an apple without understanding, at some conceptual level, what an apple is. If a child (or an animal) doesn't know what an apple is, this does not prevent it from being o-aware of apples or p-aware of their properties (this presumably happens when the child is a few months old), but it prevents it from being f-aware that the apples (she is o-aware of) are apples.

Since the account developed in §2 and §3 identifies our awareness of our own (not to mention everyone else's) experiences with f-awareness, it requires of anyone aware of the $\mathfrak{P}$ quality of her own experience an understanding, a conceptual grasp, of the property $\mathfrak{P}$ (and, thus, at some level of specificity, of P that e's having $\mathfrak{P}$ is an awareness of). If S doesn't know what it is to be $\mathfrak{P}$, then even if S has a $\mathfrak{P}$-experience (i.e., an experience of P), S cannot be aware of this. S will be "blind" to it. Since the mind's awareness of itself is always (according to this account)

---

17 I take f-awareness (of the fact) that o is P to imply knowledge (of the fact) that o is P and the latter to imply belief that o is P. Belief, in turn, requires possession of concepts corresponding to the (obliquely) occurring expressions (i.e., "P") in the factive clause that specifies what is believed. Hence, one cannot be f-aware that o is P without possessing the (or a) concept corresponding to P.

175

f-awareness, there is no way one can be aware of one's mental states without having a mastery of relevant concepts. The senses make you aware (i.e., *o*-aware and *p*-aware) of the world (and, if we can generalize, your own body) before you have developed the concepts needed for understanding what you are aware of, but, lacking a "mental sense" (a sense that allows us to become *o*-aware of the mind and *p*-aware of its properties) we must first develop suitable concepts, those that pick out properties we are *p*-aware of, before we can be made conscious of what transpires in our own minds.

This result may seem mildly paradoxical, so let me take a moment to dispel the mystery. Imagine a child completely naive about numbers and shapes who is shown brightly colored geometrical shapes. Possessing normal eyesight, the child sees differences between these figures in the sense that the pentagons look (phenomenally) different from the triangles and squares. How else explain why we could teach her to say "pentagon" when (and only when) she saw a pentagon? In the terminology we have already introduced for describing these facts, the child (before learning) is *o*-aware of circles, squares, and pentagons and *p*-aware of their shapes. The child hasn't yet been taught what a circle, a square, or a pentagon is, so she isn't (yet) *f*-aware of what these figures are, but that doesn't prevent her from being aware of the figures themselves and *p*-aware of their (different) shapes.

Is the child also aware – in *any* sense – of what its experience of these shapes is like, of what it is like to see a pentagon? No.[18] Lacking the concept of a pentagon (not to mention the concept of awareness), the *only* awareness the child has when she sees a pentagon is an awareness of the pentagon and its shape. She cannot be made aware of her experience of the pentagon until she develops the resources for understanding, at *some* level (see footnote 18), what pentagons are and what it means to be aware of (experience) them. Only then can she become aware of her pentagon experiences. In having an experience of a pentagon, the child is, to be sure, aware (i.e., *o*-aware) of a pentagon and *p*-aware of its distinctive shape. What the child lacks is not a visual awareness (experi-

---

18 If the child understands that this figure (a circle) is different from that figure (a square) it can (assuming it has the concept EXPERIENCE) be aware that its experience of this is different from its experience of that without being aware at any more determinate level of what either experience is like. If you can distinguish (by taste) wines, you don't have to know what feature(s) of the wine you are tasting (i.e., you do not need to be able to identify wines having that feature) to know that wines differing in that feature taste different.

ence) of pentagons, but an awareness of pentagon experiences. Awareness of experience awaits development of the understanding, an understanding of what property the experience is a p-awareness of. If you lack this understanding, you can still become aware of pentagons (just open your eyes in a pentagon-infested environment), but you cannot be aware of your pentagon experiences. It is like awareness of neutrinos. Being what they are (i.e., unobservable: we do not have a sense organ that makes us o-aware of them), neutrinos are objects one cannot be aware of until one learns physics. Unlike pentagons, you have to know what they are to be aware of them.

The mind becomes aware of itself, of its own conscious experiences, by a developmental process in which concepts needed for such awareness are acquired. You don't need the concepts of PENTAGON or EXPERIENCE to experience (e.g., see or feel) pentagons, but you do need these concepts to become aware of pentagon experiences. As psychologists are learning (in the case of such concepts as EXPERIENCE), this doesn't happen with children until around the age of four to five years. In most animals it never happens. The mind is the first − indeed, the *only* − thing we are aware with, but it is among the last things we are aware of.

REFERENCES

Chisholm, R. 1957. *Perceiving*. Ithaca, NY: Cornell University Press.
Damasio, A. R. 1994. *Descartes' Error: Emotion, Reason, and the Human Brain*. New York: Avon Books.
Dretske, F. 1995. *Naturalizing the Mind*. Cambridge, MA: MIT Press/A Bradford Book.
Frisby, J. P. 1980. *Seeing: Illusion, Brain and Mind*. Oxford: Oxford University Press.
Hardcastle, V. G. 1994. Psychology's Binding Problem and Possible Neurobiological Solutions. *Journal of Consciousness Studies*, 1: 1, pp. 66–90.
Jackson, F. 1986. What Mary Didn't Know. *The Journal of Philosophy*, LXXXIII, pp. 291–295.
Locke, J. 1959. *An Essay concerning Human Understanding*. Ed. A. C. Fraser. New York: Dover Publications. First published in 1689.

10

What Good Is Consciousness?

If consciousness is good for something, conscious things must differ in some causally relevant way from unconscious things. If they do not, then, as Davies and Humphreys conclude, too bad for consciousness: "psychological theory need not be concerned with this topic."[1]

Davies and Humphreys are applying a respectable metaphysical idea – the idea, namely, that if an object's having a property does not make a difference to what that object does, if the object's causal powers are in no way enhanced (or diminished) by its possession of this property, then nothing the object does can be explained by its having that property. A science dedicated to explaining the behavior of such objects would not have to concern itself with that property. That is why being an uncle is of no concern to the psychology (let alone the physics) of uncles. I am an uncle, yes, but my being so does not (causally speaking)[2] enable (or prevent) me to do anything I would not otherwise be able to do. The fact that I am an uncle (to be distinguished, of course, from my *believing* I am an uncle) does not explain anything I do. From the point of view

Reprinted from *Canadian Journal of Philosophy* 27(1) (March 1997), 1–15, by permission of the publisher.

1 Davies and Humphreys (1993), 4–5
2 There is a sense in which it enables me to do things I would not otherwise be able to do – e.g., bequeath my books to my nephews and nieces – but (I hope it is obvious) this is not a causal sense of "enable." My having nephews and nieces is necessary for my bequeathing my books to them, but nothing I do *in* bequeathing my books to them would I be disabled from doing if I did not have nephews and nieces (i.e., if I weren't an uncle). The result (of what I do) would just not be describable in this way if I were not an uncle.

    I hope the distinction between causal and other senses of "enable" is sufficiently intuitive to let me proceed without supplying an analysis. I'm not sure I could.

of understanding human behavior, then, the fact that some humans are uncles is epiphenomenal. If consciousness is like that — if it is like being an uncle — then, for the same reason, psychological theory need not be concerned with it. It has no purpose, no function. No good comes from being conscious.

Is this really a worry? Should it be a worry? The journals and books, I know, are full of concern these days about the role of consciousness.[3] Much of this concern is generated by startling results in neuropsychology (more of this later). But is there a real problem here? Can there be a serious question about the advantages, the benefits, the good of being conscious? I don't think so. It seems to me that the flurry of interest in the function of consciousness betrays a confusion about several quite elementary distinctions. Once the distinctions are in place — and there is nothing especially arcane or tricky about them — the advantages (and, therefore, the good) of consciousness is obvious.

1. THE FIRST DISTINCTION: CONSCIOUS BEINGS VS. CONSCIOUS STATES

Stones are not conscious, but we are.[4] So are many animals. We are not only conscious (full stop), we are conscious *of* things — of objects (the bug in my soup), events (the commotion in the hall), properties (the color of his tie), and facts (that someone is following me). Using Rosenthal's (1990) terminology, I will call all these *creature* consciousness. In this sense the word is applied to beings who lose and regain consciousness and are conscious of things and that things are so.

Creature consciousness is to be distinguished from what Rosenthal calls *state* consciousness — the sense in which certain mental states, processes, events, and activities (in or of conscious beings) are said to be either conscious or unconscious. When we describe desires, fears, and experiences as being conscious or unconscious we attribute or deny consciousness not to a being, but to some state, condition, or process in that being. States (processes, etc.), unlike the creatures in whom they

---

3 For recent expressions of interest, see Velmans (1991), Rey (1988), and Van Gulick (1989).
4 I here ignore dispositional senses of the relevant terms — the sense in which we say of someone or something that it is a conscious being even if, at the time we describe it this way, it is not (in any occurrent sense) conscious. So, for example, in the dispositional sense, I am a conscious being even during dreamless sleep.

occur, are not conscious of anything or that anything is so, although we can be conscious of them and (more of this in §2) their occurrence in a creature may make that creature conscious of something.

That is the distinction. How does it help with our question? I'll say how in a moment, but before I do, I need to make a few things explicit about my use of relevant terms. I have discovered that not everyone talks the way I do when they talk about consciousness. So let me say how I talk. My language is, I think, entirely standard (I use no technical terms), but just in case my readers talk funny, I want them to know how I (and, I hope, other ordinary folk) talk about these matters.

For purposes of this discussion and in accordance with most dictionaries I regard "conscious" and "aware" as synonyms. Being conscious of a thing (or fact) is being aware of it. Alan White (1964) describes interesting differences between the ordinary use of "aware" and "conscious." He also describes the different liaisons they have to noticing, attending, and realizing. Although my use of these expressions as synonymous for present purposes blurs some of these distinctions, I think nothing essential to this topic is lost by ignoring the nuances.

I assume, furthermore, that seeing, hearing, smelling, and so on are sensory or perceptual forms of consciousness. Consciousness is the genus; seeing, hearing, and smelling are species (the traditional five sense modalities are not, of course, the *only* species of consciousness). Seeing is visual awareness. Hearing is auditory awareness. Smelling burning toast is becoming aware – in an olfactory way – of burning toast. One might also see the burning toast. And feel it. These are other modalities of awareness, other *ways* of being conscious of the toast.[5] You may not pay much attention to what you see, smell, or hear, but if you see, smell, or hear it, you are conscious of it.

This is important. I say that if you see, smell, or hear it, you are conscious of it. The "it" refers to *what* you are aware of (the burning toast), not *that* you are aware of it. When one is aware of burning toast, there are two ways one might fail to be aware that one is aware of it. First, one might know one is aware of something, but not know what

5 I here ignore disputes about whether, in some strict sense, we are really aware of objects or only (in smell) odors emanating from them or (in hearing) voices or noises they make. I shall always take the perceptual object – what it is we see, hear, or smell (if there is such an object) – to be some external physical object or condition. I will not be concerned with just *what* object or condition this is.

it is. "What is that I smell?" is the question of a person who might well be aware of (i.e., smell) burning toast without being aware that it is burning toast he is aware of. Second, even if one knows what it is one is aware of – knows that it is burning toast – one might not understand what it means to be aware of it, might not, therefore, be aware that one is *aware* of it. A small child or an animal – someone who lacks the concept of awareness – can be conscious of (i.e., smell) burning toast without ever being aware that they are aware of something. Even if she happens to know that it (i.e., what she is aware of) is burning toast, she may not, therefore, be aware – that she is *aware* of it.

The language here is a bit tricky, so let me give another example. One can be aware of (e.g., hear) a French horn without being aware that that is what it is. One might think it is a trombone or (deeply absorbed in one's work) not be paying much attention at all (but later remember hearing it). If asked whether you hear a French horn, you might well (falsely) deny it or (more cautiously) say that you don't know. Not being aware that you are aware of a French horn does not mean you are not aware of a French horn. Hearing a French horn is being conscious *of* a French horn. It is not – not *necessarily* anyway – to be aware *that* it is a French horn or aware that you are aware of it. Mice who hear – and thus become auditorily aware of – French horns never become aware that they are aware of French horns.[6]

So, once again, when I say that if you see, hear, or smell something you must be conscious of it, the "it" refers to *what* you are aware of (burning toast, a French horn), not *what it is* (i.e., that it is burning toast, a French horn) you are aware or *that* you are aware of it. Animals (not to mention human infants) are presumably aware of a great many things (they see, smell, and feel the things around them). Often, though, they are not aware of what it is they are aware of and seldom (if ever) are they aware that they are aware of it.

So much for terminological preliminaries. I have not yet (I hope) said anything that is controversial. Nonetheless, with only these meager

---

6 In saying this I assume two things, both of which strike me as reasonably obvious: (1) to be aware that you are aware of a French horn requires some understanding of what awareness is (not to mention an understanding of what French horns are); and (2) mice (even if we give them some understanding of French horns) do not understand what awareness is. They do not, that is, have the concept of awareness.

resources, we are in a position to usefully divide our original question into two more manageable parts. Questions about the good, the purpose, or the function of consciousness can be questions either about creature consciousness or about state consciousness. I will, for the rest of this section, take them to be questions about creature consciousness. I return to state consciousness in the next section.

If, then, we take our question about the good of consciousness as a question about *creature* consciousness, about the advantages that consciousness affords the animals who are conscious, the answer would appear to be obvious. If animals could not see, hear, smell, and taste the objects in their environment – if they were not (in these ways) conscious – how could they find food and mates, avoid predators, build nests, spin webs, get around obstacles, and, in general, do the thousand things that have to be done in order to survive and reproduce?

Let an animal – a gazelle, say – who is aware of prowling lions – where they are and what they are doing – compete with one who is not and the outcome is predictable. The one who is conscious will win hands down. Reproductive prospects, needless to say, are greatly enhanced by being able to see and smell predators. *That*, surely, is an evolutionary answer to questions about the benefits of creature consciousness.[7] Take away perception – as you do when you remove consciousness – and you are left with a vegetable. You are left with an eatee, not an eater. That is why the eaters of the world (most of them anyway) are conscious.

This answer is so easy that I expect to be told that I'm not really answering the question everyone is asking. I will surely be told that questions about the function of consciousness are not questions about why we – conscious beings – are conscious. It is not a question about the biological advantage of being able to see, hear, smell, and feel (thus, being conscious of) the things around us. It is, rather, a question about *state* consciousness, a question about why there are conscious states,

---

7   This is not to say that consciousness is *always* advantageous. As Georges Rey reminds me, some tasks – playing the piano, pronouncing language, and playing sports – are best performed when the agent is largely unaware of the performatory details. Nonetheless, even when one is unconscious of the means, consciousness of the end (e.g., the basket into which one is trying to put the ball, the net into which one is trying to hit the puck, the teammate to whom one is trying to throw the ball) is essential. You don't have to be aware of just how you manage to backhand the shot to do it skillfully, but, if you are going to be successful in backhanding the puck into the net, you have to be aware of the net (where it is).

processes, and activities *in* conscious creatures. Why, for instance, do conscious beings have conscious experiences and thoughts?

2. THE SECOND DISTINCTION: OBJECTS VS. ACTS OF AWARENESS

If our question is one about the benefits of conscious *states*, then, of course, we have preliminary work to do before we start answering it. We have to get clear about what a conscious state is. What makes an experience, a thought, a desire conscious? We all have a pretty good grip on what a conscious animal is. It is one that is – via some perceptual modality – aware of things going on around (or in) it. There are surely modes of awareness, ways of being conscious, that we do not know about and will never ourselves experience. We do not, perhaps, understand bat phenomenology or what it is like for a dogfish to sense its prey electrically. But we do understand the familiar modalities – seeing, hearing, tasting, and so on – and these, surely, qualify *as ways* of being conscious. So I understand, at a rough and ready level, what someone is talking about when she talks about a creature's being conscious in one of these ways. But what does it mean to speak not of an animal's being conscious in one of these ways, but of some state, process, or activity *in* the animal as being conscious? States, remember, aren't conscious *of* anything. They are just conscious (or unconscious) *full stop*. What kind of property is this? Until we understand this, we won't be in a position to even speculate about what the function of a conscious state is.

There are, as far as I can see, only two options for making sense out of state consciousness. Either a state is made conscious by (1) its being an *object* or (2) its being an *act* of creature consciousness. A state of creature S is an *object* of creature consciousness by S being conscious of it. A state of S is an *act* of creature consciousness, on the other hand, not by S being aware *of* it, but by S being made aware (so to speak) *with* it – by its occurrence in S making (i.e., constituting) S's awareness of something (e.g., an external object). When state consciousness is identified with a creature's *acts* of awareness, the creature need not be aware of these states for them to be conscious. What makes them conscious is not S's awareness of them, but their role in making S conscious – typically (in the case of sense perception), of some external object.

Consider the second possibility first. On this option, a conscious experience is one that makes an animal conscious (of whatever the experience is an experience of). When a gazelle sees a lion, its visual

183

experience of the lion qualifies as a conscious experience, a conscious state, because it makes, or helps make,[8] the gazelle visually conscious of the lion. Without this experience the gazelle would not see the lion.

There are, to be sure, states of (processes and activities in) the gazelle that are not themselves conscious but that are nonetheless necessary to make the animal (visually) aware of the lion. Without photoreceptors (eyes) and the various states of these receptors, the animal would not see anything — would not, therefore, be visually aware of the lion. Yet, these electrical and chemical events occurring in the retina are not conscious. This is true enough, but it is irrelevant to an act conception of conscious experience. According to an act conception of state con-sciousness, a conscious visual state is one that (in the case of lions) is necessary to the awareness of lions and sufficient for the awareness of those aspects, features, or properties (color, shape, movement, etc.) that seeing (or hallucinating) lions makes one aware of. The eyes may be necessary for the gazelle to be conscious of external objects (i.e., lions), but they are not necessary for the gazelle to be aware of those leonine properties that seeing lions make it aware of. That is why, on an act account of state consciousness, the processes in early vision, those occur-ring in the retina and optic nerve, are not conscious. They may be necessary to a creature's visual awareness of external *objects*, but they are not essential to creature awareness of *properties*. Even without a func-tional optical system, the creature can still dream about or hallucinate the things it can no longer see. The same *acts* of awareness can still occur. They just do not have the same (according to some, they don't have *any*) objects.

If we agree about this — agree, that is, that conscious experiences are internal states that make creatures conscious of things (typically, in the case of sense perception, of external objects) — then the function, the good, of state consciousness becomes evident. It is to make creatures conscious, and if (see §1) there is no problem about why animals are conscious, then, on the *act* conception of conscious states, there is no problem about why states are conscious. Their function is to make creatures conscious. Without state consciousness, there is no creature consciousness. If there is a biological advantage in gazelles being aware of prowling lions, then there is a purpose in gazelles having conscious

---

8 In the case of external objects (like lions) the experience is necessary, but not sufficient, for awareness of (seeing) the lion. We also need a lion, of course, and whatever causal relations between the lion and the experience are required to make the experience *of* the lion.

experiences. The purpose is to enable the gazelle to see, hear, and smell the lions.

I do not expect many people to be impressed with this result. I expect to be told that internal states are conscious not (as I have suggested) if the animal is conscious *with* them, but, rather, if the animal (in whom they occur) is conscious *of* them. A conscious state is conscious in virtue of being an object, not an act, of creature awareness. A state becomes conscious, according to this orthodox line of thinking, when it becomes the object of some higher-order act, a thought or experience. Conscious states are not states that make the creatures in whom they occur conscious; it is the other way around: creatures make the states that occur in them conscious by becoming conscious of them.

Since, according to this account, the only way a state can become an object of consciousness is if there are higher-order acts (i.e., thoughts or experiences) that take it as their object, this account of what makes a state conscious has come to be called an HO (for higher-order) theory of consciousness. It has several distinct forms, but all versions agree that an animal's experience (of lions, say) remains unconscious (or, perhaps, nonconscious) until the animal becomes aware of it. A higher-order awareness of one's lion-experience can take the form of a thought (an HOT theory) – in which case one is aware *that* (i.e., one thinks that) one is experiencing a lion – or the form of an experience (an HOE theory) – in which case one is aware of the lion-experience in something like the way one is aware of the lion: one experiences one's lion-experience (thus becoming aware of one's lion-experience) in the way one is aware of (experiences) the lion.

I have elsewhere (Dretske 1993, 1995) criticized HO theories of consciousness, and I will not repeat myself here. I am more concerned with what HO theories have to say – if, indeed, they have anything to say – about the good of consciousness. If conscious states are states we are, in some way, conscious of, why have conscious states? What do conscious states do that unconscious states don't do? According to HO theory, we (i.e., creatures) could be conscious of (i.e., see, hear, and smell) most of the objects and events we are now conscious of (and this includes whatever *bodily* conditions we are proprioceptively aware of) without ever occupying a conscious state. To be in a conscious state is to be conscious of the state, and since the gazelle, for example, can be conscious of a lion without being conscious of the internal states that make it conscious of the lion, it, can be conscious of the lion – that is, see, smell, feel, and hear the lion – while occupying no conscious states at all. This being so, what is the purpose, the biological point, of conscious states? It is awareness of the lion, not awareness of lion-experiences, that is presumably useful in the struggle for survival. It is the lions, not the lion-experiences, that are dangerous.

On an object conception of state consciousness, it is difficult to imagine how conscious states could have a function. To suppose that conscious states have a function would be like supposing that conscious ball bearings – that is, ball bearings we are conscious of – have a function. If a conscious ball bearing is a ball bearing we are conscious of, then conscious ball bearing have exactly the same causal powers as do the unconscious ones. The causal powers of a ball bearing (as opposed to the causal powers of *the observer* of the ball bearing) are in no way altered by being observed or thought about. The same is true of mental states like thoughts and experiences. If what makes an experience or a thought conscious is the fact that S (the person in whom it occurs) is, somehow, aware of it, then it is clear that the causal powers of the thought or experience (as opposed to the causal powers of the thinker or experiencer) are unaffected by its being conscious. Mental states and processes would be no less effective in doing their job – whatever, exactly, we take that job to be – if they were all unconscious. According to HO theories of consciousness, then, asking about the function of conscious states in mental affairs would be like asking about the function of conscious ball bearings in mechanical affairs.

David Rosenthal (a practicing HOT theorist) has pointed out to me in correspondence that although experiences do not acquire causal powers by being conscious, there may nonetheless be a purpose served by their being conscious. The purpose might be served not by the beneficial effects of a conscious experience (conscious and unconscious experiences have exactly the same effects, according to HO theories), but by the effects of the higher-order thoughts that makes the experience conscious. Although the conscious experiences don't do anything the unconscious experiences don't do, the creatures in which conscious experiences occur *are* different as a result of having the higher-order thoughts that make their (lower-order) experiences conscious. The animals having conscious experiences is therefore in a position to do things that animals having unconscious experiences are not. They can, for instance, run from the lion they (consciously) experience – something they might not do by having an unconscious experience of the lion. They can do this because they are (let us say) aware that they are aware of a lion – aware that they are having a lion-experience.[9] Animals in which the experience of the lion is unconscious, animals in which there is no higher-order awareness that they are aware of a lion, will not do this (at least not deliberately). This, then, is an advantage of conscious experience; perhaps – who knows? – it is the function of conscious experiences.

I concede the point. But I concede it about ball bearings too. I cannot imagine conscious ball bearings having a function – simply because conscious ball bearings don't do anything nonconscious ball bearings don't do – but I can imagine there being some purpose served by *our* being aware of ball bearings. If we are aware of them, we can, for instance, point at them, refer to them, talk about them. Perhaps, then, we can replace defective ones, something we wouldn't do if we were not aware of them, and this sounds like a useful thing to do. But this is something *we* can do by being aware of them, not something *they* can do by our being aware of them. If a conscious experience was an experience we were aware of, then there would be no difference between conscious and unconscious experiences – any more than there would be a difference between conscious and unconscious ball bearings. There would simply be a difference in the creatures in whom such experiences occurred, a difference in what they were aware of.

The fact that some people who have cancer are aware of having it, while others who have it are not aware of having it, does not mean there are two types of cancer – conscious and unconscious cancers. For exactly the same reason, the fact that some people (you and me, for instance) are conscious of having visual and auditory experiences of lions, while others (parrots and gazelles, for example) are not, does not mean that there are two sorts of visual and auditory experiences – conscious and unconscious. It just means that we are different from parrots and gazelles. We know things about ourselves that they don't, and it is sometimes useful to know these things. It does not show that *what* we know about – our conscious experiences – are any different from theirs. We both have experiences – conscious experiences – only we are aware of having them; they are not. Both experiences – those of the gazelle

---

9 I assume here that, according to HOT theories, the higher-order thought one has about a lion-experience that makes that experience conscious is that it is a lion-experience (an experience *of* a lion). This needn't be so (Rosenthal 1991 denies that it is so), but if it isn't so, it is even harder to see what the good of conscious experiences might be. What good would be a thought about a lion-experience that it was . . . what? . . . simply an experience? What good is that?

and those of a human – are conscious because, I submit, they make the creature in which they occur aware of things – whatever objects and conditions are perceived (lions, for instance). Being aware that you are having such experiences is as irrelevant to the nature of the experience as it is to the nature of observed ball bearings.[10]

3. THE THIRD DISTINCTION: OBJECT VS. FACT AWARENESS

Once again, I expect to hear that this is all too quick. Even if one should grant that conscious states are to be identified with acts, not objects, of creature awareness, the question is not what the evolutionary advantage of perceptual belief is, but what the advantage of perceptual (i.e., phenomenal) experience is. What is the point of having conscious experiences of lions (i.e., lion-qualia) as well as conscious beliefs about lions? Why are we aware of objects (lions) as well as various facts about them (that they are lions, that they are headed this way)? After all, in the business of avoiding predators and finding mates, what is important is not experiencing (e.g., seeing, hearing) objects, but knowing certain facts about these objects. What is important is not seeing a hungry lion but knowing (seeing) *that* it is a lion, hungry, or whatever (with all that this entails about the appropriate response on the part of lion-edible objects). Being aware of (i.e., seeing) hungry lions and being aware of them, simply, *as* tawny objects or *as* large, shaggy cats (something a two-year-old child might do) isn't much use to someone on the lion's dinner menu. It isn't the objects you are aware of, the objects you see – and, therefore, the qualia you experience – that is important in the struggle for survival; it is the facts you are aware of, what you *know* about what

---

10 I'm skipping over a difficulty that I should at least acknowledge here. There are a variety of mental states – urges, desires, intentions, purposes, etc. – that we speak of as conscious (and unconscious) whose consciousness cannot be analyzed in terms of their being *acts* (instead of *objects*) of awareness since, unlike the sensory states associated with perceptual awareness (seeing, hearing, and smelling), they are not, or do not seem to be, states of awareness. If *these* states are conscious, they seem to be made so by being objects, not acts of consciousness (see, e.g., van Gulick 1985). I don't have the space to discuss this alleged difference with the care it deserves. I nonetheless acknowledge its relevance to my present thesis by restricting my claims about state consciousness to *experiences* – more particularly, *perceptual* experiences. Whatever it is that makes a desire for an apple, or an intention to eat one, conscious, visual (gustatory, tactile, etc.) experiences of apples are made conscious not by the creature in whom they occur being conscious of them, but by making the creature in whom they occur conscious (of apples).

you see. Being aware of (seeing) poisonous mushrooms (these objects) is no help to an animal who is not aware of the fact that they are poisonous. It is the representation of the fact that another animal *is* a receptive mate, not simply the perception of a receptive mate, that is important in the game of reproduction. As we all know from long experience, it is no trick at all to see sexually willing (or, as the case may be, unwilling) members of the opposite sex. The trick is to see which is which – to know that the willing are willing and the others are not. That is the skill – and it is a cognitive skill, a skill involving knowledge of facts – that gives one a competitive edge in sexual affairs. Good eyesight, a discriminating ear, and a sensitive nose (and the assorted qualia associated with these sense modalities) are of no help in the struggle for survival if such experiences always (or often) yield false beliefs about the objects perceived. It is the conclusions, the beliefs, the knowledge that is important, not the qualia-laden experiences that normally give rise to such knowledge. So why do we have phenomenal experience of objects as well as beliefs about them? Or, to put the same question differently: Why are we conscious of the objects we have knowledge about?

Still another way of putting this question is to ask why we aren't all, in each sense modality, the equivalent of blindsighters who appear able to get information about nearby objects without experiencing (seeing) the objects.[11] In some sense blindsighters seem able to "see" the facts (at least they receive information about what the facts are – that there is, say, an X (not an O) on the right – without being able to see the objects (the Xs) on the right. No qualia. No phenomenal experience. If, therefore, a person can receive the information needed to determine appropriate action without experience, why don't we?[12] Of what use is

---

11 For more on blindsight see Weiskrantz (1986) and Milner and Rugg (1992). I here assume that a subject's (professed) absence of visual experience is tantamount to a claim that he cannot see objects, that he has no visual experience. The question that blindsight raises is why one has to see objects (or anything else, for that matter) in order to see facts pertaining to those objects – what (who, where, etc.) they are. If blindsighters can see where an object is, the fact that it is *there* (where they point), without seeing it (the object at which they point), what purpose is served by seeing it?

12 There are a good many reflexive "sensings" (Walker 1983: 240) that involve no awareness of the stimulus that is controlling behavior – e.g., accommodation of the lens of the eye to objects at different distances, reactions of the digestive system to internal forms of stimulation, direction of gaze toward peripherally seen objects. Milner (1992: 143) suggests that these "perceptions" are probably accomplished by the same midbrain visuomotor systems that mediate prey catching in frogs and orienting reactions in rats and monkeys. What is puzzling about blindsight is not that we get information we are not aware of

phenomenal experience in the game of cognition if the job can be done without it?

These are respectable questions. They deserve answers – scientific, not philosophical, answers. But the answers – at least in a preliminary way – would appear to be available. There are a great many important facts we cannot be made aware of unless we are, via phenomenal experience, made aware of objects these facts are facts about. There are also striking behavioral deficits – for example, an inability to initiate intentional action with respect to those parts of the world one does not experience (Marcel 1988). Humphrey (1970, 1972, 1974), worked for many years with a single monkey, Helen, whose capacity for normal vision was destroyed by surgical removal of her entire visual cortex. Although Helen originally gave up even looking at things, she regained certain visual capacities.

She improved so greatly over the next few years that eventually she could move deftly through a room full of obstacles and pick up tiny currants from the floor. She could even reach out and catch a passing fly. Her 3-D spatial vision and her ability to discriminate between objects that differed in size or brightness became almost perfect. (Humphrey 1992: 88).

Nonetheless, after six years she remained unable to identify even those things most familiar to her (e.g., a carrot). She did not recover the ability to recognize shapes or colors. As Humphrey described Helen in 1977 (Humphrey 1992: 89),

She never regained what we – you and I – would call the sensations of sight. I am not suggesting that Helen did not eventually discover that she could after all use her eyes to obtain information about the environment. She was a clever monkey and I have little doubt that, as her training progressed, it began to dawn on her that she was indeed picking up "visual" information from somewhere – and that her eyes had something to do with it. But I do want to suggest that, even if she did come to realize that she could use her eyes to obtain visual information, she no longer knew how that information came to her: if there was a currant before her eyes she would find that she knew its position but, lacking visual sensation, she no longer *saw* it as being there. . . . The information she obtained through her eyes was "pure perceptual knowledge" for which she was aware of no substantiating evidence in the form of visual sensation. . . .

(these reflexive sensings are all instances of that), but that in the case of blindsight one appears able to use this information in the control and guidance of deliberate, intentional action (when put in certain forced choice situations) – the sorts of actions that normally require awareness.

190

If we follow Humphrey and suppose that Helen, although still able to see where objects were (conceptually represent them as there), was unable to see them there, had no (visual) experience of them, we have a clue about what the function of phenomenal experience might be: we experience (i.e., see, hear, and smell) objects to help in our identification and recognition of them. Remove visual sensations of X and S might still be able to tell *where* X is, but S will not be able to tell *what* X is. Helen couldn't. That is – or may be – a reasonable empirical conjecture for the purpose of experience – for why animals (including humans) are, via perceptual experience, made aware of objects. It seems to be the only way – or at least *a* way – of being made aware of pertinent facts about them.

Despite the attention generated by dissociation phenomena, it remains clear that people afflicted with these syndromes are always "deeply disabled" (Weiskrantz 1991: 8). Unlike Helen, human patients never recover their vision to anything like the same degree that the monkey did. Although they do much better than they "should" be able to do, they are still not very good (see Humphrey 1992: 89). Blindsighted subjects cannot avoid bumping into lampposts, even if they can guess their presence or absence in a forced-choice situation. Furthermore,

All these subjects lack the ability to think about or to image the objects that they can respond to in another mode, or to inter-relate them in space and in time; and this deficiency can be crippling. (Weiskrantz, 1991: 8)

This being so, there seems to be no real empirical problem about the function (or at least a function) of phenomenal experience. The function of experience, the reason animals are conscious of objects and their properties, is to enable them to do all those things that those who do not have it cannot do. This is a great deal indeed. If we assume (as it seems clear from these studies we have a right to assume) that there are many things people with experience can do that they cannot do without it, then *that* is a perfectly good answer to a question about what the function of experience is. That is why we, and a great many other animals, are conscious of things and, thus, why, on an act conception of state consciousness, we have conscious experiences. Maybe something else besides experience would enable us to do the same things, but this would not show that experience didn't have a function. All it would show is that there was more than one way to skin a cat – more than one way to get the job done. It would not show that the mechanisms that did the job weren't good for something.

Davies, M. and G. W. Humphreys. Introduction. M. Davies and G. W. Humphreys, eds., *Consciousness* (Oxford: Blackwell 1993) 1–39.

Dretske, F. "Conscious Experience," *Mind* 102 (1993) 1–21.

. *Naturalizing the Mind* (Cambridge, MA: The MIT Press 1995).

Humphrey, N. "What the Frog's Eye Tells the Monkey's Brain," *Brain, Behavior and Evolution* 3 (1970) 324–337.

"Seeing and Nothingness," *New Scientist* 53 (1972) 682–684.

"Vision in a Monkey Without Striate Cortex: A Case Study," *Perception* 3 (1974) 241–255.

A History of the Mind: Evolution and the Birth of Consciousness (New York: Simon and Schuster 1992).

Marcel, A. J. "Phenomenal Experience and Functionalism." A. J. Marcel and E. Bisiach, eds. *Consciousness in Contemporary Science* (Oxford; Clarendon Press, 1988) 121–158.

Milner, A. D. "Disorders of Perceptual Awareness – Commentary" Milner and Rugg 1992: 139–158.

Milner, A. D. and M. D. Rugg, eds. *The Neuropsychology of Consciousness* (London: Academic Press 1992).

Rey, G. "A Question about Consciousness." H. Otto and J. Tuedio, eds., *Perspectives on Mind* (Dordrecht: Reidel 1988).

Rosenthal, D. "A Theory of Consciousness." Report No. 40, Research Group on Mind and Brain, ZiF, University of Bielefeld (1990).

"The Independence of Consciousness and Sensory Quality." E. Villanueva, ed. *Consciousness* (Atascadero, CA: Ridgeview 1991) 15–36.

van Gulick, R. "Conscious Wants and Self Awareness," *The Behavioral and Brain Sciences* 8 (1985) 555–556.

"What Difference Does Consciousness Make?" *Philosophical Topics* 17 (1989) 211–230.

Velmans, M. "Is Human Information Processing Conscious?" *Behavioral and Brain Sciences* 14 (1991) 651–668.

Walker, S. *Animal Thought* (London: Routledge and Kegan Paul 1983).

Weiskrantz, L., ed. *Blindsight: A Case Study and Implications* (Oxford: Oxford University Press 1986).

"Introduction: Dissociated Issues." Milner and Rugg 1992: 1–10.

White, A. R. *Attention* (Oxford: Basil Blackwell 1964).

Part Three

Thought and Intentionality

11

Putting Information to Work

Information isn't much good if it doesn't do anything. If the fact that an event carries information doesn't help explain the event's impact on the rest of the world, then, as far as the rest of the world is concerned, the event may as well not carry information. To put it bluntly, in the way positivists liked to put it, a difference that doesn't make a difference isn't really a difference at all. If an event's carrying information doesn't make a difference – and by a difference here I mean a causal difference, a difference in the kinds of effects it has – then for all philosophical (not to mention practical) purposes, the event doesn't carry information.

Surely, though, this is not a serious threat. We all know how useful a commodity information is, how even the smallest scrap can radically alter the course of human affairs. Think about its role in business, education, and war. Or consider the consequences of telling Michael about his wife's passionate affair with Charles. Kaboom! Their lives are never again the same. A small piece of information dramatically alters a part (and – who knows? – maybe eventually the entire course) of world history. In light of such obvious examples, how can anyone seriously doubt the causal efficacy of information and, hence, its relevance to understanding *why* some things turn out the way they do?

MEANING AND INFORMATION

There is a small subset of the world's objects on which information *appears* to have this kind of dramatic effect. These objects are people,

I wish to thank the Center for Advanced Study in the Behavioral Sciences, Stanford University, the National Endowment for the Humanities FC-20060-85, and the Andrew Mellon Foundation for their support during 1987–1988 when this essay was written.

195

objects like you and me, who *understand*, or *think* they understand, some of what is happening around them. Talking to Michael has profound effects, while talking to rocks and goldfish has little or no effect because Michael, unlike rocks and goldfish, understands, or thinks he understands, what he is being told. As a consequence, he is – typically at least – brought to believe certain things by these acts of communication. The rocks and the goldfish, on the other hand, are impervious to meaning. Instead of inducing belief, all we succeed in doing by remonstrating with such objects is jostling them a bit with the acoustic vibrations we produce.

So appearances may be deceptive. It may turn out that the difference between Michael and a goldfish isn't that Michael, unlike a goldfish, responds to information, but that Michael, unlike a goldfish, has beliefs, beliefs about what sounds mean (or about what the people producing these sounds mean), and which therefore (when he hears these sounds) induce beliefs on which he acts. These beliefs are, to be sure, sometimes aroused in him by sounds that actually carry information. Nevertheless, if these beliefs in no way depend on the information these sounds carry, then the information carried by the belief-eliciting stimulation is explanatorily irrelevant. After all, rocks and goldfish are also affected by information-carrying signals. When I talk to a rock, the rock is, as I said, jostled by acoustic vibrations. But the point is that although my utterances, the ones that succeed in jostling the rock, carry information, the information they carry is irrelevant to their effect on the rock. The information in this stimulation doesn't play any explanatory role in accounting for the rock's response to my communication. From the rock's point of view, my utterance may as well not carry information. Subtract the information (without changing the physical properties of the signal carrying this information) and the effect is exactly the same.

And so it may be with Michael. To find out, as we did with the rock, whether information is doing any real work, we merely apply Mill's Method of Difference. Take away the information, leaving everything else as much the same as possible, and see if the effect on Michael changes. As we all know, we needn't suppose that his wife, Sandra, is actually having an affair with Charles to get a reaction – in fact, the very same reaction – from Michael. He will react in exactly the same way if his alleged informant is lying or is simply mistaken about Sandra's affair. As long as the act of communication is the same, as long as what the speaker says and does *means* the same thing (to Michael), it will elicit the same reaction from him. What is said doesn't have to be *true* to get this effect. Michael just has to *think* it true. Nothing, in fact, need even be said. As long as Michael *thinks* it was (truly) said, as long as he thinks something with this meaning occurred, the result will be the same.

In saying that it is Michael's beliefs, not the meaning (if any) or information (if any) in the stimuli giving rise to these beliefs, that causally explains Michael's behavior, I am assuming that we can (and should) make appropriate distinctions between these ideas – between information, meaning, and belief. Some people, I know, use these notions interchangeably. That is too bad. It confuses things that should be kept distinct. According to this careless way of talking (especially prevalent, I think, among computer scientists), information *is* meaning or (at least) a species of meaning, and a belief (or a reasonable analog of a belief) just *is* an internal state having the requisite kind of meaning. So, for instance, anything that means that Michael's wife is having an affair carries this piece of information. If I *say* his wife is having an affair, then my utterance, *whether or not it is true*, carries this information. And if I enter this "information" into a suitably programmed computer, then, whether or not Sandra is unfaithful, the "fact" that she is unfaithful becomes part of the machine's "data base," the "information" on which it relies to reason, make inferences, answer questions, and solve problems. The computer now "thinks" that Michael's wife is having an affair. Michael doesn't even have to be married for the machine to be given the "data," the "information," that, as it were, his wife is having an affair. On this usage, the facts, the information, the data, are what we say they are.

It is perfectly understandable why computer scientists (not to mention a good many other people) prefer to talk this way. After all, it is natural to suppose that a computer (or a human brain, for that matter) is insensitive to the *truth* of the representations on which it operates. Put the sentence "P" in a machine's (or a human brain's) data file, and it will operate with those data in exactly the same way whether "P" is true or false, whether it is information or misinformation. From the machine's (brain's) point, of view, anything in it that qualifies as a belief qualifies as knowledge, anything in it that *means* that P is *information* that P. The distinction between meaning and information, between belief and knowledge, is a distinction that makes sense only from the outside. But what makes sense *only from the outside* of the machine or person whose behavior is being explained cannot (according to this way of thinking) help to explain that machine's (or person's) behavior. It cannot because the machine (or person) can't get outside of itself to make the needed discriminations. So, for practical explanatory purposes, meaning *is* (or may as well be) information.

Whatever the practical exigencies may be, something that makes sense only from the outside is, nonetheless, something that makes perfectly good sense. It certainly should make perfectly good sense to those of us (on the outside) talking about such systems. Something (like a statement) that *means* that Michael's wife is having an affair need not carry this information. It needn't carry this information either because Michael's wife is *not* having an affair or because, although she is, the words or symbols used to make this statement are being used in a way that is quite unrelated to her activities. I can *say* anything I like, that Mao Tse Tung liked chocolate ice cream for instance, and the words I utter will mean something quite definite – in this case that Mao Tse Tung liked chocolate ice cream. But these words, even if they are (by some lucky accident) true, won't carry the information that Mao liked chocolate ice cream. They won't because the sentence, used merely as an example and in total ignorance of Mao's preferences in ice cream, in no way depends on Mao's likes and dislikes. These words mean something, but they do not, not at least when coming from me, inform the listener. I might succeed in getting you to believe that Mao liked chocolate ice cream. I might, by telling you this, *mis*inform you about his taste in ice cream. But misinformation is not a species of information any more than belief is a species of knowledge.

So, at least on an ordinary understanding of information and meaning, something can mean that P without thereby carrying the information that P. And someone can believe that P without ever having received the information that P. Often enough, what makes people believe that P is being told that P by someone they trust. Sometimes these communications carry information. Sometimes they do not. Their efficacy in producing belief resides, however, not in the fact that the utterance carries information, but in its meaning (or perceived meaning), who uttered it, and how. No successful liar can seriously doubt this.

So if we distinguish between an event's meaning (= what it says, *whether truly or falsely*, about another state of affairs) and the information it carries (what it, among other things, *truly* says about another state of affairs), a distinction that is roughly equivalent to Grice's (1957) distinction between nonnatural and natural meaning, the causal role of information becomes more problematic. What explains Michael's reaction to the verbal communication is his believing that his wife was having an affair with Charles. What explains his believing this is his being told it by a trusted confidant – that is, his hearing someone (he trusts) *say* this, utter words with this meaning. At no point in the explanatory proceedings do we have to mention the truth of what is said, the truth of what is believed, or the fact that information (as opposed to misinformation) was communicated. If Michael *acts* on his belief, he may, sooner or later, confront a situation that testifies to the truth of what he believes (and was told). He will then, presumably, acquire new beliefs about his wife and Charles, and these new beliefs will help determine what further reactions he has, what he goes on to do. But still, at no point do we have to speak of information or truth in our explanations of Michael's behavior. All that is needed is what Michael *thinks* is true, what he *thinks* is information, what he *believes*. Knowing whether these beliefs are true or not may be helpful in predicting the *results* of his actions (whether, for instance, he will actually find Sandra at home when he goes to look), but it is not essential for explaining and predicting what he will actually do – whether, that is, he will go home to look.

Appearances, then, *do* seem to be misleading. Despite the way things first looked, despite a variety of familiar examples in which information seemed to make a causal difference, we still haven't found an honest job for it, something information (as opposed to meaning or belief) does that constitutes *its* special contribution to the causal story.

TRUTH AND SUPERVENIENCE

It isn't hard to see why there is trouble finding a decent job for information. The information a signal (structure, event, condition, state of affairs) carries is a function of the way a signal is *related* to other conditions in the world. I have my own views (Dretske 1981) about what these relations come down to, what relations constitute information. I happen to think information requires, among other things, some relation of dependency between the signal and the condition about which it carries information. Signals don't carry information about conditions, even conditions that happen to obtain, on which their occurrence does not depend in some appropriate way. But it isn't necessary to argue about these details. I'm not asking you to agree with me about exactly what information is to agree with me that, whatever it is, as long as it (unlike meaning) involves truth, there is a special problem about how it can be put to work in a scientifically respectable way – how *it*, or the fact that something carries it, can be made explanatorily relevant.

In order to appreciate the problem it is enough to realize that since no signal, S, can carry the information that P is the case when P is not the case, you can change the information a signal carries by tinkering not with the signal itself, but with the condition, P, about which it carries information. If it is possible, as it almost always is (by tinkering with the causal mechanisms mediating P and S), to change P without changing the character of S itself (i.e., without changing any of S's nonrelational properties), then the fact that S carries information is a fact that does not (to use a piece of current jargon) supervene on its nonrelational (intrinsic) properties. Signals that are otherwise identical can be informationally different. They will be informationally different when one occurs when P is the case, while the other, a physical clone of the first, occurs when P is not the case.[1] But if this is so, and we assume, as it seems we must assume (more of this in a moment), that the causal powers of a signal are embodied in, and exhausted by, its nonrelational properties (so that two signals that are physically identical are, in the same circumstances, causally equivalent), then the information character of a signal, the fact that it carries information, is causally inert. However useful it might be (because of the correlations it exhibits) as a predictor of correlated (even *lawfully* correlated)[2] conditions, the fact that a signal carries information will *explain* absolutely nothing. The fact that a signal carries the information that P cannot possibly explain anything if a signal lacking this information has exactly the same effects. This is not to say that signals bearing information cannot cause things. Certainly they can. It just means that their carrying information does not help explain why

1 It is better to say that under such conditions they *can be* informationally different. Whether they *are* different will depend not only on whether P exists in one case but not the other, but on whether there is, in the case where P exists, the required information-carrying dependency between P and the signal.

2 In "common cause" situations, cases where A, although neither the cause nor the effect of B, is correlated with B because they have some common cause C, we may (depending on the details of the case) be able to say that B would not have happened unless A happened and, yet, deny that A in any way *explains* (causally or otherwise) B. An explanatory relation between A and B, a relation that lets us say that B happened *because* A happened, requires *more than* counterfactual-supporting generalizations between A and B.

I disagree, therefore, with Jerry Fodor (1987: 139–140) that (to put it crudely) an adequate story can be told about mental *causation* without making intentional properties (like meaning or information) determine causal roles. It isn't enough to have these intentional properties (like meaning or information) determine causal roles. It isn't enough to have these intentional properties figure in counterfactual-supporting generalizations. That (alone) won't show that people behave the way they do *because* of what they believe and desire.

they cause what they cause. Distilled water will extinguish a fire – thereby causing exactly what undistilled water causes – but the fact that the water is distilled does not figure in the explanation of *why* the fire is extinguished. It won't because undistilled water has exactly the same effects on flames. And if the information in a signal is like this, like the fact that water is distilled, then the fact that a signal carries information is as explanatorily relevant to its effects on a receiver as is the fact that the water is distilled to its effects on a flame.[3]

Coupled with the idea that a symbol's meaning is a function of its relations to other conditions (the conditions it, in some sense, signifies or means), such arguments have led to the view that it is the form, shape, or syntax – not the meaning, content, or semantics – of our internal states that ultimately pulls the levers, turns the gears, and applies the brakes in the behavior of thoughtful and purposeful agents. Semantics or meaning, the what-it-is-we-believe (and want) is causally (and, therefore, explanatorily) irrelevant to the production of behavior (which is not to say that it cannot be used to *predict* behavior). I have merely extended these arguments, applying them to information rather than meaning or content. Since information, unlike meaning, requires truth, I think these arguments are even more persuasive when applied to information. I have, in fact, assumed up to this point that there is no particular difficulty about how meaning, either as embodied in *what a person says* or as embodied in *what a person believes*, could figure in a causal explanation. But this, too, has its difficulties. Since I am convinced that belief and meaning are notions that ultimately derive from the information-carrying properties of living systems, I think these problems are, at a deeper level, connected. I think, in fact, that the central problem in this area is the causal efficacy of information. If we can find a respectable job for information, if *it* can be provided a causal job to do, if it can be put to work, then the causal role of meaning and belief (indeed, of all the other psychological attitudes), being derivative, will fall into place. But these are issues that go beyond the scope of this essay and I will not return to them here.[4]

---

3 Jerry Fodor, *Psychosemantics*, 33, nicely illustrates this with the property of being an H-particle. A particle has the property of being an H-particle (at time *t*) if and only if a dime Fodor flips (at time *t*) is heads. If the dime turns up tails, these particles are T-particles. H-particles are obviously causally efficacious, but no one supposes that their causal efficacy is to be explained by their being H-particles.

4 For a full discussion see *Explaining Behaviour: Reasons in a World of Causes* (Cambridge, MA: 1988 Bradford/MIT Press).

To put information to work will require understanding how the causal efficacy of a signal is altered by the fact that it carries information. A part of the task, then, is to see how the causal efficacy of S (the signal carrying the information that P) is changed or modified by the fact that, in a certain range of circumstances, it occurs *only when* P is the case. I say that this is *part* (not *all*) of the task since S's occurrence *only when* P is the case does not mean that S carries the information that P. It depends on what *else*, besides co-occurrence (by this I mean the occurrence of S only when P is the case), is required for S to carry the information that P. So showing the causal relevance of co-occurrence will not directly demonstrate the causal relevance of information. Nonetheless, since we are assuming, as a minimal condition on information, that S cannot carry the information that P unless P is the case, unless, that is, S and P *do* co-occur in the relevent conditions, demonstrating the causal relevance of co-occurrence will be an important step in showing that information has a causal job to do.

This isn't as easy as it looks. The job, remember, is to show how the co-occurrence of S with P, the fact that S occurs only when P is the case, makes a difference in S's causal powers. The job is not to show that S *together with* P causes things that S *alone* does not. That latter task is simple enough but quite irrelevant. It is quite obvious that Tommy and his big brother can do things that Tommy alone cannot. And if Tommy never goes anywhere without his big brother, then Tommy will be a "force" to contend with on the school playground. Strictly speaking, though, the presence of his big brother doesn't enhance *Tommy*'s prowess. It merely makes him part of a *team* that is feared by the other boys, a team whose presence is signaled by the appearance of Tommy and, thus, makes (via the beliefs of the other boys) Tommy an intimidating figure on the playground.

Such situations are familiar enough, but they are not what we are after. What we are looking for, instead, is a case where *Tommy's* punches carry increased authority because he (always) has his big brother with him.[5] How can Tommy derive added strength, increased causal powers, from the mere fact (a fact that may even be unknown to Tommy) that his big brother is always nearby? How can the (mere) fact that P is the case when S occurs, whether or not anyone – including S – realizes this

---

5 Not, mind you, because he *thinks, believes, or knows* that his big brother is backing him up. For this would, at best, only demonstrate, once again, the causal efficacy of belief.

fact, change *S*'s causal powers? Until we know how, we won't know how information can make a difference in this world.

I think we can make a beginning at understanding how this is possible by thinking about how some elements are *given* a causal job to do because of what they indicate about related conditions. Suppose we want some particular kind of movement or change (call it M) to occur when, and only when, condition P exists. I want an annoying buzzer to go on when, and only when, passengers fail to buckle their seat belts. I want the fan to go on when the engine overheats but not otherwise. I want the light to come on when anyone, or anything, crosses a threshold. The way to get what I want is to make an indicator of P — something that will activate when, and only when, P is the case — into a cause of M. To design such mechanisms is a job for engineers. Find or build something that is selectively sensitive to the occurrence of P and make it into a switch for M. Find (or build) something that is sensitive to passengers with unbuckled seat belts. Make it into a buzzer switch. This device doesn't have to be very fancy — just a little electrical-mechanical gadget that will be activated by weight (on a car seat) and electrical contact (in the seat belt buckle). Joint occurrence of the right set of conditions (P) — the condition in which we want M to occur — is then made into a switch for, a cause of, M, the buzzer. If things work right, we now get M when, and only when, P: the buzzer sounds when, and only when, there are passengers with unfastened seat belts.

Building a gadget like this (and such gadgets are all around us) is an exercise in making a more or less reliable indicator, a structure exhibiting a more or less reliable correlation with P, into a cause of M — the response to be coordinated with P. By appropriate design, manufacture, and installation, the causal powers of an indicator, an information-bearing structure, an S that occurs *only when* P is the case, is modified, and, what is most significant, it is modified *because* this indicator (or the appropriate activation of this indicator) occurs when, and only when, a certain other condition (P) occurs. The properties of this internal structure (S) that are relevant to its selection as a cause of M, and hence that explain why it (now) causes M, are not its intrinsic properties — its size, shape, weight, color, charge, and so on. These might help to explain *how* S is made to cause M, how it can be converted into a cause of M, but not why it is converted into a cause of M. It is, rather, S's relational properties that explain why it was selected (by the engineer designing the device) for this causal job. Anything, no matter what its intrinsic properties (as long as they can be harnessed to do the job), would have done as well. As long as the behavior of this element exhibits the appropriate degree of correlation with P, it is a candidate for being made into a switch for M, the behavior we want coordinated with P. If, furthermore, an element is selected for its causal role (in the production of M) *because* of its correlation with P, because it does not (normally) occur without P, we have (almost) a case of an element's informational properties explaining its causal properties: it does (or is made to do) this because it carries information about (or co-occurs with) that. It isn't the element's shape, form, or syntax that explains its conversion into a cause of M; it is, instead, its information-carrying, its semantic, properties.

This is all a little too fast, of course. We smuggled into the proceedings an engineer, with purposes and intentions of his own, soldering things here, wiring things there, because of what he knows (or thinks) about the effects to be achieved thereby. I therefore expect to hear the objection that deliberately designed artifacts do not demonstrate the causal efficacy of information. All they illustrate, once again, is the causal efficacy of belief (and purpose). In the case of artifacts, what explains the conversion of an information-bearing element (an indicator of P) into a cause of output (M) is the designer's knowledge (or belief) that it is a reliable indicator and his or her desire to coordinate M with P. To make information do some real work, it would be necessary to make the causal powers of S depend on its carrying information, or on its co-occurrence with P, *without* the intercession of cognitive intermediaries with purposes and intentions of their own. The information (correlation) alone, not some agent's recognition of this fact, must carry the explanatory burden.

INDICATORS AND LEARNING

To see how this might be accomplished, simply remove the engineer. Since artifacts do not spontaneously change the way they behave (at least not normally in a desired way) without some help from the outside, replace the seat belt mechanism with a system that *is* capable of such unassisted reconfiguration. That is, replace the artifact with an animal – a rat, say. Put the rat into conditions – a suitably arranged Skinner box will do – in which a certain response is rewarded (with food, say) when, and only when, it occurs in conditions P. The response is punished when it occurs without P. Let P be some condition that the rat can observe – a certain audible tone, say. Let the response be the pressing of a bar. What happens? Given a hungry rat, enough trials, and a tolerance for stray errors, the rat learns to press the bar when, and only when, it hears the tone. A correlation between M (bar pressing) and P (the tone) begins to emerge. The engineer got the seat belt mechanism to behave the way he wanted it to behave, to buzz when a passenger failed to buckle her seat belt, by connecting wires in the right places, by making an internal indicator of P (an unbuckled belt) into a cause of M (buzzer activation). The same thing happens to the rat without the assistance of an engineer or, indeed, *any* intentional agent. An internal indicator of P (in this case a certain tone) becomes a cause of M (in this case bar-pressing movements) not through the intercession of an outside agent, but merely by having the response, M, rewarded *when* it occurs in the right condition (P).

This kind of learning – discrimination learning – can occur only if there is some internal condition of the learner, call it S, that exhibits some degree of correlation with P (the external condition being discriminated) – unless, that is, there is some internal condition of the learner that under normal conditions carries information about the condition to be discriminated. Unless there is some internal condition that occurs when, and only when, P is the case, it will be impossible to get M, the behavior, to occur when, and only when, P, the discriminated condition, exists. You can't make a system do M when (and only when) P exists if there is nothing in the system to *indicate* when P exists, and having something in the system to indicate when P exists is, among other things, a matter of having something in the system that occurs when, and only when, P exists. So when this type of learning *is* successful, as it often is, there must be, internal to the learner, a condition S that, with some degree of reliability, occurs when (and only when) P exists. There must actually be, inside the rat, something that (under appropriate stimulus conditions) occurs when, and only when, the right tone is sounded.

Furthermore, for this type of learning to occur, there must not only *be* an internal structure, S, carrying information about P, it must, during this type of learning, actually assume control functions it did not formerly have. It must be converted into a switch for M, the behavior that (through this type of learning) becomes coordinated with P. Unless S is, through this type of learning, recruited as a cause (or partial cause) of

M, there is no way of coordinating behavior with the conditions on which its success depends. For S is, by definition, the internal element that signals *when* the conditions are right (when P exists) for the behavior (M) to achieve success (to be rewarded). So S must be made into a cause of M (at least something on which M depends) if learning is to occur. Otherwise it is sheer magic. Whatever it is in the rat – call it the rat's *perception* of the tone – that signals the occurrence of the tone, it must actually be recruited as a cause of bar-pressing movements in this kind of learning if the rat is to learn to press the bar when the tone occurs.

Not only must an internal indicator be enlisted for control duties in this kind of learning, the properties of the indicator that explain its recruitment (as a cause of movement) are its *semantic* or *relational* properties, the properties that do *not* supervene on its intrinsic neurophysiological character. What explains why the rat's perception of a tone causes it to press the bar, what explains this internal element's altered causal powers, is not the fact that it has certain neurophysiological properties – a certain electrical-chemical-mechanical profile or form. For it presumably had that form *before* learning occurred (the rat could hear the tone before it learned to respond to it in a particular way). Before learning occurred, though, this internal state, this perception of the tone, did not cause the same movements (or any movements at all). Hence, what explains why the rat's perception of the tone causes movements it did not formerly cause is the fact that it, the rat's perception of the tone, is, specifically, a perception *of the tone*, the fact that it is an internal state exhibiting the requisite correlation with those external conditions on which the success of output depends. What explains the perceptual state's newfound causal power is, in other words, its semantic, informational, or intentional properties – not what it *is*, but what it is *about*.

If this theory, sketchy as it is, is even approximately right, then we have found a place where information does some honest work: it does real work when living systems are, during learning, reorganizing their control circuits to exploit the correlations (correlations between what is happening inside and what is happening outside) that perception puts at their disposal. Whenever there is something inside a system that can, by suitable redeployment, affect output, then there exists an opportunity to put to work whatever information that element carries. Such information can be exploited if there is a range of behaviors whose benefits (to the animal) depend on their emission in those (external) conditions about which information is carried. If there is such a dependence, then, assuming the animal capable of modifying its behavior so as to better

206

coordinate it with those external conditions on which its success depends (capable, that is, of learning), the animal can exploit perceptual information by recruiting, as a cause of behavior, the internal vehicles of this information.

I say that this is an honest job for information because, unlike the artifacts discussed earlier, it is information itself, the fact that S does not normally occur unless P, and therefore (other possible conditions being satisfied) the fact that S carries the information that P, that explains the recruitment of internal elements as causes of movement (those movements whose success depends on their coordination with P). At the neuroanatomical level it may be a mystery how such recruitment takes place, how learning actually occurs, but that it *does* occur, in some animals under some circumstances, is perfectly obvious. And it is its occurrence, not details about how it occurs, that demonstrates – indeed, requires – the causal efficacy of information.

There are, it seems to me, profound implications of this fact, the fact that information begins to find a real causal and hence explanatory use only in systems capable of learning. Only here do we find the behavior of a system explicable in terms of the relational properties of the internal states that produce it. Only here do we begin to see something like *content* or *meaning*, properties (like information) that do not supervene on the intrinsic properties of the internal states that possess it, assuming a significant place in our explanations of animal and human behavior. It is here, I submit, that psychological explanations of behavior first get a real, as opposed to merely a metaphorical, purchase. It is only when information begins to do some real explanatory – hence, scientific – work that minds rightfully enter the metaphysical picture.

REFERENCES

Dretske, Fred (1981). *Knowledge and the Flow of Information*. Cambridge, MA: Bradford/MIT Press.
   (1988). *Explaining Behavior: Reasons in a World of Causes*. Cambridge, MA: Bradford/MIT Press
Fodor, Jerry (1987). *Psychosemantics*. Cambridge, MA: Bradford/MIT Press
Grice, Paul (1957). Meaning. *Philosophical Review* 66:377–378

12

If You Can't Make One, You Don't Know How It Works

There are things I believe that I cannot say — at least not in such a way that they come out true. The title of this essay is a case in point. I really do believe that, in the relevant sense of all the relevant words, if you can't make one, you don't know how it works. The trouble is I do not know how to specify the relevant sense of all the relevant words.

I know, for instance, that you can understand how something works and, for a variety of reasons, still not be able to build one. The raw materials are not available. You cannot afford them. You are too clumsy or not strong enough. The police will not let you.

I also know that you may be able to make one and still not know how it works. You do not know how the parts work. I can solder a snaggle to a radzak, and this is all it takes to make a gizmo, but if I do not know what snaggles and radzaks are, or how they work, making one is not going to tell me much about what a gizmo is. My son once assembled a television set from a kit by carefully following the instruction manual. Understanding next to nothing about electricity, though, assembling one gave him no idea of how television worked.

I am not, however, suggesting that being able to build one is sufficient for knowing how it works. Only necessary. And I do not much care about whether you can *actually* put one together. It is enough if

Reprinted from *Midwest Studies in Philosophy* 19 (1994), 468–482, by permission of the publisher.

    I read an early version of this essay at the annual meeting of the Society for Philosophy and Psychology, Montreal, 1992. I used an enlarged form of it at the NEH Summer Institute on the Nature of Meaning, codirected by Jerry Fodor and Ernie LePore, at Rutgers University in the summer of 1993. There were many people at these meetings who gave me useful feedback and helpful suggestions. I am grateful to them.

you *know how* one is put together. But, as I said, I do not know how to make all the right qualifications. So I will not try. All I mean to suggest by my provocative title is something about the spirit of philosophical naturalism. It is motivated by a constructivist's model of understanding. It embodies something like an engineer's ideal, a designer's vision, of what it takes to really know how something works. You need a blueprint, a recipe, an instruction manual, a program. This goes for the mind as well as any other contraption. If you want to know what intelligence is, or what it takes to have a thought, you need a recipe for creating intelligence or assembling a thought (or a thinker of thoughts) out of parts you already understand.

INFORMATION AND INTENTIONALITY

In speaking of parts one *already* understands, I mean, of course, parts that do not already possess the capacity or feature one follows the recipe to create. One cannot have a recipe for cake that lists a cake, not even a small cake, as an ingredient. One can, I suppose, make a big cake out of small cakes, but recipes of this sort will not help one understand what a cake is (although it might help one understand what a *big* cake is). As a boy, I once tried to make fudge by melting fudge in a frying pan. All I succeeded in doing was ruining the pan. Don't ask me what I was trying to do – change the *shape* of the candy, I suppose. There are perfectly respectable recipes for cookies that list candy (e.g., gumdrops) as an ingredient, but one cannot have a recipe for *candy* that lists candy as an ingredient. At least it will not be a recipe that tells you how to make candy or helps you understand what candy is. The same is true of minds. That is why a recipe for thought cannot have interpretive attitudes or explanatory stances among the eligible ingredients – not even the attitudes and stances of *others*. That is like making candy out of candy – in this case, one person's candy out of another person's candy. You can do it, but you still will not know how to make candy or what candy is.

In comparing a mind to candy and television sets I do not mean to suggest that minds are the sort of thing that can be assembled in your basement or in the kitchen. There are things, including things one fully understands, things one knows how to make, that cannot be assembled that way. Try making Rembrandts or $100 bills in your basement. What you produce may look genuine, it may pass as authentic, but it will not be the real thing. You have to be the right person, occupy the right office, or possess the appropriate legal authority in order to make certain things. There are recipes for making money and Rembrandts, and knowing these recipes is part of understanding what money and Rembrandts are, but these are not recipes you and I can use. Some recipes require a special cook.

This is one (but only one) of the reasons it is wrong to say, as I did in the title, that if you cannot make one, you do not know how it works. It would be better to say, as I did earlier, that if you do not know how to make one, or know how one is made, you do not really understand how it works.

Some objects are constituted, in part, by their relationships to other objects. Rembrandts and $100 bills are like that. So are cousins and mothers-in-law. That is why you could not have built my cousin in your basement, while my aunt and uncle could. There is a recipe in this case, just not one you can use. The mind, I think, is also like that, and I will return to this important point in a moment.

It is customary to think of naturalistic recipes for the mind as starting with extensional ingredients and, through some magical blending process, producing an intentional product: a thought, an experience, or a purpose. The idea behind this proscription of intentional ingredients seems to be that since what we are trying to build – a thought – is an intentional product, our recipe cannot use intentional ingredients.

This, it seems to me, is a mistake, a mistake that has led some philosophers to despair of ever finding a naturalistic recipe for the mind. It has given naturalism an undeserved bad name. The mistake is the same as if we proscribed using, say, copper wire in our instruction manual for building amplifiers because copper wire conducts electricity – exactly what the amplifiers we are trying to build do. This, though, is silly. It is perfectly acceptable to use copper wire in one's recipe for building amplifiers. Amplifier recipes are supposed to help you understand how something amplifies electricity, not how something conducts electricity. So you get to use conductors of electricity, and in particular copper wire, as a part in one's amplifier kit. Conductors are eligible components in recipes for building amplifiers even if one does not know how they manage to conduct. An eligible part, once again, is an ingredient, a part, a component, that does not already have the capacity or power one uses the recipe to create. That is why one can know what gumdrop cookies are, know how to make them, without knowing how to make gumdrops or what, exactly, gumdrops are.

The same is true for mental recipes. As long as there is no mystery – not, at least, the *same* mystery – about how the parts work as how the whole is supposed to work, it is perfectly acceptable to use intentional ingredients in a recipe for thought, purpose, and intelligence. What we are trying to understand, after all, is not intentionality, per se, but the mind. Thought may be intentional, but that is not the property we are seeking a recipe to understand. As long as the intentionality we use is not itself mental, then we are as free to use intentionality in our recipe for making a mind as we are in using electrical conductors in building amplifiers and gumdrops in making cookies.

Consider a simple artifact – a compass. If it was manufactured properly (do not buy a cheap one), and if it is used in the correct circumstances (the good ones come with directions), it will tell you the direction of the Arctic Pole (I here ignore differences between magnetic and geographic poles). That is what the pointer indicates. But although the pointer indicates the direction of the Arctic Pole, it does not indicate the whereabouts of polar bears even though polar bears live in the Arctic. If you happen to know this fact about polar bears, that they live in the Arctic (not the Antarctic), you could, of course, figure out where the polar bears are by using a compass. But this fact about what you could figure out *if you knew* does not mean that the compass pointer is sensitive to the location of polar bears – thus indicating *their* whereabouts – in the way it indicates the location of the Arctic. The pointer on this instrument does not track the bears; it tracks the pole. If there is any doubt about this, try using Mill's Methods: move the bears around while keeping the pole fixed. The pointer on your compass will not so much as quiver.

Talking about what a compass indicates is a way of talking about what it tracks, what information it carries, what its pointer movements are dependent on, and a compass, just like any other measuring instrument, can track one condition without tracking another even though these conditions co-occur. Talk about what instruments and gauges indicate or measure creates the same kind of intensional (with an "s") context as does talk about what a person knows or believes. Knowing or believing that *that* is the North Pole is not the same as knowing or believing that that is the habitat of polar bears even though the North Pole is the habitat of polar bears. If we regard intensional (with an "s") discourse, referentially opaque contexts, as our guide to intentional (with a "t") phenomena, then we have, in a cheap compass, something we can buy at the local hardware store, intentionality. Describing what such an instrument indicates is describing it in intensional terms. What one is describing is, therefore, in this sense, an intentional state of the instrument.

211

It is worth emphasizing that this is not derived or in any way second-class intentionality. This is the genuine article – *original* intentionality, as some philosophers (including this one) like to say. The intentional states a compass occupies do not depend on our explanatory purposes, attitudes, or stances. To say that the compass (in certain conditions *C*) indicates the direction of the Arctic Pole is to say that, in these conditions, the direction of the pointer depends in some lawlike way on the whereabouts of the pole. This dependency exists whether or not we know it exists, whether or not anyone ever exploits this fact to build and use compasses. The intentionality of the device is not, like the intentionality of words and maps, *borrowed* or *derived* from the intentionality (purposes, attitudes, knowledge) of its users. The power of this instrument to indicate north *to* or *for* us may depends on our taking it to be a reliable indicator (and, thus, on what we believe or know about it), but its *being* a reliable indicator does not itself depend on us.

"Intentionality" is a much abused word, and it means a variety of different things. But one thing it has been used to pick out are states, conditions, and activities having a propositional content the verbal expression of which does not allow the substitution, *salva veritate*, of coreferring expressions. This is Chisholm's third mark of intentionality.[1] Anything exhibiting this mark is about something else under an aspect. It has, in this sense, an aspectual shape.[2] Compass needles are about geographical regions or directions under one aspect (as, say, the direction of the pole) and not others (as, say, the habitat of polar bears). This is the same way our thoughts are about a place under one aspect (as where I was born) but not another (as where you were born). If having this kind of profile is, indeed, one thing that is meant by speaking of a state, condition, or activity as intentional, then it seems clear that there is no need to naturalize intentionality. It is already a familiar part of our physical world. It exists wherever you find clouds, smoke, tree rings, shadows, tracks, light, sound, pressure, and countless other natural phenomena that carry information about how other parts of the world are arranged and constituted.

Intentional systems, then, are not the problem. They can be picked

---

1 Roderick M. Chisholm, *Perceiving: A Philosophical Study* (Ithaca, N.Y., 1957), chap. 11.
2 This is John Searle's way of putting it; see his *The Rediscovery of Mind* (Cambridge, Mass., 1992), 131, 156. I think Searle is wrong when he says (p. 161) that there are no aspectual shapes at the level of neurons. Indicators in the brain, those in the sensory pathways, are as much about the perceived world under an aspect as is the compass about the Arctic under an aspect.

up for a few dollars at your local hardware store. We can, therefore, include them on our list of ingredients in our recipe for building a mind without fear that we are merely changing the shape of the candy or the size of the cake. What we are trying to build when we speak of a recipe for building a mind is not merely a system that exhibits intentionality. We already have that in systems and their information-carrying states that are in no way mental. Rather, what we are trying to build is a system that exhibits that peculiar array of properties that characterizes thought. We are, among other things, trying to build something that exhibits what Chisholm describes as the first mark of intentionality, the power to say that something is so when it is not so, the power to misrepresent how things stand in the world. Unlike information-providing powers, the capacity to misrepresent is *not* to be found on the shelves of hardware stores. For that we need a recipe.

MISREPRESENTATION

Let us be clear about what we seek a recipe to create. If we are trying to build a thought, we are looking for something that cannot only say that x is F without saying that x is G despite the coextensionality of "F" and "G"[3]; thus being about x under an aspect, we are looking for something that can say this, as a thought can say it, even when x is not F. Unless we have a recipe for this, we have no naturalistic understanding of *what it is* that we think, no theory of meaning or content. Meaning or content, the what-it-is that we think, is, like intelligence and rationality, independent of truth. So a recipe for thought, where this is understood to include what one thinks, is, of necessity, a recipe for building systems that can misrepresent the world they are about.

---

3 Despite even the *necessary* coextensionality of "F" and "G." A thought that x is F is different from a thought that x is G even if F-ness and G-ness are related in such a way that nothing *can* be F without being G. This, too, is an aspect of intentionality. In *Knowledge and the Flow of Information* (Cambridge, Mass., 1981), 173, I called this the second (for nomic necessity) and third (for logical necessity) orders of intentionality. Although measuring instruments exhibit first-order intentionality (they can indicate that x is F without indicating that x is G even when "F" and "G" happen to be coextensional), they do not exhibit higher levels of intentionality. If (in virtue of a natural law between F-ness and G-ness) Fs *must* be G, then anything carrying information that x is F will thereby carry the information that it is G. Unlike thoughts, compasses cannot distinguish between nomically equivalent properties.

My discussion has so far passed over this important dimension of intentionality. Although I will return to it briefly, the point raises too many complications to be addressed here.

Without the capacity to misrepresent, we have no capacity for the kind of representation that is the stuff of intelligence and reason.

Jerry Fodor focused attention on what he calls the disjunction problem for naturalistic theories of representation.[4] The problem is one of explaining how, in broadly causal terms, a structure in the head, call it R, could represent, say, or mean that something was F even though (if misrepresentation is to be possible) non-F-ish things are capable of causing it. How, in roughly causal terms, can R mean that something is F (the way a thought can be the thought that something is F) when something's being F is (at best[5]) only one of the things capable of causing R? For someone trying to formulate an information-based recipe for thought, this is, indeed, a vexing problem. But I mention the problem here only to point out that this problem is merely another way of describing the problem (for naturalistic theories) of misrepresentation. For if one could concoct a recipe for building systems capable of misrepresentation – capable, that is, of saying of something that was not F that it was F – then one would have a recipe for meaning, for constructing structures having a content that was independent of causes in the desired sense. This is so because if R can misrepresent something as being F, then R is, of necessity, something whose meaning is independent of its causes, something that can mean COW even when it is caused by a distant buffalo or a horse on a dark night. It is, therefore, something whose meaning is less than the disjunction of situations capable of causing it. In the words of Antony and Levine, it is something whose meaning has been "detached" from its causes.[6] A naturalistic recipe for misrepresentation, therefore, is a recipe for solving the disjunction problem.[7] One way of solving problems is to show that two problems are really, at bottom, the same problem. We are making progress.

For this problem artifacts are of no help. Although clocks, compasses, thermometers, and fire alarms – all readily available at the corner hardware store – can misrepresent the conditions they are designed to deliver

---

4 Jerry Fodor, *A Theory of Content and Other Essays* (Cambridge, Mass., 1990) and, earlier, *Psychosemantics* (Cambridge, Mass., 1987).
5 "At best" because, with certain Fs ("unicorn," "miracle," "angel," etc.) something's being F will not even be *among* the things that cause R.
6 Louise Antony and Joseph Levine, "The Nomic and the Robust," in *Meaning in Mind: Fodor and His Critics* (Oxford, 1991), 1–16.
7 Fodor puts it a bit differently, but the point, I think, is the same: "Solving the disjunction problem and making clear how a symbol's meaning could be so insensitive to variability in the causes of its tokenings are really two ways of describing the same undertaking" (*A Theory of Content and Other Essays*, 91).

information about, they need our help to do it. Their representational successes and failures are underwritten by – and, therefore, depend on – our purposes and attitudes, the purposes and attitudes of their designers and users. *As* representational devices, *as* devices exhibiting a causally detached meaning, such instruments are not therefore eligible ingredients in a recipe for making thought.

The reason the representational powers of instruments are not, like their indicative (information-carrying) powers, an available ingredient in mental recipes is, I think, obvious enough. I will, however, take a moment to expand on the point in order to set the stage for what follows.

Consider the thermometer. Since the volume of a metal varies lawfully with the temperature, both the mercury in the glass tube and the paper clips in my desk drawer carry information about the local temperature. Both are intentional systems in that minimal, that first, sense already discussed. Their behavior depends on a certain aspect of their environment (on the temperature, not the color or size, of their neighbors) in the same way the orientation of a compass needle depends on one aspect of its environment, not another. The only difference between thermometers and paper clips is that we have given the one volume of metal, the mercury in the glass tube, the job, the function, of telling us about temperature. The paper clips have been given a different job. Since it is the thermometer's job to provide information about temperature, it (we say) misrepresents the temperature when it fails to do its assigned job, just as (we say) a book or a map might misrepresent the matters of which they (purport to) inform us about. What such artifacts say or mean is what we have given them the job of indicating or informing us about, and since they do not lose their job – at least not immediately – merely by failing to satisfactorily perform their job, these instruments continue to mean that a certain condition exists even when that condition fails to exist, even when some other condition (a condition other than the one they have the job of informing about) is responsible for their behavior. For such measuring instruments, meanings are causally detached from causes for the same reason that functions are causally detached from (actual) performance. This is why thermometers can, while paper clips cannot, misrepresent the temperature. When things go wrong, when nothing is really 98°, a paper clip fails to say, while the broken thermometer goes right on saying, that it is 98°.

But, as I said, thermometers cannot do this by themselves. They need our help. We are the source of the job, the function, without which the thermometer could not say something that was false. Take us away and all you have is a tube full of mercury being caused to expand and contract by changes in the temperature – a column of metal doing exactly what paper clips, thumb tacks, and flag poles do. Once we change our attitude, once we (as it were) stop investing informational trust in the instrument, it loses its capacity to misrepresent. Its meaning ceases to be detached. It becomes, like every other piece of metal, a mere purveyor of information.

NATURAL FUNCTIONS

Although representational artifacts are thus not available as eligible ingredients in our recipe for the mind, their derived (from us) power to misrepresent is suggestive. If an information-carrying element in a system could somehow acquire the function of carrying information, and acquire this function in a way that did not depend on our intentions, purposes, and attitudes, then it would thereby acquire (just as a thermometer or a compass acquires) the power to misrepresent the conditions it had the function of informing about. Such functions would bring about a detachment of meaning from cause. Furthermore, since the functions would not be derived from us, the meanings (unlike the meaning of thermometers and compasses) would be original, underived meanings. Instead of just being able to build an instrument that could, because of the job we give it, fool *us*, the thing we build with these functions could, quite literally, *itself* be fooled.

If, then, we could find naturalistically acceptable functions, we could combine these with natural indicators (the sort used in the manufacture of compasses, thermometers, pressure gauges, and electric eyes) in a naturalistic recipe for thought. If the word "thought" sounds too exalted for the mechanical contraption I am assembling, we can describe the results in more modest terms. What we would have is a naturalistic recipe for representation, a way of building something that would have, quite apart from its creator's (or anyone else's) purposes or thoughts, a propositional content that could be either true or false. If that is not quite a recipe for mental béarnaise sauce, it is at least a recipe for a passable gravy. I will come back to the béarnaise sauce in a moment.

What we need in the way of another ingredient, then, is some natural process whereby elements can acquire, on their own, apart from us, an

216

information-carrying function. Where are these natural processes, these candyless functions, that will let us make our mental confections?[8]

As I see it, there are two retail suppliers for the required natural functions: one phylogenetic, the other ontogenetic.

If the heart and kidneys have a natural function, something they are *supposed* to be doing independently of our knowledge or understanding of what it is, then it presumably comes from their evolutionary, their selectional, history. If the heart has the function of pumping blood, if (following Larry Wright[9]) that is why the heart is there, then, by parity of reasoning, and depending on actual selectional history, the senses would have an information-providing function, the job of "telling" the animal in which they occur what it needs to know about the world in which it lives. If this were so, the *natural* function of sensory systems would be to provide information about an organism's optical, acoustic, and chemical surroundings. There would thus exist, inside the animal, representations of its environment, elements capable of saying what is false. Although I have put it crudely, this, I take it, is the sort of thinking that inspires biologically oriented approaches to mental representation.[10]

There is, however, a second, an ontogenetic, source of natural functions. Think of a system with certain needs, certain things it must have in order to survive.[11] In order to satisfy those needs it has to do *A* in

---

8 For the purpose of this essay, I ignore skeptics about functions – those who think, for example, that the heart only has the function of pumping blood because this is an effect in which we have (for whatever reason) a special interest. See, for example, John Searle, *The Rediscovery of Mind*, p. 238, and Dan Dennett's "Evolution, Error and Intentionality" in *The Intentional Stance* (Cambridge, Mass., 1987).

9 Larry Wright, "Functions," *Philosophical Review* 82 (1973): 139–168, and *Teleological Explanations* (Berkeley, 1976).

10 E.g., Ruth Millikan, *Language, Thought, and Other Biological Categories: New Foundations for Realism* (Cambridge, Mass., 1984) and "Biosemantics," *Journal of Philosophy* 86, no. 6 (1989); David Papineau, *Reality and Representation* (New York, 1987) and "Representation and Explanation," *Philosophy of Science* 51, no. 4 (1984): 550–572; Mohan Matthen. "Biological Functions and Perceptual Content," *Journal of Philosophy* 85, no. 1 (1988): 5–27; and Peter Godfrey Smith, "Misinformation," *Canadian Journal of Philosophy* 19. no. 4 (December 1989): 533–550 and "Signal, Decision, Action," *Journal of Philosophy* 88, no. 12 (December 1991): 709–722.

11 This may sound as though we are smuggling in the back door what we are not allowing in the front: a tainted ingredient, the idea of a *needful* system, a system, that, given its needs, has a use for information. I think not. All that is here meant by a need (for system of type *S*) is some condition or result without which the system could (or would) not exist as a system of type *S*. Needs, in this minimal sense, are merely necessary conditions for existence. Even plants have needs in this sense. Plants cannot exist (*as* plants) without water and sunlight.

conditions C. Nature has not equipped it with an automatic A-response to conditions C. There is, in other words, no hard-wired, heritable instinct to A in circumstances C. Think of C as a mushroom that has recently appeared in the animal's natural habitat. Although attractive (to this kind of animal), the mushroom is, in fact, poisonous. The animal can see the mushrooms. It has the perceptual resources for picking up information about (i.e., registering) the presence of C (it looks distinctive), but it does not yet have an appropriate A response (in this particular case, A = avoidance) to C.

We could wait for natural selection, and a little bit of luck, to solve this problem for the species, for the descendants of this animal, but if the problem – basically a coordination problem – is to be solved at the individual level, by *this* animal, learning must occur. If *this* animal is to survive, what must happen is that the internal sign or indicator of C – something inside this animal that constitutes its perception of C – must be made into a cause of A (avoidance). Control circuits must be reconfigured by inserting the internal indicators of C (the internal sensory effects of C) into the behavioral chain of command. Short of a miracle – the fortuitous occurrence of A whenever C is encountered – this is the only way the coordination problem essential for survival can be solved. Internal indicators must be harnessed to effector mechanisms so as to coordinate output A to the conditions, C, they carry information about. Learning of this kind achieves the same result as do longer-term evolutionary solutions: internal elements that supply needed information acquire the function of supplying it by being drafted (in this case, through a learning process) into the control loop because they supply it. A supplier of information acquires the function of supplying information by being recruited for control duties because it supplies it.[12]

Obviously this ingredient, this source of natural functions, whether it be phylogenetic or ontogenetic, cannot be ordered from a Sears catalog. There is nothing that comes in a bottle that we can squirt on thermally sensitive tissue that will give this tissue the natural function of indicating temperature, nothing we can rub on a photosensitive pigment that will give it the job of detecting light. If something is going to get the function, the job, the purpose, of carrying information in this natural way, it has to get it on its own. We cannot "assign" these functions, although we can (by artificial selection or appropriate training) encour-

12 This is a short and fast version of the story I tell in *Explaining Behavior* (Cambridge, Mass., 1988).

age their development. If the only natural functions are those provided by evolutionary history and individual learning, then, no one is going to build thinkers of thoughts, much less a mind, in the laboratory. This would be like building a heart, a real one, in your basement. If hearts are essentially organs of the body having the biological function of pumping blood, you cannot build them. You can wait for them to develop, maybe even hurry things along a bit by timely assists, but you cannot assemble them out of ready-made parts. These functions are the result of the right kind of history, and you cannot – not *now* – give a thing the right kind of history. It has to have it. Although there is a recipe for building internal representations, structures having natural indicator functions, it is not a recipe you or I, or anyone else, can use to build one.

THE DISJUNCTION PROBLEM

There are, I know, doubts about whether a recipe consisting of information and natural teleology (derived from natural functions – either phylogenetic or ontogenetic) is capable of yielding a mental product – something with an original power to misrepresent. The doubts exist even with those who share the naturalistic impulse. Jerry Fodor, for instance, does not think Darwin (or Skinner, for that matter) can rescue Brentano's chestnuts from the fire.[13] He does not think teleological theories of intentionality will solve the disjunction problem. Given the equivalence of the disjunction problem and the problem of misrepresentation, this is a denial, not just a doubt, that evolutionary or learning-theoretic accounts of functions are up to the task of detaching meaning from cause, of making something say COW when it can be caused by horses on a dark night.

I tend to agree with Fodor about the irrelevance of Darwin for understanding *mental* representation. I agree, however, not (like Fodor) out of the general skepticism about teleological accounts of meaning, but because I think Darwin is the wrong place to look for the teleology, for the functions, underlying *mental* representations (beliefs, thoughts, judgments, preferences, and their ilk). *Mental* representations have their place in explaining deliberate pieces of behavior, intentional acts for which the agent has reasons. This is exactly the sort of behavior that evolutionary histories are unequipped to explain. We might rea-

13   Fodor, *A Theory of Content and Other Essays*, 70.

219

sonably expect Darwin to tell us why people blink, reflexively when someone pokes a finger at their eye, but not why they deliberately wink at a friend, the kind of behavior we invoke beliefs and desires (*mental* representations) to explain. I do not doubt that the processes responsible for blink (and a great many other) reflexes are controlled by elements having an information-providing function (derived from natural selection). After all, if the reflex is to achieve its (presumed) purpose, that of protecting the eye, there must be something in there with the job of telling (informing) the muscles controlling the eyelids that there is an object approaching. But the representations derived from these phylogenetic functions are not mental representations. We do not blink because we believe a finger is being jabbed at our eye. And even if we do believe it, we blink, reflexively, *before* we believe it and independent of believing it. So even if there are representations whose underlying functions are phylogenetic, these are not the representations we would expect to identify with *mental* representations, the representations that serve to explain intentional behavior. For that, I submit, one needs to look to the representations whose underlying functions are ontogenetic.

Nonetheless, wherever we get the teleology, Fodor thinks it is powerless to solve the disjunction problem and, hence, hopeless as an account of thought content. I disagree. There are, to be sure, some problems for which teleology is of no help. But there are, or so I believe, some aspects of the naturalization project for which functions are indispensable. Whether teleology helps specifically with the disjunction problem depends on what one identifies as the disjunction problem. Since I have heard various things singled out as *the* disjunction problem, I offer the following two problems. Both have some claim to be called the disjunction problem. I will indicate, briefly, the kind of solution I favor to each. Teleology helps with only one.[14]

1. If a token of type R indicates (carries the information that) A, it also indicates that A or B (for any B). If it carries the information that x is a jersey cow, for instance, it carries the information that x is either a jersey cow or a holstein cow (or a can opener, for that matter). It also carries the information that x is, simply, a cow – a jersey cow, a holstein cow, and so on. This being so, how does an information-based approach to meaning get a token of type R to mean that A rather than A or B?

14 I was helped in my thinking about these problems by Peter Godfrey-Smith's "Misinformation."

220

How can an event have the content JERSEY COW rather than, say, COW when any event that carries the first piece of information also carries the second? To this problem functions provide an elegant answer. A token of type R can carry information that it does not have the function of carrying – that it does not, therefore, mean (in the sense of "mean" in which a thing can mean that P when P is false). Altimeters, for instance, carry information about air pressure (that is *how* they tell the altitude), but it is not their function to indicate air pressure. Their function is to indicate altitude. That is why they represent (and can misrepresent) altitude and not air pressure.

2. If tokens of type R can be caused by both A and B, how can tokens of this type mean that A (and not A or B)? If R is a type of structure tokens of which can be caused by both cows and, say, horses on a dark night, how can any particular token of R mean COW rather than COW OR HORSE ON A DARK NIGHT? For this problem I think Fodor is right: teleology is of no help. What we need, instead, is a better understanding of information, how tokens of a type R can carry information (that x is a cow, for instance) even though, in different circumstances and on other occasions, tokens of this same type fail to carry this information (because x is not a cow; it is a horse on a dark night). The solution to this problem requires understanding the way information is relativized to circumstances, the way tokens of type R that occur in broad daylight at 10 feet, say, can carry information that tokens of this same type, in *other* circumstances, in the dark or at 1200 feet, fail to carry.[15]

The problem of detaching meaning from causes – and thus solving the problem of misrepresentation – occurs at two distinct levels, at the level of types and the level of tokens. At the token level the problem is: how can tokens of a type all have the same meaning or content, F, when they have different causes (hence, carry different information)? Answer: each token, whatever information it happens to carry, whatever its particular cause, has the same information-carrying function, a function it derives from the type of which it is a token. Since meaning is identified with information-carrying function, each token, whatever its cause, has the same meaning, the job of indicating F. Teleology plays a crucial role here – at the level of tokens. The problem at the type level is: how can a *type* of event have, or acquire, the function of carrying

---

15 In *Knowledge and the Flow of Information* I called these circumstances, the ones to which the informational content of a signal was relative, "channel conditions."

221

information F when tokens of this type occur, or *can* occur (if misrepresentation is to be possible), without F? Answer: certain tokens, those that occur in circumstances C, depend on F. They would not occur unless F existed. These tokens carry the information that F. It is from them that the type acquires its information-carrying function. At the type level, then, teleology is of no help. Information carries the load. Both are needed to detach meaning from causes.

There is a third problem, sometimes not clearly distinguished from the preceding two problems, that has still a different solution (why should different problems have the same solution?). How can R represent something as F without representing it as G when the properties F and G are equivalent in some strong way (nomically, metaphysically, or logically)? How, for instance, can R have the function (especially if this is understood as a *natural* function) of indicating that something is water without having the function of indicating that it is H_2O? If it cannot, then, since we can obviously believe that something is water and not believe that it is H_2O, a theory of representation that equates content with what a structure has the natural function of indicating is too feeble to qualify as a theory of belief. It does not cut the intentional pie into thin enough slices.

I mention this problem here (I also alluded to it in footnote 3), not for the purpose of suggesting an answer to it,[16] but merely to set it apart as requiring special treatment. The problem of distinguishing representational contents that are equivalent in some strong way is surely a problem for naturalistic theories of content, but it is not a problem that teleology (at least not a naturalistic teleology) can be expected to solve. To discredit a teleological approach to representation because it fails to solve this problem, then, is like criticizing it because it fails to solve Zeno's Paradoxes.

THE RECIPE

We have, then, the following recipe for making a thoughtlike entity. It does not give us a very fancy thought – certainly nothing like the thoughts we have every day: that tomorrow is my birthday, for example, or that I left my umbrella in the car. But one thing at a time. The recipe will do its job if it yields *something* – call it a "proto-thought" – that has

---

16   I tackled that in *Knowledge and the Flow of Information*, 215ff.

222

belieflike features. I, personally, would be happy with a crude de re belief about a perceived object that it was, say, moving.

Recipe: Take a system that has a need for the information that *F*, a system whose survival or well-being depends on its doing *A* in conditions *F*. Add an element, or a detector system that produces elements, that carries information about condition *F*. Now, stir in a natural process, one capable of conferring on the *F*-indicator the *function* of carrying this piece of information. One does not quite "stir" these processes in (the metaphor is getting a bit strained at this point). Once you have got the right system, adding functions is more like *waiting* for the dough to rise. There is nothing more one can do. You sit back and hope that natural processes will take a favorable turn. Just as one cannot expect everything in which one puts yeast to rise (it does not work in sand), one cannot expect to get representational "bread" from everything in which needed indicators are placed. You need a reasonably sophisticated system, one with a capacity to reorganize control circuits so as to exploit information in coordinating its behavior to the conditions it gets information about. You need a system, in other words, capable of the right kind of learning. These are special systems, yes, but they are *not* systems that must already possess representational powers. We are not, in requiring such systems in our recipe, smuggling in tainted ingredients.

If all goes well, when the process is complete, the result will be a system with internal resources for representing – and, equally important from the point of view of modeling the mind, *mis*representing – its surroundings. Furthermore, that this system represents, as well as what it represents, will be independent of what we know or believe about it. For we, the cooks, are not essential parts of this process. The entire process can happen "spontaneously" and, when it does, the system will have its own cache of *original* intentionality.

RATIONALITY: THE FUNCTIONAL ROLE OF THOUGHT

Whether this is really *enough* to have supplied a recipe for thought depends, of course, on just what one demands of thought. What does it take to *be* a thought? If all it takes is possession of content, then, perhaps, we have supplied a recipe of sorts for making a thought. But the product is pretty disappointing, a mere shadow of what we know (in ourselves and others) to be the fullest and richest expression of the mind. What I have described might be realized in a snail. What we want (I expect to hear) is something more, something exhibiting the complex dynamics, both inferential and explanatory, that our thoughts have. To have a cow thought it is not enough to have an internal, isolated cow representation. To be a cow thought, this representation must actually *do* what cow thoughts do. It must be involved in reasoning and inference about cows. It must, together with cow-directed desires, explain cow-directed behavior and rationalize cow-related attitudes and intentions.

There is validity to this complaint. If we are going to make a thought, we want the product to both look and behave like a thought. What we have so far devised may (to be generous) look a bit like a thought. At least it has representational content of the sort we associate with thought. Nonetheless, there is nothing to suggest that our product will behave like a thought. Why, then, advertise the recipe as a recipe for thought? I have, after all, already conceded that there may be representations of this sort, mechanisms in the body having an indicator function, that are not mental representations at all. When the underlying functions are phylogenetic (e.g., in the processes controlling various reflexes), the representations are not thoughts. They have a content, yes, but they do not *behave* like thoughts. They do not, for instance, interact with desires and other beliefs to produce intelligent and purposeful action. Why, then, suppose that when the functions are ontogenetic, when they develop in learning, the results are any better qualified to be classified as mental?

Since I have addressed this issue elsewhere,[17] I will merely sketch an answer. A system that acquires, in accordance with the recipe, and in its own lifetime, the power to represent the objects in its immediate environment will also, automatically, be an intelligent system, one capable of behaving (at least insofar as these representations are concerned) in a rational way. To see why this is so, consider a process by means of which an indicator of *F* might acquire the function of carrying information about the *F*-ness of things – becoming, thereby, a representation (possibly, on occasion, a misrepresentation) that something is *F*. In order to acquire this status, the element must acquire the job of supplying information about the *F*-ness of things. The only way an element can acquire this job description, I submit, is by being recruited to perform control-related services *because* it supplies this needed information. If *R* is drafted to shape output because it supplies needed information about

---

17 *Explaining Behavior*, Chapters 4 and 5.

when and where that output is appropriate, then, no matter what further services may be required of R, part of R's job, its function, is to supply this needed information. That is why it is there, directing traffic, in the way that it is.

In achieving its representational status, then, R becomes a determinant of need-related behavior, behavior that satisfies needs when R carries the information it is its function to carry. Since R represents the conditions (F) in which the behavior it is called upon to cause is need-satisfying, R must, when it is doing its job, produce intelligent (i.e., need-satisfying) output. Even when it is not doing its job, even when it misrepresents, the behavior it helps produce will be behavior that is rationalized by the F-facts that R (mis)represents as existing. According to this recipe for thought, then, something becomes the thought that F by assisting in the production of an intelligent response to F.

Something not only becomes the thought that F by assisting in the production of an intelligent response to F, it assists in the intelligent response *because* it signifies what it does. When the capacity for thought emerges in accordance with the preceding recipe, not only do thoughts (together with needs and desires) conspire to produce intelligent behavior, they produce this behavior because they are the thoughts they are, because they have *that* particular content. It is their content, the fact that they are thoughts that F, not thoughts that G, that explains why they were recruited to help in the production of those particular responses to F. This, it seems to me, vindicates, in one fell swoop, both the explanatory and rationalizing role of content. We do not need "rationality constraints" in our theory of content. Rationality emerges as a by-product from the process in which representational states are created.

Our recipe yields a product having the following properties:

1. The product has a propositional content that represents the world in an aspectual way (as, say, F rather than G even when Fs are always G).
2. This content can be either true or false.
3. The product is a "player" in the determination of system output (thus helping to explain system behavior).
4. The propositional content of this product is the property that explains the product's role in determining system output. The system not only does what it does because it has this product, but what it is about this product that explains why the system does what it does is its propositional content.
5. Although the system *can* behave stupidly, the normal role of this product

(the role it will play when it is doing the job for which it was created) will be in the production of intelligent (need and desire satisfaction) behavior.

This, it seems to me, is about all one could ask of a naturalistic recipe for thought.

13

The Nature of Thought

A state or activity is *extrinsic* if an agent cannot occupy this state or engage in this activity, unless there exists (or existed) some wholly distinct object. Hitting a home run, watching a sunset, and paddling a canoe are extrinsic activities. Being watched, surrounded, and ignored are extrinsic states.

If, as some of these examples suggest, this other object must be a person, a conscious being of some sort, I will say that the extrinsic state or activity has a social character. A person can be surrounded by trees or water, but you need another conscious being to be ignored or watched. Marrying, divorcing, and tangoing are also social: it takes two. Killing, kidnapping, and stealing, although not exactly sociable, are also social. You simply cannot do these things alone, without there existing (either then or at some earlier time) another conscious being. Being a father and a widow are also social in this minimal sense. Fathers must have children and widows must have had husbands.

If this is what it means to have a social character, and I do not see how anything less could qualify, then it seems plausible – nay, obvious – that language has a social character. Communication, the heart and soul of language, requires senders and receivers. Without a set of reciprocal intentions and agreements, without a network of shared conventions

Reprinted from *Philosophical Studies* 70 (1993), 185–199, by permission of the publisher. Copyright © 1993 by Kluwer Academic Publishers, with kind permission from Kluwer Academic Publishers. This essay was written for a conference on The Social Character of Language and Thought sponsored by the University of California, Riverside, May 15–16, 1992. Tyler Burge and Pat Suppes also gave papers. I am grateful to them, to many people in the audience, and especially to my commentator, Richard Fumerton, for stimulating criticism and discussion.

that confer meaning on our acoustic productions, nothing we do *counts* as saying anything.

I do not mean to suggest that we cannot talk to or communicate with ourselves. Hermits can scribble reminders to themselves. And even without a natural language (whose origin, if not the present use of, might require other people) a person might cut notches in trees so that she can later find her way out of the forest. Isn't she communicating with herself – saying, in effect, "Go this way!" to a later time slice of herself? If this isn't language, it certainly looks like communication.

We could, I know, quarrel about this, but I'm not going to. That language – at least in origin, if not always in application or use (as in the case of the hermit) – has a social character strikes me as plausible enough to accept on its face without niggling over what, exactly, is to be counted as a language and what, exactly, is meant by the "cannot" in my definition of a social phenomenon.[1] Since everything we in fact call a language, at least a natural language, is the product of social factors, I am content to leave the matter there – content, that is, to acknowledge that language has a social character. You can talk to yourself, or to a rock, but the capability of doing so presupposes the existence – if not at the present time, then at some past time – of other conscious beings.

I am quick to concede this point because, frankly, I am more inter-ested in thought, and the possibility of *its* having a social character, than I am in language. For thought is not, at least not on the surface, a social phenomenon. Quite the reverse. Language may be public – maybe even essentially public – but thought is surely private, maybe even essentially so.[2] My ability to *say* I am hungry may depend on the existence of shared conventions that give meaning to the sounds I produce, but my ability to *think* I am hungry does not seem to depend on anyone else. Just as I could, all alone in the universe, *be* hungry, so I could, or so it seems, also *think* I was hungry. Why not?

Well, a number of philosophers have told us, or tried to tell us, why

1 Tyler Burge (1990: 113) suggests that, if nothing else, language is social in that interaction with other persons is psychologically necessary to learn language.
2 Those who argue for the social character of thought are not, of course, denying that thought is private, something that goes on *in* the head of the thinker. I can make out my Federal income tax return in the privacy of my home, but in order for this to be a correct description of what is gong on in my home, there has to be something (a federal govern-ment) outside my home.

not.[3] I don't believe them. I go halfway but no further. Thought is extrinsic, yes, but it is not social.[4] Thinking that P, for any value of P, requires the existence of objects wholly distinct from the thinker, yes, but it does not require that any of these objects be another person. Even if a solitary speaker is a contradiction, a solitary thinker is not.

Let me say a word about philosophical motivations before I go on to say why I believe this, why I am convinced that the content of thought – what we think – although extrinsic to the thinker, is not essentially social. I have in mind the sorts of considerations that dominate current thinking about the causal efficacy, and hence the explanatory role, of thought. These considerations have convinced many philosophers that thought cannot even be extrinsic, let alone social. The reasoning goes something like this: if we are to retain the familiar doctrine that much of what we do is not only rationalized, but explained, by what we think, then it seems that what it is we think has to be intrinsic to (or supervene on states that are intrinsic to) the agent whose behavior it helps explain.[5] For, as our definitions reveal, extrinsic (and therefore social) facts about A depend on the existence and character of some other, wholly distinct, object B. Remove B, change B, or simply imagine A the same in every other respect (a twin A, if you will) related to a different B, and A no longer occupies the same extrinsic state. Hilda is a widow. This is an extrinsic condition of Hilda. It is also a condition that, because extrinsic, does not explain anything about Hilda's impact on, her power to affect, the rest of the world.[6] The causal story from this point forward in time, at least with regard to Hilda's contribution to it, would be exactly the

---

3   Donald Davidson (1975), for example. Also D. W. Hamlyn (1990). I do not include Tyler Burge (1979, 1982) in this class, despite the prominence of his arguments against an individualistic treatment of thought, because Burge does not claim that thought has a social character (in the sense defined earlier), but that "many" (1990: 116) or "virtually" all (1982: 117) thoughts have this character. He is careful to say (1979: 540) that he prefers to "leave open precisely how far one can generalize" his argument for the social character of thoughts. Burge should be understood not as arguing that thought cannot occur in the absence of the social, but that thought *can* be affected by the social without affecting the intrinsic physical state of the thinker.

4   Putnam's (1975) Twin Earth examples have convinced many that thought, at least thoughts involving natural kinds, are extrinsic (whether or not they are, in addition, social).

5   This, basically, is the assumption that drives the currently orthodox idea that if thoughts are relevant to explaining behavior, their content must be *narrow* (i.e., intrinsic to the system whose behavior it helps explain). See Fodor (1980, 1987).

6   Other people, or Hilda herself, *believing* that Hilda is a widow, can make a difference, a causal difference, of course, but this is quite a different mater.

229

same if we imagined that, because of a legal technicality, she was not married to the deceased and is, therefore, technically not a widow. Extrinsic conditions are like that: you can change them, remove them, or imagine them to be different in various respects without ever changing the causal powers of the object or person that is in this extrinsic condition. This being so, how can extrinsic and, therefore, social facts about A, depending as they do on factors that are temporally and spatially remote from A, help explain A's current behavior? Surely what explains, causally explains, A's raising her arm or pushing a button (and, therefore, the "richer" behaviors these basic acts help constitute: e.g., voting for a candidate or blowing up a bridge) are intrinsic, not extrinsic, facts about A.

According to this line of reasoning, then, if what we think is causally relevant to what we do, then what we think, and hence the thoughts themselves, *have* to be intrinsic states of the thinker. If thoughts are to fulfill their familiar role as both rationalizers and explainers of behavior, they *cannot* have a social character. If they do, then, like Hilda's widowhood, they are irrelevant to understanding what goes on in the world. They are, in particular, irrelevant to understanding why the thinker behaves the way she does.

Since I have already indicated my sympathy for the view that thought has an extrinsic character, this argument cuts as deeply against my own position as it does against those who believe that thought has a social character. I will return, later, to indicate why I am not deterred by this fact. I mention the argument now, however, to suggest some of what is at stake in this controversy. It is not simply a matter of thought having, or lacking, a social character. Matters do not end there. For if thought has a social character, if what one thinks somehow depends on the existence of other human beings in the world, then it becomes a mystery how what one thinks can explain what one does. I do not like mysteries. I also believe that, sometimes at least, what I do is explained by what I think. That is my motive for resisting the socialization of thought.[7]

In rejecting the social (although not the extrinsic) character of thought, I do not, of course, reject the idea that many, perhaps most, conceivably even *all*, thoughts can be expressed or described in such a way as to imply the existence of other conscious agents. All I reject is

---

7 As remarked earlier, it is also a good reason to resist the externalization of thought. I will try to indicate later why I do not believe it is *as good* a reason.

the view that they *have* to be expressed that way to capture the psychological reality of the thought being described.

To illustrate this important point, suppose I describe Clyde as thinking that my wife is a good cook. What I say (not just my saying it) implies that I have a wife. Clyde cannot think this thought unless I have a wife, unless, therefore, there is someone else in the world besides Clyde. He can, of course, think some other thought, a thought he might express by the words "Your wife is a good cook," but if I do not have a wife, this would not be the thought that my wife is a good cook. It would be the thought that X is a good cook where "X" picks out someone, or something, that Clyde mistakenly takes to be my wife and thinks, mistakenly or not, is a good cook. This something needn't be a human being; it could be a robot or a figment of Clyde's imagination. So Clyde can have a thought that he would express this way without my having a wife, but he cannot have a thought fitting this description, the thought that my wife is a good cook, without my having a wife.

What this tells us is that we can describe what someone thinks in a way that implies the existence of other people even though the thought being described remains, so to speak, socially uncommitted. Our *attributions* of thought have, or may have, a social character while the thoughts themselves lack it.[8]

So what must be shown if one is to show that thought has a social character is not merely that our attributions of thought, our thought ascriptions, have a social character, but that the thoughts themselves are such that they cannot be thought, cannot possess the kind of psychological identity that makes them the thoughts they are, without the existence of other beings. It may turn out, as Brian Loar (1985) argues, that the that-clauses we use to ascribe thoughts are shot through with social presuppositions but that the thoughts themselves, the content that we

---

8   In 1979 (76) and 1982 (98) Burge is careful to point out that the individuation of thoughts is bound up primarily with the obliquely occurring expressions in the content-clauses (the that-clauses) we attribute to a person. Other differences (mainly involving personal pronouns, possessive adjectives, demonstrative pronouns and indexical adverbs and pronouns like "here," "now," "there," etc.), although they make for differences in *ascription*, do not constitute differences in psychological content.

Woodfield (1982a: vi) makes the same distinction and says that in considering the social (or extrinsic) character of thought we are concerned with whether these thoughts are *intrinsically* social – whether, that is, it is the thought itself that is existentially committed or merely our ascriptions of thought. What we are after (Woodfield 1982b: 263) is "the whole content and nothing but the content *as it presented itself to S*."

ordinarily use to individuate thoughts, and on which we rely to understand the behavior of the person in whom they occur, is free of such social implications.

Since this is a moderately tricky point, let me dwell on it a moment longer. It would be silly to say that action has a social character, that you cannot *do* anything in isolation, because we can describe every action in a way that implies the existence of other human beings. Clyde touched my car. That is one way of describing what Clyde did, and describing what he did in this way implies that someone else (me) exists. Maybe I can always manage to describe what Clyde and everyone else does by words that imply that I (or some other human being) exists. Susan stepped on a rock that I once stepped on. Andrew bought a jacket the same color as mine. And so on. The possibility of doing this proves nothing. It shows nothing about action itself (as opposed to these actions) because there are other descriptions that are equally correct descriptions of actions Clyde performed that do *not* imply that there are other human beings. Clyde not only touched my car, he touched a car. That, too, is an action of his, and it does not imply that anyone else exists. So action does not have a social character. If you want to show that action has a social character, you have to show not that actions *can* be described in a way so as to imply the existence of other human beings, but that they *have to be*, that unless this implication is present the thing being described is not really an action. This is what it takes to show that thought has a social character. Not that thoughts can be, perhaps always are, described in such a way as to imply the existence of other beings, but that unless this implication is present, what is being described is not really a thought.

This is a very tall order. I do not know how anyone can hope to argue it without a fully developed theory of what it takes to have a thought.

There are, I know, shortcuts. You don't need a complete theory of the mind. To establish the social character of thought, all you need is a necessary condition for thought that itself has a social character. Ever since Descartes, one of the favorite candidates for this necessary condition has been language. You can't think *anything* if you don't have a language since thought is, as it were, an internalization of the spoken word (or, as with behaviorists, a linguistic disposition). If, then, language is social, something I have already conceded, then so is thought. You cannot develop the capacity to think, hence cannot think, unless there are (or *were* – they may all have died) other people. You can have a solitary thinker of thoughts, but only if he or she acquired this capacity in a social framework.[9]

I think it fairly obvious that some thoughts depend intimately on language. I cannot imagine myself thinking that the day after tomorrow is Sunday, that the cube root of 27 is 3, and that I have arthritis in my thigh without the resources of a public language. These are thoughts that infralinguistic creatures, dogs and cats, simply cannot have. I am quite happy to admit, that is, that some thoughts, perhaps a great many thoughts, perhaps, indeed, all the thoughts I have each day, are language dependent.[10] But this does not tell us what we (or I) want to know. The question is whether thought – not *my* thoughts, not *your* thoughts, not *our* thoughts, but thought – is language dependent and, therefore, has a social aspect. Is it possible for a creature that does not possess a language to think and, if so, is it furthermore possible for it to do so in total isolation? That is the question an answer to which would tell us something not just about the thoughts that people in fact have, but about thought itself.

I have a view about the nature of thought that makes the existence of such infralinguistic and socially isolated thought not only possible, but, if I may risk an empirical conjecture, widespread. Such thought exists in certain animals and in prelinguistic children. The view I am talking about conceives of thought as a species of representation, and representation, in turn, as a natural phenomenon bearing no essential relation to language and social context. Some thoughts may have a social character, and others may depend on language, but that is because they are (like Clyde's thoughts about my car and my thoughts about the day after tomorrow) the thoughts that they are. Thought itself is socially neutral.

---

9 Norman Malcolm (1973: 460) accepts the Cartesian doctrine ("I agree, therefore, with the Cartesians that thoughts cannot be attributed to animals that are without language") but maintains that this is consistent with saying that animals think. Thinking, for Malcolm, is not the same as having thoughts.

10 At times Burge seems to be suggesting that although thought may not have a social character (it may not, for example, in nonlinguistic animals or infants), it does in creatures that speak a language: "Crudely put, wherever the subject has attained a certain competence in large relevant parts of his language and has (implicitly) assumed a certain general commitment or responsibility to the communal conventions governing the language's symbols, the expressions the subject uses take on a certain inertia in determining attributions of mental content to him. In particular, the expressions the subject uses sometimes provide the content of his mental states or events even though he only partially understands, or even misunderstands, some of them" (1979: 562).

The only way I know to argue that thought lacks a social character is to provide an example of an internal state of an animal that in no way depends on the existence of other animals and is, arguably at least, a thought. In order to give this example, in order to make it convincing, I have to say something about what a representation is and why it is plausible to regard thought as a kind of internal representation.

Representations are produced by objects or (in the case of biological entities) organs by way of performing an indicator or information-providing function. Think about an ordinary instrument – the speedometer in your car, for instance. This device has the job of telling you how fast the car is moving. It has the function of supplying this information. The way it performs its job is by means of a mobile pointer on a calibrated scale. When things are working right, the position of the pointer indicates, carries the information, that the car is going, say, 60 mph. When things are not working right, the gauge misrepresents the speed of the car: it "says" the car is going 60 mph when the car is not going this fast. The way the instrument "says" this, the way it performs its job, is by adjusting the orientation of the pointer. Different positions of the pointer are the instrument's representations, its (as it were) "thoughts" about how fast the car is going. The instrument's power to misrepresent the speed of the car, a power that any system must have in order to qualify as an appropriate model for thought (since thoughts are the sorts of things that can be false), is a power that derives from the instrument's information-carrying function. A device that does not have the function of indicating speed (even if it happens to indicate speed) cannot misrepresent speed. That is why paper clips cannot, while thermometers can, misrepresent the temperature. Although both the mercury in the thermometer and the paper clips in my desk carry information about temperature, the thermometer has the function of providing this information, while the paper clips do not. Thermometers can lie, at least about the temperature; paper clips cannot.

If we think, then, of thoughts as something like internal representations, internal pointer readings, having an information-carrying function, we can see how thoughts could be either true or false, depending on whether they were doing their job right or not. This is grossly over-simplified, of course, because we are dealing with only the crudest possible situations. But the basic idea, I hope, is clear.

In the case of artifacts (like instruments, diagrams, gauges, and language), the functions that convert an otherwise eligible event or condition (one that *can* carry the relevant information) into a representation come from us. They are conventional in the same way that all symbols are conventional. *We* determine what the function of these artifacts will be and, hence, whether they will produce representations and, if so, of what. Since thought is not conventional, at least not in this way, the functions that convert otherwise eligible internal events and conditions in the nervous system into representations (and, hence, thoughts) are natural, not conventional. Just as they give the heart a certain blood-pumping function, evolutionary histories give various sense organs their information-providing function – thereby making our experience of the world, the product these organs produce by way of performing their function, a (sensory) representation of the world. Learning (or so I have argued in Dretske 1988) also gives rise to elements that have an informational function. Such items are the concepts essential to thought. Thoughts are the internal representations whose information-providing function has been acquired in learning, the kind of learning wherein is acquired the concepts needed to have these thoughts.

This is a stripped-down version of a view about the nature of thought. It happens to be *my* view, but that is irrelevant for the purposes to which I want to put it. I haven't, I know, given you enough of the view to convince you of its many and fulsome merits. But that, too, isn't necessary. I have given enough of it, I hope, to provide the backdrop of the example that I now want to develop. For with this theory in the background, what I hope to give you is the example I promised – an example of something that is, arguably at least, a thought and that is free of all social implications. What I will provide is a description of a normal learning process in which an internal structure develops that has representational content. It not only has an appropriate content, it helps explain the actions of the animal in which it occurs. If you agree with me that this is, indeed, what I have succeeded in describing, then I hope you will also agree with me that what I have described is, *arguably* at least, a thought. It will also be something that is devoid of all social character. If you do not agree with me that what I have described is a thought, I hope you will at least agree with me that it is thoughtlike in character, the sort of thing that, if it got enough companions of the right kind, a (so to speak) critical mass of such representational neighbors, then it would be a thought. I'll settle for this.

Consider, then, the following story about a generic animal I will call Buster. Buster lives in a place where there are furry worms. I will call them (naturally enough) furms. Furms come in all sizes and colors, but they all are furry (F) and they are all shaped like worms (W). Since they are the only things in Buster's habitat that are both furry and worm-shaped, the properties F and W suffice to identify an object as a furm in this environment.

Furms and their salient features are observable by Buster. By this I mean that, thanks to evolution, Buster comes into the world equipped with sensory mechanisms that register such things as the shape and color, the movement and orientation, the texture and size of middle-sized objects like furms. Although he might have to learn where to look for them, Buster doesn't have to learn to see them. Since they are all around him, all he has to do to see them is open his eyes.

But although Buster is, from birth, equipped to see furms, he has no instinctive, no genetically programmed, reaction to them. They are not, in this respect, like bright lights, hot surfaces, loud noises, and fleas on the rump, objects to which he has an instinctive, a genetically deter-mined, response. Buster doesn't withdraw or hide from, snarl or stare at, attack or bite furms. Or, if he does, this is not to a furm *as* a furm, but as (say) an obstacle in his path, something blocking his line of sight, or as something moving in the grass. Buster might, out of curiosity, sniff at a furm, poke at it, step on it, or watch it if it does something unusual, but a furm for Buster, initially at least, is much what a tree, a bush, or a rock is to us: just one of the many uncategorized things in our environ-ment that we cannot help see when our eyes are open but to which, prior to learning, we pay little attention.

What I am asking you to imagine, of course, is an animal who can and does experience objects of a particular kind (furms) but an animal who as yet has developed no capacity to respond to them *as* objects of a particular type. Buster does not yet have the concept FURM. Although he can experience furms, and in this sense (if this is a sense) internally represent them, he does not yet have beliefs of the sort: that is a furm. There is a difference, as we all (I hope) know, between seeing a furm and having a belief that it (what one sees) is a furm, a difference that only learning is capable of bridging.[11] If Buster is to develop the capacity to believe *of* the furms he sees *that* they are furms, if he is to see them *as* furms, he has to develop a *new* way of representing them. Unlike Buster's experiences of furms, the sensory mechanisms for which are

---

11   If the reader doubts this, think about (say) trapezoids. You could see trapezoids (the ones the teacher drew on the board) long before you could see them *as* trapezoids, long before you were able to recognize or identify them as trapezoids (see *that* they were trapezoids).

innate, nature did not equip Buster to have furm beliefs. He has to get that for himself.

One day, out of idle curiosity, Buster sniffs at a large red furm and thereupon experiences a painful stinging sensation in his nose. Buster thereafter avoids large red furms. The same thing happens again with a small green furm. In a short time we find Buster behaving in a way we would all agree is intelligent: he avoids furms. He no longer sniffs at them. When they approach, he quickly retreats. Why? How is one to explain Buster's behavior?

Let me put this explanatory question in a special context so as to clarify just what we are seeking when we ask to have Buster's behavior explained. Imagine that we put Buster in a contrived, an artificial, situation in which there are fake furms (caterpillars or, if you like, mechanical furms), objects that are both furry and wormlike but not furms. Buster spots a fake furm approaching, and he quickly withdraws. A newly arrived observer wants to know why. Why did Buster retreat? He didn't do this before. What is the explanation of Buster's behavior?

First Try: Buster withdrew because he saw a furm coming toward him.

This cannot be the right answer since Buster did not see a furm coming toward him. It was not a furm.

Second Try: Buster withdrew because he saw what looked like a furm (something that was both F and W) coming toward him.

Once again, this explanation (like the first explanation) attempts to explain Buster's behavior without invoking a belief that Buster has about the object he sees. He retreats, we are told, because he sees something fitting a certain description, just as one might pull one's hand away from a surface fitting a certain description – "hot."

But this, too, cannot be the right explanation. At least it cannot be the full explanation. Prior to his painful encounters with furms, Buster saw what looked like furms coming toward him (in this case they actually were furms), objects that were both F and W, and Buster did not withdraw. He had exactly the same experience then, before learning, that he is having now, after learning, the sort of experience that constitutes his seeing an approaching furm. Now he withdraws; then he did not. Now the experience triggers withdrawal movements; then it did not. Why? What is the difference? That, surely, is the question we need answered in order to understand *why* Buster is withdrawing, and that question is not answered by describing what Buster sees. It sounds more like the kind of question that is answered by describing what Buster believes about what he sees.

The attempt to explain Buster's behavior by mentioning what he sees is an attempt to explain his behavior in terms of what I have called a triggering cause. Typically, in this sort of situation, a triggering cause is some environmental event that causes a person to believe something. In seeking explanations of behavior, though, we seek what I called a structuring, not a triggering, cause of the behavior we are trying to understand. We often mention triggering causes in giving an explanation of a person's behavior, but the explanation succeeds, works, only if it suggests or implies something about what the triggering cause causes the person to believe. You understand why I ran if I tell you I ran because I saw a lion coming after me. This explanation works, though, only because you assume that seeing a lion coming at me caused me to *believe* that a lion was coming at me. If I was not caused to believe this, then you do not know why I ran even if you know that an approaching lion (or my seeing an approaching lion) *caused* me to run.

This is why the second attempt at an explanation fails. It doesn't tell us what, if anything, Buster believes about what he sees. It only tells us what he sees. But he saw furry worms before and he didn't run. So it cannot be seeing furry worms that explains his running.

Third Try: Buster withdraws because he thinks it is a furm and he is afraid of furms.

If, at this early stage of learning, this description sounds a bit too fancy for Buster, we can say that he withdraws because he thinks it (the approaching object) is one of those furry (F), wormy (W) objects that stings his nose (S) when it gets too close. Call this the FWS (furry-wormy-stinger) concept of furms. Buster runs because he thinks it (the furry worm he sees) is a FWSer and he does not want to get stung.

We have been drawn, irresistibly, into new territory. We are now giving rational explanations of Buster's behavior, explanations in terms of what Buster thinks and what Buster wants (or fears). We may suppose that Buster was motivated to avoid pain, wanted to avoid it, long before his painful encounters with the furms. This, we may assume, is a long-standing, a more or less fixed, instinct or desire. But if we want to credit a belief to Buster, and it seems hard to resist this temptation, we must suppose that such a belief, or the capability of holding such a belief, emerged in his learning experience with the furms.

All this strikes me as fairly obvious. This is what concept formation is all about. A brief learning episode of this sort is enough to credit an animal like Buster with a rudimentary concept, a concept essential for the holding of the sort of belief that will, when a relevant piece of behavior occurs, and in association with appropriate motivational states and other beliefs, explain why Buster does what he does.

What Buster develops during his brief but painful encounter with furms is a way of representing them that goes beyond the sensory mechanisms he was given at birth, beyond what it takes to see furms. Buster (we are assuming) was always getting information about the furms in his environment. They have a distinctive look, a look that only furms have, and he could see them, could see the features (F and W) that set furms apart from other objects. Although he was getting this information, he wasn't, before learning, doing anything with it. That changed. Now the information sufficient unto identifying something as a furm is being put to work. It has, as it were, been given a job to do, the job of getting Buster out of range. It has been harnessed to control mechanisms so as to coordinate Buster's behavior with the environmental conditions in which such behavior is beneficial. Something in Buster, his experience of furms, that earlier, before learning, indicated the presence of F (furriness) and W (wormyness) has come to have the function of indicating furms: F, W, *and* S. On a representational model of beliefs, this is to say that something in Buster has come to play the part of a belief, the belief that that object (the one he sees) is a furm (or a FWSer).

If we accept this account of things, then, since Buster thinks it is a furm approaching, and the process wherein he came to think this does not require the existence of any conscious being (the fact that furms are animals plays no essential part in this story; they could as well have been thorny tumbleweeds), the conclusion is inescapable: thought, the development of representational powers of this sort, does not require a social context. Buster could have this thought even if he was the only conscious being in the universe.

The moral of the story about the extrinsicness of belief is not, however, so clear. For in this story Buster acquired his concept of a furm by interacting with furms. Take away the furms (or imagine the FW's without the S) and you take away Buster's concept of a furm (a FWSer) – hence, his belief that approaching objects are furms. This, of course, is exactly the moral I would like to draw. Concepts, in the first instance at least, have an origin in the learning experiences with the kinds of which they are concepts. Since, however, I have no argument that this learning process is necessary for *all* concept formation I have no argument that thought is essentially extrinsic. I leave that as a more or less plausible conjecture.

In closing, however, let me return to motivations, the problem I described at the beginning. If you will recall, I suggested that one reason for denying that thought was extrinsic, and therefore social, was the difficulty in seeing how thought, if it had this character, could figure in the explanation of behavior. I think Buster's story helps one to understand how this is possible. The internal elements in Buster that become representations (of furms) by acquiring the function (of indicating their presence) do so in the very process in which control circuits governing the reaction to furms are reconfigured. Internal elements become thoughts about, representations of, furms at the same time as are created the neural structures underlying the production of output (hence, the kind of future behavior that thought will be called upon to explain). The representational aspect of thought, although extrinsic, is causally relevant to behavior because what is represented determines what it is that these representations end up doing in the system. Change what these internal structures represent and, through the learning process, you change the causal organization of the system in which these structures occur. You thereby change what these structures *do*. That is how thought content is made relevant to behavior.

Thoughts have been described as maps by means of which we steer. I like this metaphor. Maps are representations, and their power to steer is their role in the determination of output. What we see in Buster's case is the way an internal map, the power of thought, is created in the very process in which that map gets its hand on the steering wheel. Such, I submit, is the way thoughts, qua thoughts, are relevant to what we do.

REFERENCES

Burge, T. 1979: "Individualism and the Mental," in Peter A. French, Theodore Uehling, Jr., and Howard K. Wettstein (eds.), *Midwest Studies in Philosophy*, vol. IV, Minneapolis: University of Minnesota Press; reprinted in Rosenthal (1991). All page references in the text are to Rosenthal.

Burge, T. 1982: "Other Bodies," in Andrew Woodfield (ed.), *Thought and Object: Essays on Intentionality*, Oxford: Clarendon Press.

Burge T. 1990: "Wherein Is Language Social?" in C. Anthony Anderson and Joseph Owens (eds.), *Propositional Attitudes*, Stanford, Calif.: CSLI.

Davidson, D. 1975: "Thought and Talk," in Samuel Guttenplan (ed.), *Mind and Language: Wolfson College Lectures 1974*, Oxford: Oxford University Press.

Dretske, F. 1988: *Explaining Behavior: Reasons in a World of Causes*, Cambridge, Mass.: MIT Press.

Fodor, J. 1980: "Methodological Solipsism Considered as a Research Strategy in Cognitive Science," *Behavioral and Brain Sciences*; reprinted in Jerry A. Fodor, *Representations*, Cambridge, Mass.: MIT Press, 1981.

Fodor, J. 1987: *Psychosemantics*, Cambridge, Mass.: MIT Press.

Hamlyn, D. W. 1990: *In and Out of the Black Box: On the Philosophy of Cognition*, Oxford: Basil Blackwell.

Loar, B. 1985: "Social Content and Psychological Content," in Robert Grimm and Daniel Merrill (eds.), *Contents of Thought*, Tucson: University of Arizona Press.

Malcolm, N. 1973: "Thoughtless Brutes," *Proceedings and Addresses of the American Philosophical Association* 46 (1972–1973); reprinted in Rosenthal (1991). All page references in the text are to Rosenthal.

Putnam, H. 1975: "The Meaning of 'Meaning,' " in Keith Gunderson (ed.), *Language, Mind and Knowledge: Minnesota Studies in the Philosophy of Science*, vol. VII, Minneapolis: University of Minnesota Press.

Rosenthal, D. M. 1991: *The Nature of Mind*, Oxford: Oxford University Press.

Woodfield, A. 1982a: "Foreword," in Andrew Woodfield (ed.), *Thought and Object: Essays on Intentionality*, Oxford: Clarendon Press.

Woodfield, A. 1982b: "On Specifying the Contents of Thoughts," in Andrew Woodfield (ed.), *Thought and Object: Essays on Intentionality*, Oxford: Clarendon Press.

14

Norms, History, and the Constitution of the Mental

No one doubts that the mind evolved. What would be surprising is if it *had* to evolve – if the mind not only had a history, but a history essential to its very existence.

Surprising though it is, some people think this is so.[1] Of those who think it so, some think it because they discern, or think they discern, a normative quality to mental affairs, a way mental states and activities (qua mental) are *supposed to be*, that can be understood only by conceiving of them as products of a historical process. Without a process like natural selection or learning, processes capable of grounding a difference between how things are and how they are supposed to be, there is nothing to provide the requisite contrast with existing fact, the sort of contrast we normally invoke by speaking of how things *should* be or behave. Objects that materialize wholly by accident, for instance, have, at the first moment of their existence (before acquiring an appropriate history), no purpose, no way they are supposed to be or behave. Such objects (so it is said) can harbor no meaning or content – hence, no capacity for reason, judgment, or experience – states and activities that

My thanks to the participants of the Notre Dame Conference on Varieties of Dualism (March 1998) for useful feedback and criticism on an earlier draft of this essay. I specially want to thank John O'Leary-Hawthorne, Fritz Warfield, Al Plantinga, and Marian David for helpful comments.
1 Certainly Millikan (1984, 1995), Papineau (1993) and Dretske (1986, 1995), and, depending on which way they go on representation, probably also Lycan (1997 – see p. 75, where he expresses sympathy with a teleological view of representation) and Tye (1995 – see Sections 5.4 and 7.4). Neander (1995) insightfully explores a teleological (thus, historical) view of representation without actually defending it.

presuppose norms. History is to minds what it is to fossils. Without the right history, there aren't any.

Since the arguments for this view are not entirely convincing – even to someone like me who accepts their conclusion – and the consequences of the view, I keep being told, are preposterous,[2] I take this occasion to reexamine the matter. If I am to continue believing not just that the mind is a product of historical development (we all believe that), but, like a fossil, can exist *only* in that way, I need better reasons than I've already got. I'm not sure I can produce them, but I hope the exercise of looking for them will prove philosophically useful. It was for me.

1. NORMATIVE CONCEPTS

Philosophers of science used to worry a lot about theory-laden concepts. A theory-laden concept is one whose correct application to an object presupposes that a certain theory, or fragment of a theory, is true of that object. There cannot be objects of that sort, objects to which the concept applies, unless the theory, or theory-fragment, is true. Showing the theory false has the consequence that a concept loaded with it (and, therefore, implying the truth of it) applies to nothing. There are no such objects.

Norwood Russell Hanson (1958) did much to sensitize philosophers to theory-laden concepts and the role they played in science. He used the ordinary concept of *wound* to illustrate the idea. To be a wound it is not enough to be a cut or incision in a person's flesh, the sort of gash an assailant might make in wounding a person. To qualify as a wound, the cut must have a particular origin, a certain kind of history. Surgeons do not wound patients on whom they perform appendectomies (not, at least, if they are doing their job right) even though the cuts they make may be indistinguishable from genuine wounds. When made by a surgeon for an approved medical reason, the incision is not made with the

2 A favored way of dramatizing this is by invoking Swampman, a creature imagined by Donald Davidson (1987), who materializes by chance when a bolt of lightning strikes a decaying log in a swamp. Miraculously, Swampman is, molecule for molecule, the same as Davidson. Since Swampman has no significant history – certainly none of the kind that would (according to historical accounts of the mind) give him thoughts and (maybe even) experiences – he lacks these mental states even though he is physically and (therefore) behaviorally indistinguishable from Davidson. Swampman is a zombie.

right purpose to qualify as a wound. It has the wrong history. Having the right history is, if you will, the "theory" the concept *wound* is loaded with.

Concepts come laden with norms as well as theories and history.[3] Think of the difference between *murdering* and *killing*. *Murder* is a norm-loaded concept because it requires the killing to be done in a morally or legally objectionable way. To murder X is to kill X wickedly, with malice aforethought, inhumanely, or barbarously. That is why you can't murder (although you can kill) someone accidentally or while trying to save her life. When accidental (or when done with benevolent motives), the killing isn't bad, wrong, wicked, or malicious[4] – hence, not murder. People may disagree about whether abortion is murder, but, often, the disagreement isn't about whether abortion involves killing a fetus. It is a disagreement about whether the killing is morally wrong. Thus, *murder* is, while *killing* is not, norm-laden.

This is not to say that killings can't be wrong. Of course they can. It is just that killings are not – whereas murders are – *necessarily* wrong. Murders depend on norms for their very existence. Killings do not. Take away norms and, in one stroke, you extinguish murder, just as wounds are eliminated by removing their history. Killings and cuts remain, yes, but not wounds and murder.

The evaluations implied by describing an act as *murder* are moral (or perhaps legal) evaluations. There are other kinds of norms. Being *broken*, for instance, is one of a cluster of terms that imply something about how objects to which it applies are, in some nonmoral and nonlegal sense, *supposed*, or *supposed not*, to be. To say that a bone (leg, toy, window) is broken implies that the bone (leg, toy, window) is not in the condition it is supposed to be in. If it was designed (e.g., the toy), it is not in the condition it was designed to be in. Aside from the intentions of its designer (or, perhaps, a certain kind of history – more of this later), nothing is broken. If you or I (or God) deliberately make a thing the

---

3 The following discussion of norm-loaded concepts is, I think, independent of what view one takes of the embedded norms. If one is a subjectivist about these things – thinking, perhaps, that to say that something is wrong (bad, not the way it ought to be, etc.) is merely to assert (or evince) personal feelings and attitudes toward it (e.g., that you don't like or approve of it), then norm-laden concepts are concepts that S cannot correctly apply to x unless S (not necessarily anyone else) has the right feelings or attitudes toward x. For a recent defense of an "expressivist" analysis of norms see Gibbard (1990).

4 Although something else may be bad or wrong – e.g., the negligence (driving while drunk) that led to the accident. Thus, the result may still be labeled murder.

way it is in order to illustrate a point, as a prototype, or as a work of abstract art, it isn't broken. If it materialized randomly that way out of cosmic dust, it isn't broken no matter how much it looks and behaves like an object that (with a different history or created with different intentions) is broken. Broken things *have to* have a history. If they don't, they aren't broken.

Injury, healthy, strained, stretched, diseased, defective, flawed, ill, sick, damaged, spoiled, ruined, marred, contaminated, defiled, corrupted, infected, malformed – they are all like that. Nothing can be any of these things unless it, or the processes leading up to it, are subject to norms. If something is marred or damaged, for instance, it departs in some degree from a standard that defines how it *should* be. Many of these standards come from us, the designers and makers of devices. It is our purposes, the way we want or intend things to be, that makes them – when they fail to be that way – damaged, spoiled, malformed, flawed, and so on. If a gadget is my creation, if I made it do a certain task, then it is broken, flawed, defective, or broken if it doesn't do what I want it to do. If I want the clock I build to lose time, if that was my purpose in building it this way, then it isn't working right, it is broken or defective, if it doesn't lose time.[5] I am the origin of this norm.

Things are subject to multiple standards. Sometimes, for example, we intend things to be in a condition they are not – relative to some other standard – supposed to be in. There is no inconsistency in saying that an object is supposed to be in a state that (relative to another standard) it is not supposed to be in.

2. ARE MENTAL CONCEPTS NORMATIVELY LOADED?

If mental concepts are normatively loaded, then minds (or those parts of the mind that we pick out with norm-laden concepts) cannot exist without norms. This gives rise to a problem: where do these norms come from? They certainly cannot come from us – from our intentions, purposes, and desires – the way the norms governing our own creations (e.g., my slow-running clock) come from us since the norms we now seek are ones on which intentions, purposes, and desires themselves

---

5   If one thinks of clocks as functional devices – objects that are supposed to tell the *right* time – then the gadget I build, not having that function, is not a clock. Whatever it is, though, it is supposed to run slowly – i.e., more slowly than a proper clock.

depend for their existence. So the norms constituting these mental states have to come from somewhere else. Where?

This is a problem *if* mental concepts are norm-laden. But are they? Some of them seem to be. *Mistakes*, after all, are (according to my dictionary) beliefs, judgments, or takings that are in some way wrong, bad, or improper. One cannot believe, perceive, or infer without risking misrepresentation, illusion, and fallacy. That is part of the game. Maybe cognition can occur (in an omniscient being?) without error, but the possibility of mistake, the possibility of getting it wrong, of committing a fallacy, is part of what we mean when we speak of someone as judging, inferring, or concluding that so-and-so is true. If, then, the possibility of mistake (if not mistakes themselves) is part of what we mean in describing an act or practice as cognitive, then *cognition* is norm-laden in the sense that nothing merits this description unless there are, somewhere in the background, norms relative to which states and activities can be deemed wrong, bad, or incorrect. If you *can't* make a mistake, if what you are doing isn't the sort of thing in which mistakes are possible, then what is happening might be described as digestive or immunological, but it isn't cognitive. It is not believing, judging, reasoning, perceiving, or inferring.

At one time this line of reasoning seemed right to me, and I took it to show that there was a problem for naturalistic accounts of the mind. The problem – or what seemed to me a problem – was to determine the source of these cognitive norms. Where did they come from? How does one get a mental OUGHT, a SUPPOSED TO BE, from a biological IS? David Hume taught us that it is a fallacy to conclude that something ought (morally) to be so from premises describing only what is (as a matter of fact) so. Why isn't it also a fallacy to suppose (as naturalistic theories of the mind do) that normatively loaded mental states arise from, and are thus reducible to, the norm-free facts of physics and biology?

One response to this problem (championed by Ruth Millikan, 1984, 1993) is that the facts of biology are not norm free. An organ's or a trait's proper function – roughly speaking, what it is selected to do – is, Millikan insists, itself a normative concept.[6] If it is a thing's proper function to do F, then it is supposed to do F. Thus, norm-laden cogni-

6   See also Neander (1995, p. 112), who says that biological norms underwrite semantic norms. Not everyone agrees, of course, that natural selection yields norms. Foder (1996, p. 252), Bedau (1993), Matthen (1997), and others are skeptics.

tive discourse (Millikan 1993, p. 72, speaks of false beliefs as *defective* and "true" and "false" as normative terms) can be grounded in biological norms. There is no fallacious derivation of a cognitive OUGHT from a biological IS, only a transformation of a biological into a cognitive OUGHT. She describes her purpose (1993, p. 10) as defending this biological solution to "the normativity problem," the problem of accounting for false beliefs, misperceptions, bad inferences, errors, and so on. This, indeed, is why she speaks (in the title of her first book) of language and thought as biological categories (Millikan 1984).

The problem to which Millikan's biological solution is a solution no longer seems like a problem to me. Beliefs and judgments must be either true or false, yes, but there is nothing normative about truth and falsity. What makes a judgment false (true) is the fact that it fails (or succeeds) in corresponding to the facts, and failing (or succeeding) in corresponding to the facts is, as far as I can see, a straightforward factual matter. Nothing normative about it. An arrow (on a sign, say) can point to Chicago or away from Chicago. There is a difference here, yes, but the difference is not normative. Aside from our purposes in putting the sign there or in using the sign as a guide, there is nothing right or wrong, nothing that is supposed-to-be or supposed-not-to-be, about an arrow pointing to Chicago. The same holds for beliefs. Aside from our purposes in forming beliefs or in using beliefs as guides to action, there is nothing they should or shouldn't be. Chris Peacocke (1992, p. 126) claims that "correct" and "incorrect" are normative notions because whether X is correct or not depends on the way the world is. But whether X is pointing at Chicago also depends on the way the world is. It depends on where Chicago is. That doesn't make "pointing at Chicago" a normative expression.

For understandable reasons we dislike false beliefs and do our best to avoid them. This dislike and avoidance leads us to describe false beliefs in ways that are heavily normative – as, for example, *mistakes* or *misrep*resentations where the prefix "mis" signifies that the judgment or belief has gone amiss, that it is wrong, bad, or improper in some way. But the practice of describing false beliefs in this normative way doesn't show that there is anything *essentially* normative about false beliefs any more than it shows that there is something essentially normative about the weather (e.g., a blizzard) on the day of our picnic because we describe it as awful. The fact that cognition requires the possibility of error, and that errors are bad, does not mean that cognition *requires* norms – not unless errors are *necessarily* bad. But why should we believe this? Bad, yes, at least most of the time, but not necessarily bad. The only *fault* with fallacious reasoning, the only thing *wrong* or *bad* about mistaken judgments, is that, generally speaking, we don't like them. We do our best to avoid them. They do not – most of the time at least – serve our purposes. This, though, leaves the normativity of false belief and fallacious reasoning in the same place as the normativity of foul weather and bad table manners – in the attitudes, purposes, and beliefs of the people who make judgments about the weather and table behavior.

Some have argued that it isn't *truth* and *falsity* that are norm-laden, but the concept of *belief* itself. Beliefs by their very nature, and unlike wishes, hopes, desires, and doubts (not to mention bicycles and rocks), are mental states that aspire to truth and, therefore, fail or are defective in some way when they are not true. A belief can be false, yes, just as a (defective) heart can fail to pump blood, but a belief, even when false, is *supposed* to be true, just as the defective heart is supposed to pump blood. Beliefs aspire to truth; that is their job, their purpose, their raison d'être. Anything lacking this purpose just isn't a belief any more than a device that isn't supposed to tell the right time is a clock. So if, in the natural world, there are no OUGHTS, neither are there any beliefs.

I know this view is aggressively promoted,[7] but I do not find it plausible. I agree that beliefs are necessarily true or false. If I didn't understand what it was to *be* true or false, I could hardly understand what it was to be a belief. But I do not see that I need go further than this. This seems like enough to distinguish beliefs from other mental states like wishes, desires, hopes, doubts, and pains – not to mention bicycles and rocks.[8] Why, in order to understand what a belief is, do I also have to think of a belief as something that is *supposed to be* true? If I deliberately deceive you, is the resulting belief supposed to be true?

---

7 Paul Boghassian defended it at a conference in Palermo, Sicily, in August 1997, but I do not attribute specific arguments to him since, lacking a copy of the paper, I am forced to rely on my feeble memory of an oral presentation. Peacocke (in 1992, Chapter 5) argues that content (hence, belief) is normative and Kripke (1982) that meaning (and presumably, therefore, also thought) is. Also see Brandom (1994), in which a Kantian (vs. a Cartesian) view is defended according to which mental states like judgment and belief (involving concepts) are inherently normative. On the Kantian view of things, concepts have the form of *rules* that bring with them entitlements and commitments. Peacocke and Brandom distinguish different kinds of norms (Peacocke's "normative liaisons" are similar to Brandom's "consequential commitments"), but I think my arguments against the *essential* normativity of mental content apply to both.

8 Although it may not be enough to distinguish believing P from entertaining the thought (or hypothesis) that P. For that we may need additional functional properties.

248

Aren't people supposed to be deceived by a well-executed trompe l'oeil, a magician's trick, or a clever disguise? My inclination is to say that such beliefs are supposed to be false. My reason for saying this is the same as my reason for saying that anything that one deliberately brings about (e.g., a slow-running clock) is (given one's purposes) supposed to be the way one intends it to be. So if I design a device to be (or produce) F, if that is my purpose, the device, given my purpose, is supposed to be (or produce) F. If F happens to be a false belief in you (or even in me), then your (my) belief is supposed to be false in the same way my "clock" is supposed to tell the wrong time.[9]

This debate (about the normativity of meaning or content) is sometimes put in terms of a concept's extension and the "rules" (hence, norms) governing its application (see Kripke 1982). Concepts have extensions: cows and only cows are in the extension of the concept *cow*. This concept can be correctly applied only to cows. If someone falsely applies it (on a dark night) to a horse (i.e., believes of the horse that it is a cow), this is an incorrect (i.e., false) application of the concept. So far, so good. Aside from our desires and intentions to avoid what is false, though, why is the false application of a concept something that is wrong, bad, or improper? What rule or norm does it violate? A belief that 37 plus 84 is 111 is certainly false; it does not correctly pick out a trio of numbers that is in the extension of *plus*, but what rule is broken by applying *plus* to these three numbers?

It will be said that if we do not care whether we get the right (correct, true) answer – or if we deliberately try to get a wrong answer – then what we are doing is not *adding* 37 and 84. We are fooling around, doodling, or, perhaps, trying to make some observer think we don't know how to add. But we are not adding. We can add 37 and 84 and get the wrong answer, yes, just as we can break the rules of chess (unintentionally or in an effort to cheat) and still be playing chess, but in order to be properly described as adding two numbers (or playing chess), we have to view ourselves as falling within the purview of the rules (hence, norms) constituting the activity we are engaged in. We must feel constrained by, a commitment to, the rules of arithmetic that determine what the right answer is, just as, when playing chess, we are supposed to follow the rules of the game. If we do not feel bound by

---

9   Recalling our early remark (about multiple standards), it may be objected that although the belief, *given my intentions*, is supposed to be false, it is, *given (merely the fact) that it is a belief*, supposed to be true. Perhaps, but what reason is there to think this is so?

these rules, if we take to be irrelevant the criticism (in the case of addition) that we forgot to carry the 1, then we are not really adding. In this sense, *addition* is a rule (norm)-constituted activity – as much so as chess or baseball. The same is true of all concepts. Norms are built into – some would say they constitute – the concepts we apply. If we do not respect these norms, do not feel the entitlements and commitments they give rise to, then we are not really applying these concepts.[10]

This, it seems to me, is a confusion between two quite different things – the norm-free concepts (meanings) we intentionally apply, on the one hand, and, on the other, the norm-laden intentions with which (or the actions in which) we apply them. All intentional acts, in virtue of being intentional (or goal directed[11]), are subject to norms. You cannot be hiding from a predator, driving to Chicago, or ironing your shirt[12] without intending to do all the things that you believe necessary to do these things. You are not really hiding from X (although you may be pretending to hide from X) if you have no care about whether X can see you or if you deliberately make attention-grabbing noise. You are not driving to Chicago if you ignore or take to be irrelevant information to the effect that *that* isn't the way to Chicago. All intentional acts, in virtue of being intentional, bring the actor under the purview of norms in the sense that the actor is obliged (ought) to adopt the means she believes necessary (in the circumstances) to do what she intends to do. If the actor feels no constraints or obligation to do what she acknowledges to be necessary for doing A, then she is not – not really –

10 I am grateful to Tim Schroeder for helpful discussion on this point. He convinced me that what I said (in an earlier draft) on this point was much too superficial to capture the position I was arguing against.

11 What I say in the text is probably better said about goal-directed activities and the means one adopts to achieve these goals (some things one does intentionally are not goal directed in the relevant sense; one does them intentionally – e.g., destroys the children's hospital – but that isn't one's goal; the goal is the destruction of the nearby munitions plant), but I skip over these complications here. I am grateful to Michael Bratman for clarification here.

12 Some verbs (like "hide") have the relevant intentions already built in. Unlike driving to Chicago (which you can do without intending to get to Chicago), you can't be hiding from X without intending or trying to conceal yourself from X. I think adding is more like hiding; you can't do it unintentionally. My intuitions about these matters (admittedly shaky) tell me that if you unintentionally add two numbers (while trying to multiply them, say), you were not (at the time you added them) adding them. You were multiplying them. I shall here assume that the actions I describe (e.g., driving to Chicago, ironing your shirt) are intentional in the relevant sense – directed at a goal (of, e.g., getting to Chicago, ironing your shirt).

intending to do A. The same is true in applying concepts. If the act (of applying the concept) is intentional, it will come under the purview of norms, not because concepts or their application is a norm-governed activity, but because the act of applying them, *when it is intentional,* generates a set of norms associated with the actor's intentions and desires. Doing A intentionally *commits* the actor to doing the things she believes necessary to doing A and, thus, exposes the actor to the norms (the shoulds and supposed-tos) that such commitment brings with it. If the application of concepts is not an intentional act – as it isn't in the case of perceptual judgment (e.g., seeing that the bottle is empty) – then, as far as I can see, norms are absent. All that is left is truth or falsity.

This, by the way, is why conceptual role semantics (generally speaking, meaning as *use*) is so much more plausible for language than thought. Saying (asserting, claiming) that P (unlike believing that P) is, generally speaking, a purposeful, goal-directed action and, thus, the language of entitlements, commitments, rules, and norms more easily finds a home here. But, even here, I submit, the norms emerge from the associated intentions, not from the meanings applied in the act.

There is, however, a tempting argument that purports to show that a certain class of beliefs – in fact, perceptual beliefs – are norm-laden. The argumentative strategy is a bit different from the one we have so far considered in that it argues not that history is needed to explain the essential normativity of cognition, but, rather, that normativity is a consequence of the kind of history that cognition is (independently) laden with. The argument goes like this. Perception has the job, the function, the purpose of providing information to (higher) cognitive centers for the guidance of action. Since this is the job of perceptual systems, they are not doing their job, not doing what they are supposed to be doing, if they do not deliver information. If, then, one thinks (as it is natural to think) of information as something requiring a more or less reliable correspondence between input (world) and output (experience and belief), then it follows that the output of perceptual processes – perceptual experiences and beliefs – is supposed to correspond in some reliable way to the world about which it provides information. Experiences are, in this sense, supposed to be veridical and beliefs are, in this sense, supposed to be true. If they are not, the systems producing them are not doing what they are supposed to be doing. The normativity of perceptual beliefs and experiences derives from the teleofunctions of the mechanisms producing them, and the teleofunctions have their origin in the historical (selectional) process that shaped those mechanisms.

251

I came close to endorsing this argument in (Dretske 1995) — see especially p. 4 — but, as it stands, it doesn't pass muster. Given the fact that perceptual systems have an evolutionary history, it may in fact *be* their job (= biological function) to provide the brain (and resident control mechanisms) with information about the environment in and on which actions are to be performed, but that, by itself, isn't enough to show that perceptual concepts are norm-laden. It isn't enough to show that perceptual beliefs and experiences *cannot* exist without norms and the historical (selectional) processes that ground those norms. For we don't yet have an argument that the teleofunctions that give rise to those norms are *essential* to perceptual experiences and beliefs. Why, in other words, can't we agree that perceptual systems (just like the kidneys, heart, and lungs) have biological functions that they obtain from a process of natural selection and, given these functions, are supposed to do various things — whatever it is their function to do? If they don't do those things, they are broken, malfunctioning, diseased, or impaired in some way. They fail to measure up to the norms that their historical development makes applicable to them. Why can't we say all this and still deny that such a historical development is *necessary* to the beliefs and experiences, qua beliefs and experiences, that these systems produce? Why is the history essential? If an organ actually supplies information to Swampman's brain in the usual way (as it will if Swampman is molecularly indistinguishable from Donald Davidson), and this information is actually used (as it will be) to negotiate Swampman's way through his environment, why should we deny that this is perception simply because the information is being provided by organs that (lacking an appropriate history) lack the biological function of supplying it? Lacking the relevant functions, they are not supposed to supply it, yes, but why is that critical to the mentality of the process and its products? That is exactly what the arguments we have so far been examining (those that appeal to the norm-laden character of cognition) were attempting to supply, and, given their failure, what we still lack convincing arguments for.

3. INTENTIONALITY

What we have so far concluded is that although we may need history to explain norms, we do not need history to explain mentality because mentality, although subject to norms, is not constituted by them. At least we do not yet have an argument that it is. Mistakes are bad, yes, and, generally speaking, given our cognitive purposes, beliefs ought to be true and experiences veridical. But the norms implied by these evaluative judgments are the norms we bring to cognitive affairs. They have the same source – current attitudes and purposes – as do the norms applied to the weather on the day of a picnic and rude behavior at the dinner table. Take away these attitudes and purposes and you eliminate the norms that make false beliefs mistakes, but you do not eliminate false beliefs. A belief – just like the weather – is independent of the norms we apply to it. As we have seen, there are norms that are independent of our purposes and attitudes. We can still say that, given their evolutionary history, and independent of what we may happen to desire and intend, perceptual mechanisms are supposed to provide us with information about our environment and that, therefore, perceptual beliefs are supposed to be true. We can say this in the same way we say that the heart is supposed to pump blood and the liver is supposed to aid in digestion and excretion. But the norms implied in these judgments, although historically grounded, are not essential to the cognitive products of these historical processes. We do not need to suppose – at least we have not yet found a reason to suppose – that such an evolutionary history is essential to the perceptual processes and states that are its products.

There is, however, the possibility that history, although not required for the normativity of cognition, is required for some other aspect of our mental life.[13] This is a possibility I mean to raise in the remainder of this article. The upshot of this brief look will be that although we do not need history to explain the normativity of mental affairs, we may

---

13 The fact that history may be needed to explain the intentionality, not the normativity, of the mental is not always clearly distinguished. Neander (1995, p. 110), for example, speaks of grounding intentionality in biological facts (functions) but then (p. 112) says that functions are needed to underwrite the normative notion of mental (semantic) content. Millikan moves back and forth between intentionality and normativity as the feature of mental affairs that proper functions are supposed to ground. MacDonald (1989, especially p. 189), has a clear discussion of these matters.

Incidentally (in Dretske 1986) I described misrepresentation as a problem for a naturalistic approach to the mind, but I did not clearly specify whether I thought this problem was a normative problem or just a problem about intentionality. I don't think I was clear about it then. History, I would now say, is necessary for misrepresentation, not because representation (or misrepresentation) is essentially normative, but because it is essentially intentional.

need it – at least it is an attractive possibility – to explain another fact that is essential to cognitive affairs: the aboutness or intentionality of cognitive states.[14]

Thought and experience are intentional in the philosopher's sense of this word; that is, they are about things, and the things they are about need not exist in order for one to think about or experience them. If one need not stand in any actual relation to orange things in order to think about them, what makes one's thoughts about them? What makes a thought that pumpkins are orange a thought that they are orange rather than yellow or blue? What makes perceptions (dreams, hallucinations) of orange things phenomenally so different from perceptions (dreams, hallucinations) of blue things? If we begin by assuming, as I do, that experiences and thoughts are resident in the brain – some condition of or activity in this gray neural mass – what makes some conditions of this gray matter about orange, while others are about blue and still others are about nothing at all?

One attractive answer to this question is that although intentional relations (i.e., aboutness, meaning, reference) are not real relations (real relations require the existence of their relata), intentional relations (I will call them "semantic connections") can be analyzed into real relations if (only if?) the relationships that ground semantic connections are realized in the past. What makes this bit of stuff, A, about that bit of stuff, B, what establishes the semantic connection between them, is not that A and B *stand* in some relation to one another (that can't be right since B need not even exist for A to be about it), but, instead, that A (or appropriate ancestors – earlier tokens – of type A) and B (or earlier tokens of B) *stood* in appropriate relations to each other. If no existing relationship makes this bit of brain matter about orange pumpkins, then maybe it is the brain's past relationship to orange pumpkins (or orange things and pumpkins) that fixes this semantic connection.

The thought here (I'm putting it pretty crudely; but I'm trying to capture an intuition, not construct airtight arguments) is that if I, a thinker and experiencer, can get myself connected to things that don't exist (perhaps never existed), and if such connections are not secured by

14   I do not assume (although I argue for it elsewhere – Dretske 1995) that intentionality is the "mark of the mental." Arguably, at least, itches, tickles, and pains (mental states in good standing) do not possess it. Nonetheless, I do assume (without here arguing) that intentionality is an essential characteristic of *cognitive* states. Such mental states and processes as perception, memory, judgment, and inference involve representation, and representation, I assume, is intentional.

actual relations to the sort of thing I am now connected with, then actual relations might have done their work in the past. Being "connected" to orange pumpkins – thinking about or experiencing them – might require an appropriate history because that is the only way existing connections with (possibly) nonexisting objects can be grounded in nonintentional (i.e., real) relations. If some bit of gray matter is about the color orange (in the way an experience is of the color orange) and there does not exist, at the time of the experience, anything that is orange, then, just possibly, what makes this gray matter about orange (rather than red or blue) is its past relations to orange things.[15]

This, I admit, is a pretty creaky argument. Those who do not share my reductionistic proclivities (or my blinkered vision of what it takes to properly ground a semantic connection) will not be attracted by it.[16] It depends on a philosophically questionable assumption that semantic connections must be grounded in real relations to existing objects. It depends, that is, on the assumption that if S (a conscious being) is V to ϕ (where V is a verb describing S's semantic connection to ϕ), then this connection between S and ϕ must be the result of relations S (or a relevant ancestor of S) bore to ϕ-ish objects in the past. This is not an assumption that is likely to go unchallenged. It is a variant of the

15 I skip over complications relating to primitive vs. complex concepts. Obviously one can think about a unicorn without ever having been related to a unicorn in the past. But the idea (an old idea) is that one's capacity to think about unicorns (a complex concept) depends on past relations to the constituents of that concept – *horse, one,* and *horn.*

16 Nor will those, like Jerry Fodor (1990), who think that semantic connections can be established by real relations between universal properties (assuming that counterfactual supporting dependency relations count as real relations). I don't have the space to say why I think this doesn't work. It would take at least another essay. Suffice it to say that I do not think Fodor's (Asymmetric Dependence) theory of mental content avoids the relevance of history to mental content. It merely hides it. I have two reasons for thinking this: (1) To counter objections to his "pure" theory, Fodor offers (1990, p. 121) a modified theory. The second condition of this modified theory *is* a historical condition: Some "Xs"(symbols in the head) are actually caused by Xs (the external conditions they are symbols of). (2) Even if Fodor should retreat to his "pure" theory (which contains no such explicit historical condition), I think the dependency he speaks of is, in fact, a dependency between actual conditions in the world and not, as he alleges, a dependency between nomic relations. Such dependencies, I would argue, are *historical* dependencies: A depends on B because A was caused by B and would not (as a matter of historical fact) have occurred if B had not occurred. How can there be a law between Xs (a kind of worldly event) and causing "Xs" (where "X" is a condition of the brain) when the relation between these two properties depends on the actual constitution of an animal's nervous system? Clearly, it seems to me, there is no law here, only a condition (of a nervous system) that supports a causal relation, a condition whose dependency relations to other conditions are historically derived.

methodological idea (reductionism) that Jerry Fodor expressed by saying that if intentionality is real, it is really something else. Nonetheless, I find it plausible. But then I would. I'm a reductionist. I think this assumption – or something close to it – is probably true.

The manner in which concepts like *thought* and *experience* are, according to this approach, history-laden is, I admit, different from the way that concepts like *murder* and *impaired* are norm-laden. Certain necessary connections lie on the surface; others do not. Almost anyone, after a few minutes' reflection, will agree that if something is broken or impaired, it is not in a condition, or not behaving, the way it should be. Everyone, not just philosophers, will agree that *murder* has, while *killing* lacks, an evaluative character. That, it seems, is just part of what we all mean – and would, furthermore, readily admit to meaning – in describing a killing as murder. But not everything that is necessary for the correct application of a concept lies so close to the surface. Some connections are more deeply buried. The relations between intentional concepts and history are like that. Although they are deeply buried, they are, I submit, recoverable. They are recoverable in the same way the (for me) less obvious historical implications of concepts like *wound, broken*, and *impaired* are recoverable. Or (if causal theorists are right – as I believe they are) the way that the relation between *seeing* (X) and *causation* (of perceptual experience by X) is recoverable. If it is, indeed, true that you cannot see (hallucinate and dream of, yes, but not *see*) the Eiffel Tower unless the Eiffel Tower is actually (part of) the cause of your experience, and if it is also true (as it appears to be) that this fact is not evident on casual – not even prolonged – reflection to many people, then I see no reason why the relationships between intentional concepts and their historical antecedents must be evident. The fact that they are not evident is no more an objection to the historical nature of intentional (representational, semantic) concepts than it is to the causal character of perceptual concepts.

Where does that leave us? It leaves us with a conclusion – that intentional concepts are history-laden – the plausibility of which depends, critically, on the questionable premise that semantic connections must be grounded in genuine relationships. There are other questionable premises, but this one, I think, is the most contentious. I think it is true, but others will surely disagree. I do not know how to convince them I'm right. All I can do is ask what else, besides historical antecedents, could ground a semantic connection. If nothing else could, then intentional concepts are history-laden. Swampman is a zombie. If something else could, what is it?

REFERENCES

Bedau, M. 1993. Naturalism and teleology. In *Naturalism: A Critical Appraisal*, S. J. Wagner & R. Warner, eds. Notre Dame, IN; University of Notre Dame Press, pp. 23–51.

Brandom, R. 1994. *Making It Explicit*. Cambridge, MA; Harvard University Press.

Coates, P. 1997. Meaning, mistake and miscalculation. *Minds and Machines*, 7.2, pp. 171–197.

Davidson. D. 1987. Knowing one's own mind. *Proceedings and Addresses of the American Philosophical Association*, 60, 441–458.

Dennett, D. 1996. Granny versus Mother Nature – No contest. *Mind and Language*, 11.3, pp. 263–269.

Dretske, F. 1986. Misrepresentation. In *Belief: Form, Content, and Function*, R. Bogdan, ed. Oxford; Clarendon Press.

Dretske, F. 1995. *Naturalizing the Mind*. Cambridge, MA; MIT Press.

Fodor, J. 1990. *A Theory of Content and Other Essays*. Cambridge, MA; MIT Press.

Fodor, J. 1996. Deconstructing Dennett's Darwin. *Mind and Language*, 11.3, pp. 246–262.

Gibbard, A. 1990. *Wise Choices, Apt Feelings*. Cambridge, MA; Harvard University Press.

Hanson, N. R. 1958. *Patterns of Discovery*. Cambridge; Cambridge University Press.

Kitcher, P. 1993. Function and design. *Midwest Studies in Philosophy*, XVIII. Notre Dame, IN; University of Notre Dame Press, pp. 379–397.

Kripke, S. 1982. *Wittgenstein on Rules and Private Language*. Oxford; Blackwell.

Lycan, W. 1997. *Consciousness and Experience*. Cambridge, MA; MIT Press.

Lycan, W. 1990a. Introduction (to Part II). *Mind and Cognition: A Reader*. Oxford; Blackwell, pp. 59–62.

Lycan, W. 1990b. *Mind and Cognition: A Reader*. W. Lycan, ed. Oxford; Blackwell.

MacDonald, G. 1989. Biology and representation. *Mind and Language*, 4.3, pp. 186–199.

Matthen, M. 1997. Teleology and the product analogy. *Australasian Journal of Philosophy*, 75.1, pp. 21–37.

Millikan, R. 1984. *Language, Thought, and Other Biological Categories*. Cambridge, MA; MIT Press.

Millikan, R. 1989. In defense of proper functions. *Philosophy of Science* 56.2, pp. 288–302. Reprinted in *White Queen Psychology and Other Essays for Alice*.

Millikan, R. 1993. Introduction. *White Queen Psychology and Other Essays for Alice*. Cambridge, MA; MIT Press.

Neander, K. 1991a. Functions as selected effects: the conceptual analyst's defense. *Philosophy of Science*, 58.2, pp. 168–184.

Neander, K. 1991b. The teleological notion of function. *Australasian Journal of Philosophy*, 69.4, pp. 454–468.

Neander, K. 1995. Misrepresenting and malfunctioning. *Philosophical Studies*, 79: 109–141.

Papineau, D. 1993. *Philosophical Naturalism*. Oxford: Blackwell.

Peacocke, C. 1992. *A Study of Concepts*. Cambridge, MA; MIT Press.

Tye, M. 1995. *Ten Problems of Consciousness*. Cambridge, MA; MIT Press.

van Gulick, R. 1990. Teleological views of intentionality. In Lycan 1990b, pp. 107–128.

15

Minds, Machines, and Money: What Really Explains Behavior

According to a prevalent philosophical picture of the way mind and body are related, the mind is to intentional action what money is to the behavior of a vending machine. Just as coins are in (or get deposited in) vending machines, beliefs, desires, and intentions are in, or get produced in, us. And just as the right coins deposited in the machine cause it to behave in a certain way – to yield its contents: Coca-Cola, cigarettes, or candy, as the case may be – so the right mental entities occurring in us cause us to perform various actions. Furthermore, just as what makes money money is not its intrinsic character – shape, size, and density of the coins, for example – but certain extrinsic or relational facts about these coins (the fact that they possess monetary value), so too what makes a belief a belief is not its intrinsic neurobiological character but, rather, certain extrinsic facts about it – the fact that it has a certain meaning or content, the fact that it has certain *intentional* properties.

If we take this analogy seriously, it suggests that beliefs, qua beliefs, are as irrelevant to animal behavior as is money, qua money, to the behavior of vending machines. Since it is facts about the shape and size of coins, not facts about their monetary value, that explain why coins cause a machine to yield its contents, the analogy, if we take it seriously – and a good many philosophers do – compels us to conclude that it is the intrinsic features of beliefs, their neurobiological properties, not their extrinsic properties, their meaning or content, that explains why we do

Reprinted from *Human Action, Deliberation and Causation, Philosophical Studies Series* 77, ed. Jan Bransen and Stefan Cuypers, pp. 157–173, copyright © 1998 by Kluwer Academic Publishers, with kind permission from Kluwer Academic Publishers.

what we do. We thus seem driven to the conclusion that what we believe is causally irrelevant to what we do.

I do not think we are *driven* to this conclusion, although, I admit, some people seem willing to drive there. It is the purpose of this essay to say why this conclusion is not forced on us. Let me begin, then, by enlarging the analogy.[1]

1. MONETARY-MACHINE INTERACTIONS

The United States government does its best to make the (legal) monetary value of objects supervene on the intrinsic properties of the objects that have that value. In the case of paper money, special watermarks, high-quality paper, intaglio printing, and security strips (visible only with transmitted light to frustrate photocopying) make successful counterfeiting difficult and increasingly rare. There are no (at least not many) non-$20 bills that look and feel exactly like real $20 bills. The same is true, of course, of other denominations and coins. This is no accident. The entire system of monetary exchange depends on it. For understandable reasons, then, the U.S. Treasury Department is dedicated to maintaining the strictest supervenience.

The monetary value of an object is a relational property of that object. It has to do with its *history* – was it produced in a mint or in someone's basement? – and the economic practices of the community in which it exists – are such objects generally accepted as a medium of exchange in the community? Since the usefulness of money depends on its easy identification, governments make every effort to see to it that this extrinsic property of money supervenes on the observable (intrinsic) properties of money – size, shape, markings, weight, and so on. If two objects are observationally indiscernible, if they *look* and *feel* the same, then (if the government is doing its job) they are indiscernible with respect to monetary value. If it *looks* like a $20 bill, it *is* a $20 bill. Another way of expressing this[2] is to say that (as long as counterfeiting is kept in check) monetary values (V) are necessarily realized (usually multiply realized) in an object's intrinsic properties (S), and each value

---

1 After writing this essay I came across Allen (1995), in which a similar anlogy is developed to reach a similar conclusion.

2 Corresponding to Kim's second formulation of weak supervenience (1984a). Although citations are to individual articles, all page references to Kim are to Kim (1993b), in which the individual essays are collected.

260

of S has the same value of V. This corresponds to what Kim calls *weak supervenience*.[3]

As a result of this (normally) widespread supervenience and the correlation associated with it, we can (and regularly *do*) use the fact that something is money to predict and "explain" (more about the scare quotes in a moment) the effects money has in transactions of various sorts. Why did the cashier give me $8 in change? Because lunch cost $12 and I gave her $20. Why didn't the vending machine give me the candy I selected? Because I deposited only $0.55 and the candy bars cost $0.65.

Are these familiar explanations really correct? Is the fact that I gave the cashier $20 really the (or part of the) explanation of why she gave me $8 change? Is the monetary value of the paper I gave her a causally relevant property? The coins I deposited in the vending machine are worth only $0.55, but is this fact relevant to why the machine did not give me a candy bar? Is the value, the legal worth, of these coins a causally causally relevant fact about them? I know we talk this way. I know that everyday explanations of such results are replete with references to monetary value, but is this extrinsic property the causally relevant property?

It is important to understand that these are questions about the causal relevance of an object's properties (its being worth $20), not the causal efficacy of the objects (the $20 bills) that have these properties. These are, in other words, questions about what *explains* the result, not what *causes* it. Giving the cashier an object with a monetary value of $20 *caused* her to give me $8 change. About that there is no argument. The question we are asking, though, is not whether a $20 bill is a causally effective *object*, but whether its being a $20 bill explains its effectiveness. Is the value of the paper I give her a fact about the paper that explains the result of giving her the paper? What if I, instead, give her a piece of paper that looks and feels exactly like a real $20 bill? Would the result be different if we suppose the bill was a perfect counterfeit? No, of course not. If she can't tell the difference, how could it be? Well, if we

---

3 At least it is a form of *local* weak supervenience – local to a given nation or economic unit. Although it would complicate monetary exchanges, there is no reason why two countries might not assign the same (type of) object different monetary values. If this happened, then, even without counterfeiting, there would be local (i.e., national), but not global (international), supervenience. In speaking of monetary value supervening on the intrinsic properties of an object, I should, therefore, be understood as referring to a given country or economic unit.

really believe this, as I assume we all do, then why say that the cashier gave me $8 change *because* I gave her $20? Giving her $20 is the cause, but that it was $20 is not the explanation of her giving me $8 change. The correct explanation is that I gave her a piece of paper that looked and felt (to her) like a $20 bill. The causally effective properties, those that explain why the effect occurs, are the intrinsic, the observable, properties of the paper on which its being $20 supervenes, the properties you and I, cashiers and machines, use to *tell* whether it is $20.

I am not, mind you, recommending that we change explanatory practice. Although I am convinced that its being money is (in most imaginable cases) totally irrelevant to the results obtained, I will go right on explaining the results of monetary transactions in terms of the money exchanged. Although we predict the behavior of vending machines by mentioning the value of the money we put in them ("You have to deposit $0.75 to get a Coke") we all know that it isn't the value of the money that explains the result. It is the shape, size, weight, and (for machines that take bills) visible marks of the objects we put in them that explains why machines behave the way they do. An object with the same S and a different V (a slug) would produce the same behavior. Vending machines (not to mention store clerks) are equipped to detect the shape, size, and density, but surely not the economic history, of the objects they receive. We nonetheless pretend to explain machine behavior by mentioning the historical-social properties ($0.75) of the internal objects (coins) that cause behavior. We ignore the intrinsic properties that are causally relevant. We ignore them because, often enough, we don't even know what they are. Nonetheless, given the facts of supervenience, we know that, normally, inserting $0.75 will get you a Coke even if we don't know which properties of the $0.75 are responsible for this effect (is density relevant?). V is, after all, multiply realizable in S. We can use a variety of different coins, of different shapes and sizes, to make $0.75. The machine will give us a Coke, it will behave in the same way, if we insert quarters, dimes, and a nickel; or seven dimes and a nickel; or fifteen nickels. As long as the coins add up to $0.75 we get the same result. So it is simpler and much more convenient in our explanations of machine behavior to mention the extrinsic V all the different Ss have in common even though we know it is S, not V, that explains the result. Convenience explains the explanatory pretense.

This, incidentally, is why I am suspicious of philosophical appeals to our ordinary explanatory practice, or to the explanatory practices in the special sciences, to support accounts of what causally explains what (see, for example, Burge 1986, 1989, 1993, 1995; Baker 1995). Our explanatory practice is often governed by practical convenience and, sometimes, theoretical ignorance. I know, for example, that we commonsensically invoke beliefs and desires to explain human (and sometimes animal) behavior. That, I am willing to concede, is the accepted practice. Even in cognitive psychology and computer science (presumably special sciences) there are a variety of intentional ideas (e.g., data structures, information, representation) that regularly appear in causal explanations. But *saying* that x's having P causally explains x's Q-ing, when P is a relational or – even worse – an intentional property of x, doesn't make it so. Even if *everyone* says it. If I trusted explanatory practice this blindly, I would have to conclude that the monetary value of objects explains their effect on vending machines. It will take more than our explanatory practice to convince me of this.

It may be thought that I am constructing a false dichotomy, that the two explanations of a cashier's or a vending machine's behavior – one in terms of intrinsic S properties, the other in terms of extrinsic V properties – do not (as I have been assuming) really compete. They aren't mutually exclusive. They can *both* be correct. The explanation in terms of a coin's intrinsic properties is a *proximal* explanation of its effect on the vending machine, while the explanation in terms of monetary value is a more *remote* explanation of this same result. It is like explaining a behavioral deficit (stuttering, say) by describing the brain damage that produces the stutter (explanation by intrinsic properties of the stutterer) or by mentioning the incident – being dropped on the head as an infant – that causally explains this brain damage (an explanation by extrinsic – i.e., historical – properties). The first is a proximal, the second a remote, explanation of the stuttering. Similarly, if we think of the fact that the paper I give the cashier has a monetary value of $20 – that it has the kind of history and use that makes it $20 – as the causal explanation of its having the observable properties it now has, then social-historical V properties causally explain intrinsic S-properties and, thus, explain (in a more remote way) whatever the S-properties causally explain – why, for example, the cashier gave me $8 change for my $20.

This objection, although it gets at something interesting about the connection between extrinsic and intrinsic properties in explanations of this sort, is not, as it stands, correct. The facts that give coins and bank notes their value (the V-facts) do not causally explain why these objects have the size, shape, and markings they have (the S-facts). The reason why $20 bills have Andrew Jackson's picture on them while $5 bills

263

have Abe Lincoln's picture, the reason they have *these* particular observable features,[4] is not that these bills have the value they have. It has to do, rather, with the various decisions and policies of administrators in the U.S. Treasury Department. The pictures on U.S. coins and bank notes might well have been different. If everybody (including the government) agreed, we could, in fact, *make* $20 bills (the bills that are *now* worth $20) into bills worth $5, and vice versa.

Nonetheless, although I think the objection mistaken, it raises an interesting possibility, the possibility that the explanatory efficacy of an object's extrinsic properties lies in the complex causal relations between an object's extrinsic properties and its intrinsic nature. I will return to this point later in order to explore this possibility. Pending deeper investigation, though, I assume that the output of people and vending machines in monetary exchanges is not to be explained, not even remotely, by the extrinsic value of the money that produces that output. The causal efficacy of money is not explained by its being money.

When externally individuated properties (like V) supervene on intrinsic properties (S), and the supervenient property is *multiply* realized in S (thereby making it practically convenient to express generalizations in terms of V rather than S), talk of the supervenient properties begins to dominate explanatory contexts and one finds little or no mention of S.[5] Imagine trying to explain why Clyde got a Coke not by saying he deposited the required $0.75, but by describing the S-properties that were actually causally relevant. If we happen to be ignorant of exactly which coins Clyde deposited in the machine, the explanation would, of necessity, be radically disjunctive: fifteen coins of this sort; or two coins of this sort and seven coins of that sort; and so on and so on. Nobody gives *those* kinds of explanations. What does this show? Nothing. Or, perhaps, only that we are lazy or ignorant.

Despite this undeniable tendency in explanatory practice to drift to the most conveniently expressible generalizations, V-generalizations are not the sort that will support explanations. Predictions, yes, but not explanations. In more careful moments – when, for instance, we are

---

4 I understand, of course, that having X's picture on Y is an extrinsic, not an intrinsic, property of Y, but I think my point (about differences in observable markings) is clear enough without going into these fussy details.

5 We advert to S only when the V (and design) stance fails – when, for example, there is a breakdown or malfunction in the machine: e.g., the machine didn't give us a candy bar because the coin was bent. See Dennett (1987) for the same point about the intentional stance.

doing metaphysics – we realize that it is the object's being S, not its being V, that explains its impact on the system in which it exists. Our explanatory practice does not respect metaphysical scruples. There is no reason it should. In giving and receiving explanations we are not doing metaphysics. We take explanatory shortcuts. We leave the metaphysics for later. Or never.

That concludes my example. Its intended purpose, of course, is as an analogy with mind–body interactions. What I hope to do is to draw some useful lessons from the analogy. For convenience, I will refer to causal interactions between coins and vending machines as *monetary–machine* interactions. If we stopped here, if we looked no deeper, then, despite common explanatory practice, we would have to conclude that, with respect to machines, money was epiphenomenal. That is, the fact that money is money does not *explain* the effects of money on machines (or people, for that matter). It is the S-facts that do all the explanatory work. What explains machine behavior are not "broad" facts about the value of internal coins, but "narrow" facts about their size, shape, and density. Once we have the analogy fully in place, though, I will return to the analysis of these interactions and take a deeper look. What I hope to show is that, contrary to what I have just been arguing, there is a sense in which monetary facts about money *are* causally relevant to machine behavior.[6] The form of this relevance is, I think, suggestive about the way the mind is causally relevant to human and animal behavior.

2. THE ANALOGY

There is a prevalent view in the philosophy of mind that the propositional attitudes (including belief) are something like internal coins. What you believe (intend, desire, conclude, regret, etc.) is an extrinsic property of the internal belief (intention, etc.) in the same way that the value of coins is extrinsic to the coins in a machine. For a materialist (who is not an eliminativist) a belief (some brain state, say) has intrinsic (neurobiological) properties, but it also has a content or meaning (= what it is one believes), and this is determined, in part at least, by the relations this

---

6   To machine behavior, *not* to machine output. This distinction between output and behavior is a distinction that figures importantly in my account of the way reasons explain behavior in *Explaining Behavior* (1988). Here I merely note the distinction. I return to it later.

internal state bears to external affairs. The relational individuation of belief is why the same belief can occur in much different heads; what makes it *that* belief is not the brain state that realizes it (this can be quite different), but the way that brain state is related to the rest of the world. Putnam's (1975) and Burge's (1979) examples have convinced many that, in this respect, beliefs are "internal money."

I will call this view the *Standard Theory*. I call it the Standard Theory not just because it is widely accepted but because, if you are a materialist,[7] it is hard to see how something like this view could fail to be true. Beliefs (just like coins) have to be inside the system whose behavior they causally explain. How else could they cause the behavior they are said to explain? Nonetheless, what gives these internal states their content (just like what gives coins their value) is not inside the head. The representational (intentional) character of a belief, what makes it a belief about football rather than philosophy, is a matter of how that internal state is related to external affairs. Surely there is nothing *in the brain* that makes one neurological event about football and another about philosophy. What a person believes – its meaning or representational content – must, it seems, be extrinsic to the believer. It is the same with words. Words and sentences are printed in books, but what makes some words about football and others about philosophy is not in a book.

3. THE PROBLEM: EPIPHENOMENALISM

The Standard Theory is commonly thought to have the kind of epiphenomenal implications we uncovered in examining monetary–machine interactions. Although the content of a belief – *what* one believes – is routinely mentioned in explanations of behavior (just as the value of coins is mentioned in explanations of machine behavior), this content is, according to Standard Theory, as irrelevant to what we do as is the value of coins to what a machine does. If you want to know what makes vending machines dispense Cokes and candy bars, look to the intrinsic properties of the internal causes – the shape, size, and weight of the internal coins that trigger its responses. For the same reason, if you want to know what makes people do the things they do, look not to the relational properties of belief (those that constitute *what* we believe) but to the intrinsic (i.e., neurobiological) properties of the belief. Look to

---

7 And a realist (i.e., not an eliminativist) about the mind.

the "shape" and "size" – that is, the syntax – of these internal "coins," not their semantics.

This is a form of epiphenomenalism because although beliefs, on this view, turn out to be causally active (just as the coins deposited in vending machines are causally active), the properties of the internal cause that make it mental, the extrinsic properties that give it content (and thus make it into a belief), are not relevant to the causal efficacy of the belief. Thus, the Standard View, while denying neither the reality nor the causal efficacy of the mental, leaves little or no room for understanding the causal efficacy of the mental qua mental. Beliefs, qua beliefs, have as much effect on the behavior of persons as do quarters, qua quarters, on the behavior of vending machines.

4. SOLUTIONS

Standard theorists are aware of this problem, of course, and they have adopted a variety of different strategies to neutralize its impact. Some (e.g., Campbell 1970; Stich 1978, 1983) simply accept the implication and try to live with it. Others (e.g., Burge 1986, 1989, 1993, 1995; Baker 1995) insist that it should be actual explanatory practice, not a priori metaphysical principles, that determines what is a causally relevant property. So if, in ordinary causal explanations of behavior, we invoke what is believed to explain what is done, then what is believed – content – is causally relevant to behavior and that is an end to the matter – metaphysical principles to the contrary be hanged. Still others (e.g., Fodor 1987) concede the irrelevance of extrinsic or broad content and look for a satisfactory substitute – an intrinsic content, narrow content. Or, like Davidson (1980), one takes comfort in the fact that beliefs are causes and refuses to worry about what it is about them that explains their effects (on Davidson's theory it turns out to be the intrinsic physical properties of the belief – the ones that figure in strict laws). It is hard to see why some of these strategies (e.g., Fodor's and Davidson's) for vindicating the *explanatory* role of belief are not so much ways of solving the problem as (like the first) gritty ways of learning to live with (and talking around) it.

In a series of insightful articles, Jaegwon Kim (1984a, 1984b, 1987, 1989, 1990, 1991, 1993a) has explored the idea that mental causation is a form of supervenient causation (I denote supervenient causation by "causation$_s$"). One macroevent (increasing the temperature of a fixed volume of gas, for instance) causes, another macroevent (an increase in the gas's pressure) in virtue of the fact that both macroproperties – temperature and pressure – supervene on causally related microstates of the gas. Kim offers this as a model for the way mental states cause behavior: beliefs causally, explain behavior by supervening on "microstates" of the believer (neurophysiological states) that cause bodily movements. If mental causation is really causation, if the mental really supervenes on the physical states of the body, then, he says, "mental causation does take place, but it is reducible to, or explainable by, the causal processes taking place at a more basic physical level" (1984a, p. 107) If we assume that mental states supervene on biological states of the brain, then, Kim suggests (1984a, p. 107), this (i.e., causation) would redeem the causal powers we attribute to mental states. Mental properties (the content of the propositional attitudes) would be as efficacious on this account as are temperature, pressure, heat, and a variety of other physical macroproperties that derive their efficacy from the microevents on which they supervene.

This account of mental causation is plausible in the case of those mental states that supervene (or are thought by some philosophers to supervene[8]) on the intrinsic (biological) constitution of a person: for example, pains, itches, tingles, sensations, and feelings. This, no doubt, is why Kim chose pain and the sensation of fear (1984a, p. 106) to illustrate the theory.[9] For such mental states – call them *phenomenal* states – there is a strong intuition (most philosophers seem to have it) that physically indiscernible individuals *must* be in the same phenomenal state. Even if physical twins (as a result of much different histories) might be having different beliefs, they must (or so the intuition dictates) be having the same sensations (pains, etc.). If this is, indeed, so, then there is no particular obstacle to supposing that phenomenal states derive their causal efficacy from the physical states on which they supervene. For phenomenal mental states might – who knows? – *strongly*

---

8 Not all philosophers think this. Some (including myself – see Dretske 1995) have a representational view of sensations that identifies experienced qualities (qualia) with representational properties. Thus, just like beliefs, the mental properties of sensations turn out to be extrinsic or relational properties of internal states: see Harman (1990), Lycan (1987, 1997), Tye (1994, 1995).

9 This is confirmed by his doubts a few pages later (p. 107) about whether the account of supervenient causation will work for *intentional* states – states (like belief) that have a propositional content.

supervene[10] on the intrinsic physical properties of an individual, and it is *strong* supervenience (of the macro on the micro) that Kim requires (1989, p. 283; 1984a, pp. 104, 106) to support causal relations between macroevents. Only if the macro supervenes on the micro in the way temperature supervenes on molecular motion or being water supervenes on being H_2O is it plausible to attribute the causal efficacy of the micro to the macro.

But however plausible supervenient causation may be as an account of the way *phenomenal* states bring about their effects, it does not seem to be available as an account of the way intentional states bring about their effects.[11] For intentional states, according to Standard Theory, do not, like phenomenal mental states, strongly supervene on the intrinsic biological properties of the person who occupies these states.[12] Intentional states, unlike phenomenal states, are relational states of an individual, and it is difficult to see how such relational properties could strongly supervene on an object's nonrelational, its intrinsic, properties. Our monetary example illustrates the way, under ideal circumstances (no counterfeiting), a relational property might *weakly* supervene on intrinsic properties: as a matter of fact, thanks to the government's efforts, every piece of paper that has a particular set of intrinsic properties is a genuine $20 bill. But weak supervenience is clearly not enough for supervenient causation. Even though the value of money supervenes on its shape and size, its being money does not share in the glory of causing what its having that shape and size causes. Temperature shares (in a derivative but nonetheless real enough way) in the glory of causing whatever the events on which it supervenes causes, but the monetary value of a quarter does not share – not even derivatively – in the glory of causing

<hr>

10 Unlike weak supervenience, strong supervenience requires that anything with a given base property *necessarily* has the property that supervenes on it. This requires, as Kim notes, some kind of nomological *dependence* between the supervenient property and those properties on which it supervenes. If water (in this world) is H_2O then, if being water strongly supervenes on being H_2O, then nothing *can* be H_2O without being water. Contrast this with being a $20 bill. If pieces of paper of this size and shape (in this world) are $20 bills, this does *not* imply that things of that size and shape *in other possible worlds* are also worth $20 (i.e., are *necessarily* worth $20).

11 Despite Kim's suggestion (1991) of supervenient causation as a possible replacement for my own theory (see Dretske 1988). My own theory is explicitly about the explanatory status of *intentional* (not phenomenal) states, and, as noted earlier, Kim himself seems dubious about whether supervenient causation applies to extrinsic mental states (beliefs and desires).

12 Kim seems to agree with this; see Kim (1987).

what the coin's shape and size cause – for example, an elliptical shadow in obliquely falling light. The value (being extrinsic) and the physical appearance (intrinsic) remain distinct attributes of the coin with different causal powers. To get supervenient causation we need strong supervenience, but what could it mean to suppose that the monetary value of a piece of paper or the value of a quarter was *necessarily* tied up with its having a particular shape, size, and set of marks? This, it seems, could be the case only if the monetary value of the paper, its being a genuine $20 bill, was not in fact relational at all but, rather, reducible to the paper's having just that set of intrinsic properties.[13] This, though, is precisely what Standard Theory denies.

I do not think, therefore, that supervenient causation is a viable account of the causal powers of extrinsic mental states.[14] If what I believe is a genuine relational property of me, then it might, in some local way,[15] weakly supervene on my intrinsic physical properties, but I do not see how it can display the kind of *dependence* on my intrinsic physical properties that would tempt us to say that *it* explains whatever the physical states on which it supervenes explains.

5. A BETTER SOLUTION

We have, however, neglected an important aspect of the causal relations at work in both monetary–machine and mind–body cases. In the monetary–machine interaction, for instance, there is the fact that the machines on which coins have a causal impact were designed and manufactured to be sensitive to objects having those intrinsic properties (S) on which monetary value supervenes, and they were made that way precisely *because* V supervenes on S. Business being what it is, machines that dispense commodities like cigarettes, food, and drink would not be designed to yield their contents to objects having S *unless* objects having S had V. Remove the fact of supervenience (as a result of widespread

13 Kim (1989) makes exactly this point – the point, namely, that strong supervenience – the kind necessary for supervenient causation – occurs only when there is a possibility of reduction of the macroproperties to the micro. That is the basis of his argument that *nonreductive* materialists should derive no comfort from supervenient causation as a way to give the mental some causal punch in the material world.

14 Despite his suggestion (1991) that supervenient causation be considered a "modified" version of my own theory (of belief and desire), I suspect Kim would agree with this.

15 Kim stresses the need to localize the supervenience (the supervenience base for your thoughts may not be the same as mine) in Kim (1991).

counterfeiting, say) and S objects will soon lose their causal power. They will no longer produce the effects they now produce. They will lose their causal power because machines will no longer be built to respond to objects having S. The causal efficacy of intrinsic S (on machines – not to mention people) depends on the supervenience of extrinsic V on S. Let V supervene on a different set of properties, T, and T-objects will, quickly enough, assume the causal powers of S-objects.

This additional dimension to the causal story does not show that a vending machine's output is explained by the monetary value of the coins deposited in it. No, the Cokes come rolling down the chute not because an object with a certain value is deposited in the machine, but because an object with a certain size and shape is. Nonetheless, if what we want to explain is not why a Coke came sliding down the chute (the shape and size of the coins deposited will explain that), but why objects having the size and shape of nickels, dimes, and quarters *cause* Cokes to come rolling down the chute, why objects of that sort have effects of this sort, the answer lies, in part at least, in the fact that there is a reliable (enough) correlation between objects having that size and shape and their having a certain monetary value. It lies, in other words, in the fact that there is a supervenience (*weak* supervenience) of V on S. The value doesn't explain why the Cokes come out, but it does explain why coins – objects of that size and shape – cause Cokes to come out.

When we turn to the mind–body case, this dimension of the causal story is suggestive. If we think of ourselves as "vending machines" whose internal causal structure is designed, shaped, and modified not, as with vending machines, by engineers, but, in the first instance, by evolution and, in the second, by learning, then we can say that although it is the "size" and "shape" (the syntax, as it were) of the internal causes that make the body move the way it does (just as it is the size and shape of the coins that releases the Cokes) it is, or may be, the fact that a certain extrinsic property supervenes on that neurological "size" and "shape" that explains why internal events having these intrinsic properties have the effect on the body that they have. What explains why a certain neurological event in the visual cortex of a chicken – an event caused by the shadow of an overhead hawk – causes the chicken to cower and hide is the fact that such neurological events have a significant (to chickens) extrinsic property – the property of normally being caused by predatory hawks. It is, or may be, possession of this extrinsic property – what the internal events *indicate* about external affairs – that explains why objects having those intrinsic properties cause what they do.

271

There is but a short step from here to the conclusion that it is the extrinsic, not the intrinsic, properties of internal events that causally explain behavior. All that is needed to execute this step is the premise that behavior is not the bodily movements that internal events cause, but the *causing* of these movements by internal events. All that is required, that is, is an appropriate distinction between the behavior that beliefs explain and the bodily movements that (in part) constitute that behavior. For if moving your arms and legs (behavior) is not the same as the movements of the arms and legs, but it is, rather, some internal event causing the arms and legs to move, then although the intrinsic properties of our internal "coins" will explain (via activation of muscles) the movements of our arms and legs, the extrinsic properties, properties having to do with what external conditions these internal events are correlated with, will explain why we move them.

This is not the place to amplify this account. I tried to do this in Dretske (1988). The only point I want to make here is that the account I gave there of how reasons explain behavior depends on a correlation between the extrinsic (informational) and the intrinsic (biological) properties of reasons. It depends on weak supervenience of the extrinsic on the intrinsic. Without that supervenience, reasons cannot get their hand on the steering wheel. This is not because the extrinsic causally, explains the movements of the body. No. That would require strong supervenience, and the relational properties underlying mental content do not strongly supervene on neurobiological properties any more than the value of coins strongly supervenes on their size and shape. It is rather because supervenience – *weak* supervenience – explains why the internal events that cause the body to move cause it to move the way it does. If I am right about behavior, that is exactly what we want beliefs to explain – viz., behavior, what a person *does*.

So to our series of opening questions, the answers are as follows: Yes, beliefs stand to human behavior in something like the way money stands to vending machine behavior. Does this show that what we believe is causally irrelevant to what we do? No, it does not show this any more than it shows that the fact that nickels, dimes, and quarters have monetary value is irrelevant to the behavior of vending machines. The fact that these coins have monetary value, the fact that they are a widely accepted medium of exchange, explains why the machines (are built to) dispense their contents when objects of this sort are placed in them. In this sense, the fact that these coins have monetary value explains why machines behave the way they do when the coins are in them. The same is true of belief: the extrinsic properties of these beliefs – *what it is we believe* – explains why we behave the way we do when these beliefs occur in us.

REFERENCES

Allen, C. 1995. It Isn't What You Think: A New Idea About Intentional Causation. *Nous*, 29, pp. 115–126.

Baker, L. 1995. *Explaining Attitudes: A Practical Approach to the Mind*. Cambridge: Cambridge University Press.

Burge, T. 1979. Individualism and the Mental. *Studies in Metaphysics (Midwest Studies in Philosophy 4)*, Peter A. French, Theodore E. Uehling, and Howard K. Wettstein, eds. Minneapolis: University of Minnesota Press, pp. 73–122.

Burge, T. 1986. Individualism and Psychology. *The Philosophical Review*, XCV, No. 1, pp. 3–45.

Burge, T. 1989. Individuation and Causation in Psychology. *The Pacific Philosophical Quarterly*, 70, pp. 303–322.

Burge, T. 1993. Mind – Body Causation and Explanatory Practice. *Mental Causation*, John Heil and Alfred Mele, eds. Oxford: Clarendon Press, pp. 97–120.

Burge, T. 1995. Reply: Intentional Properties and Causation. *Philosophy of Psychology: Debates on Psychological Explanation*, Cynthia Macdonald and Graham Macdonald, eds. Oxford: Blackwell, pp. 226–235.

Campbell, K. 1970. *Body and Mind*. New York: Doubleday.

Crane, T., ed. 1992. *The Contents of Experience*. Cambridge: Cambridge University Press.

Davidson, D. 1980. *Essays on Actions and Events*. Oxford: Clarendon Press.

Dennett, D. 1987. *The Intentional Stance*. Cambridge, MA: MIT Press.

Dretske, F. 1988. *Explaining Behavior*. Cambridge, MA: MIT Press/A Bradford Book.

Dretske, F. 1995. *Naturalizing the Mind*. Cambridge, MA: MIT Press/A Bradford Book.

Fodor, J. 1987. *Psychosemantics*. Cambridge, MA: MIT Press.

Harman, G. 1990. The Intrinsic Quality of Experience. Reprinted in Tomberlin 1990.

Kim, J. 1982. Psychophysical Supervenience. *Philosophical Studies*, 41, pp. 51–70. Reprinted in Kim 1993b.

Kim, J. 1984a. Concepts of Supervenience. *Philosophy and Phenomenological Research*, 45, pp. 153–176. Reprinted in Kim 1993b.

Kim, J. 1984b. Epiphenomenal and Supervenient Causation. *Midwest Studies in Philosophy*, 9, pp. 257–270. Reprinted in Kim 1993b.

Kim, J. 1987. "Strong" and "Global" Supervenience Revisited. *Philosophy and Phenomenological Research*, 48, pp. 315–326. Reprinted in Kim 1993b.

Kim, J. 1989. The Myth of Non-reductive Materialism. *Proceedings and Addresses of the American Philosophical Association*, 63, pp. 31–47. Reprinted in Kim 1993b.

273

Kim, J. 1990. Supervenience as a Philosophical Concept. *Metaphilosophy*, 21, pp. 1–27. Reprinted in Kim 1993b.

Kim, J. 1991. Dretske on How Reasons Explain Behavior. *Dretske and His Critics*, ed. Brian McLaughlin. Oxford: Blackwell, pp. 52–72. Reprinted in Kim 1993b.

Kim, J. 1993a. The Nonreductivist's Troubles with Mental Causation. *Mental Causation*, John Heil and Alfred Mele, eds. Oxford: Oxford University Press, pp. 189–210. Reprinted in Kim 1993b.

Kim, J. 1993b. *Supervenience and Mind: Selected Philosophical Essays*. Cambridge: Cambridge University Press.

Lycan, W. G. 1987. *Consciousness*; Cambridge, MA: MIT Press/A Bradford Book.

Lycan, W. G. 1990. What Is the "Subjectivity" of the Mental? Reprinted in Tomberlin 1990.

Lycan, W. G. 1997. *Consciousness and Experience*. Cambridge, MA: MIT Press.

Putnam, H. 1975. The Meaning of "Meaning." *Language, Mind and Knowledge: Minnesota Studies in the Philosophy of Science*, vol 7, K. Gunderson, ed. Minneapolis: University of Minnesota Press.

Stich, S. 1978. Autonomous Psychology and the Belief-Desire Thesis. *The Monist*, 61, pp. 573–591.

Stich, S. 1983. *From Folk Psychology to Cognitive Science*. Cambridge, MA: MIT Press/A Bradford Book.

Tomberlin, J. E., ed. 1990. *Philosophical Perspectives, 4: Action Theory and Philosophy of Mind, 1990*. Atascadero, CA: Ridgeview.

Tye, M. 1992. Visual Qualia and Visual Content. Reprinted in Crane 1992.

Tye, M. 1994. Qualia, Content, and the Inverted Spectrum. *Nous*, 28, pp. 159–183.

Tye, M. 1995. *Ten Problems of Consciousness*. Cambridge, MA: MIT Press/A Bradford Book.

Index

absolute concepts, 50–2
acceptance, 86n7, 91n13
access consciousness, 153n44
action: social character of, 232
acts of awareness: objects vs., 183–8
advanced knowledge, 85, 88
agnosia, 141n8
Aldrich, Virgil, xi, 97–8, 100–1, 105,
  106n14, 109–10, 111n20, 112n21
Allen, C., 260n1
Alpha/Beta constellations, 125–32, 134
altimeter example, 65–6, 68, 70, 73, 74,
  221
analysis of knowledge, 89, 90
animals: and awareness, 181, 185; beliefs in, xii, 70, 86, 87n8, 144; conclusive reasons in, 22; conceptual sophistication of, 69–70; conscious
  experiences, 186–8; consciousness,
  142–4, 183, 185, 191; knowledge in,
  x, 80, 81, 82, 83–4, 85, 86–8, 89, 92,
  93; lack of concepts, 142–3 177;
  learning in, 204–5, 218; object/fact
  awareness, 189; perception of objects
  and events, 140; perceptual experiences, 151; thought in, 233, 234;
  worth of consciousness to, 182
Antony, Louise, 214
Armstrong, David, xi, 123–4, 146,
  148
artifacts, 85–6, 211; functions, 234–5;

indicators and, 203–4; misrepresentation, 214–15
aspectual shape, 212
attitudes: norms independent of, 253
Austin, J. L., 88–9
awareness, 180; confusion between
  awareness/the something of which
  we are aware, 173; of conscious experiences, 159–60, 165, 177; of experiences, 174–5, 177; of facts/of
  things, 114–20, 130; (see also fact [ƒ]-
  awareness; object [o]-awareness;
  property [p]-awareness); mind of itself, 158–77; modes of, 183; of perceptual experience, 166, 167–8, 170–
  1, 172; of properties, 174
awareness of/awareness that, 139, 140,
  142, 144

Bedau, M., 246n6
behavior: beliefs and, 145–6, 236, 237,
  238, 239, 267, 272–3; causal explanation, 271–3; caused by mental
  states, 268; changed with indicators,
  203, 204–7; effect of information on,
  197, 199; explaining, 259–73; meaning and, 201; perceptual awareness of
  facts and, 116; psychological explanations of, 207; social character of
  thought and, 240
behaviorism, 103, 112

275

sions of, 249; higher-order mental state involves, 133; information-processing resources and, 78–9; primitive vs. complex, 255n15; required for mind's awareness of itself, 175–7; rules governing application of, 249–50, 251

conceptual role semantics, 251

conclusive reasons, 3–29, 58; counterfactual analysis of, 92n14

concrete objects vs. abstract objects, 117–18

confirmation theory, 34

conscious beings: vs. conscious states, 179–83

conscious experience(s), xi, 113–37, 138, 147, 149–57, 183–5, 186–7; awareness of, 159–60, 163, 165, 177; without consciousness of having experience, 114, 121, 125, 128, 129, 132; distinguishing between, 125–32; function of, 187; purpose of, 188

conscious states, 182, 183; conscious beings vs., 179–83; identified with acts, 188; object of creature awareness, 185; purpose of, 185–6

consciousness, 113–14, 135–6, 138, 140n6, 180; in animals and infants, 142–4; differences in, 123–4, 139; of facts/of things, 113, 114–20; good of, 178–92; hard problem of, xi, 158–9; Multiple Drafts model of, 142; role of, 179; theory of, 115, 137, 142, 143

Consciousness Explained (Dennett), 139, 142, 144, 145, 148, 149n34

content, 207, 214; of beliefs, 266; explanatory and rationalizing role of, 225; independent of truth, 213; naturalistic theories of, 222; normativity of, 248n7, 249; relevant to behavior, 267; of thought, 223, 224, 225, 229n5

Content and Consciousness (Dennett), 139

contextual relativity, 50

contrast consequences, 38–40, 42–4, 46–7

Contrasting Set (CS), 56–8, 60

contrastive focusing, 58–9

conversational implicatures, 141

counterfactuals, 92n14; relevant conditions associated with, 11n9

creature consciousness, 121–2, 123, 124, 127, 129, 131, 134, 179, 180, 182, 183; state consciousness and, 184

Damasio, A. R., 174

Danto, Arthur, 22n15

Darwin, Charles, 219–20

Davidson, Donald, 229n3, 243n2, 252, 267

Davies, M., 178

de re beliefs, 105

Dennett, Daniel, xi, 114, 138–9, 140, 142, 143–4, 145, 147–8, 151, 152; on conscious experience, 149–50; on qualia, 153, 155, 156

Descartes, René, 64–5, 81, 138, 143, 144, 232

desires, 172; in explanatory practice, 263

discrimination learning, 205

disjunction problem, 214, 219–22

dissociation phenomena, 191

dolphin learning example, 68–9, 73

dreams, 25, 53, 121n13, 159, 254

Einstein, Albert, 81–2

embedded norms, 244n3

emotions, 172–5

empirically conclusive reasons (ECR), 17, 19

emptiness, 63; as absolute concept, 51, 52, 58

epiphenomenalism, 266–7

epistemic logic, 34

epistemic operators, 30–47; are semipenetrating operators, 32–3, 34, 40

epistemology, 139; of belief, 64–79; naturalized, ix-x, xi-xii

events, 115; being conscious of, 179

illusion(s), 35, 147, 246
implication vs. implicature, 117
indicators: and artifacts, 203–4; and learning, 204–7
indirect realism, 167
ineffability, 150, 154–5
infants: consciousness, 142–4; knowledge in, 82, 83, 85, 86; seeing non-epistemically, 102
information, ix, x, xi–xii, 82, 195; causal efficacy of, 198–9, 201, 202, 204, 207; counterfactual analysis of, 92n14; delivered by sensory systems, 110–11; delivery of, in seeing, 111–12; distinct from belief and judgment, 149n34; from environment, 239; and intentionality, 209–13; in knowledge/beliefs, 79, 87–8, 90, 91–2; in learning, 69, 70–2, 73, 77; meaning and, 195–9; provided by perception, 251–2; putting to work, 195–207; sources of, 60, 92, 93, 108–9; see also sensory information
information-carrying function, 215, 216–17, 218–19, 220, 221–2, 223, 224–5; of sense organs, 235; of thoughts, 234; of representations, 234
information pickup and processing capabilities: determine representational powers, 70, 72, 76–9
inner-sense theory, 133–4
inner spotlight theory of consciousness, 114, 133, 134
instruments, 148–9; information-providing function of, 234; knowledge in, 85; reliability of, 61; representational powers of, 65–7, 70, 215–16
intelligence, 209, 211
intentional action: mind and, 259
intentional acts: subject to norms, 250–1
intentional concepts: are history-laden, 256–7
intentional relations, 254
intentional states: effects of, 269–70

intentionality, 252–7; first mark of, 213; information and, 209–13; original, 212, 223; teleological theories of, 219; third mark of, 212
internal states, 172; conscious, 185; correlated with external conditions, 203–4, 205–7; and external affairs, 266; form, shape, or syntax of, 200
internalists/internalism, 82, 83, 84, 86n5, 87n8, 88, 91
intrinsic properties: of beliefs, 265–7; explaining behavior, 271, 272; intentional states and, 269, 270; of internal causes, 266; of money, 260–2, 263–4, 270–1
introspection, 135, 155
introspective awareness, 123–4, 134
introspective knowledge: psychological immediacy of, 170
inverted-spectrum problem, 155n49
irrelevant alternatives, 57, 63

Jackson, F., 170–1
judgment(s), xi, 139, 149–50, 151–2, 153, 157, 254n14; mistaken, 248; perception and, 140, 141; truth/falsity of, 247
justification, xi, 26, 57, 88–9; implied threshold of, 49, 50; optimal, 53; required for knowledge, 51; standards of, 58, 59
justified true belief, 18n13, 35, 49

Kantian view: concepts in, 248n7
killing (concept), 244, 256
Kim, Jaegwon, 260n2, 267–8, 269, 270nn13,14,15
Kinsbourne, M., 148
knowledge, ix, x–xi; absolute character of, 48–51, 52, 53; accounts of, 35; analysis of, 52–6; basis of, 5–6; and beliefs, 86–7, 90–3, 197; causal account of, 7–8, 42n4; characteristically human, 83, 84–5; conclusive reasons in, 4, 18, 20, 21–9; conditions necessary for, 26–8, 29; connection with

monkeys: thing-awareness/fact-awareness example, 131–2
moods, 172–5
Moore, G. E., 34–5
motivations, 240
movement, 162, 165, 166n10, 172–3, 203–4; experiences of, 169–70; illusion of, 163–4; internal elements as causes of, 206, 207
Multiple Drafts model of consciousness, 142
murder (concept), 244, 256

narrow content, 229n5, 267
Natsoulas, T., 140n6
natural functions, 216–19, 222, 223
natural selection, 218, 220, 242, 252
naturalism, ix-x, xi-xii, 209, 210
naturalistic accounts of mind: source of cognitive norms in, 246–7
naturalistic basis for epistemological theory, 80–1
naturalistic theories of representation, 213, 214, 216, 219, 226
Neander, K., 246n6, 253n13
neuropsychology, 179
nonpenetrating operators, 32, 37, 41
normative concepts, 243–5
normativity, 249, 251
normativity problem, 247
norms, 242–58: source of, 245–52
noticing, 145
Nozick, R., 54, 82

object (o)-awareness, 160–5, 166, 167, 168, 172, 173, 175, 176, 184; vs. fact awareness, 188–91; vs. acts of awareness, 183–8; being conscious of, 179; perception of, 140; seeing of, 98, 99, 101, 102, 106, 107, 112, 139, 142
O'Hear, 143
ontogenetic source of natural functions, 217–18, 219, 220, 224
ontological kinds: differences in, 159–60
operators, 30, 40–5; see also epistemic operators

pains, 172–5
Peacocke, Chris, 247, 248n7
penetrating operator, 30–2, 33, 35, 38
perception, ix, x, xi, 80, 90–100, 140–1, 182, 206, 254; in animals, 144; without belief, 146; causal analysis of, 108; in cognitivism, 144, 145; complex causal process, 149; of complex scenes, 151; and conception, 97, 107; everyday, 164; function of, 251–2; nonepistemic, 139–40; of objects and events/of facts, 140; veridical, 168
perceptual awareness, 150; of facts, 116–17
perceptual belief(s), 188; distinct from perceptual experience, 113, 124, 131, 152–3; norm-laden, 251–2; perceptual experience assimilated to, 146; truth of, 253
perceptual consciousness, 140, 147
perceptual experiences, 101, 102, 140, 147–9, 150–2, 165–71, 175, 188, 191, 251–2; assimilated to perceptual belief, 146; awareness of, 166, 167–8, 170–1, 172; conscious, 158, 159, 172; distinct from perceptual belief, 113, 124, 131, 152–3; phenomenology of, 164–5
perceptual object(s), 106, 107, 108
perceptual systems, 104, 251; biological functions of, 252
phenomenal character: of bodily sensations, 174; of experiences, 175; of f-awareness of experience, 167
phenomenal consciousness, 153n44, 155
phenomenal experience, 153; function of, 189, 190, 191; nature of, 158–9, 160; of or about things, 172
phenomenal properties, 153, 155
phenomenal states, xi, 268–9
phenomenology: of perceptual experience, 164–5
philosophy of mind, x, 64, 140, 145, 265; naturalized, xi-xii
phylogenetic source of natural functions, 217, 218, 219, 220, 224

sensations: representational view of, 268n8
sense data, 154, 156
sense-data theories, 166–7
Sense-Datum Fallacy, 156, 163
senses, 176; information-providing function, 217
sensory experience, 112, 124
sensory forms of consciousness, 180
sensory information: coded, 150–3; processing of, 122–3; simple seeing in gathering and utilizing, 105–6, 110–11
sensory phenomena: undestood in cognitive/conceptual terms, 145, 146
sensory systems, 60, 104, 109, 110
sentential operators, 30, 31
shape, 166n10, 176–7
signal(s): causal efficacy of, 202–3; information carried by, 199, 100–1, 202
simple seeing, 97–112; information-theoretical account of, 109, 111
skeptic(s), x; and absolute comcepts, 51; and belief/knowledge gap, 65, 79; and conclusive reasons, 24–6
skeptical arguments: knowledge claims, 38–9, 40, 46; penetrability thesis, 34–5; pragmatic dimension of knowledge, 53–4, 58, 62
skepticism, xi, 55–6, 81, 85n4
Skinner, B. F., 219
Skyrms, Brian, 18n13
Sleigh, Robert, 22n16
smelling, 159n2; and conscious experience, 115–16, 121; form of consciousness, 180–1, 182, 185
social character, 227–8; of language, 232–3; of thought, 228–34, 235–40
speckled hen example, 118
speedometer example, 66, 234
spot, consciousness of, example, 126, 127, 128–9, 130, 133, 134
Standard Theory, 266, 267, 269, 270
state consciousness, 121–2, 124, 127, 129, 131, 134, 179–80, 182–4,

188n10, 191; act conception of, 184; inner sense version of, 133–4; object conception of, 186
structuring cause, 238
supervenience: strong 269, 270, 272; truth and, 199–203; of value, 260–1, 262, 264, 269–71; weak, 260n2, 261, 269, 270, 272
supervenient causation, 267–9, 270, 271–2
suppressed inclinations, 147, 148, 156, 157
Swampman, 243n2, 252, 257
symbols, 235; meaning of, 200

tasting, 159n2; and conscious experience, 121; form of consciousness, 182, 183
teleofunctions, 251, 252
teleological theories of intentionality, 219
teleology, 220–2; natural, 219
testimony, 5–6
theory-laden concepts, 243–4
theory of knowledge, 90, 93
thimble example, 140–1, 142–3, 145–6, 147, 149
thing-awareness, 119–20, 125, 126, 127, 130, 131, 135; distinct from fact-awareness, 133–4
things: consciousness/awareness of, 113, 114–20, 130; seeing of, 98, 99, 110
thought(s), 172, 173, 183, 209; causal efficacy of, 229–30; conscious, 186; conscious states in, 185; externalization of, 230n7; functional role of, 223–6; intentional, 254; intentional ingredients for, 210, 211; as internal representations, 234, 235; as maps, 240; nature of, 227–41; recipe for, 209, 213, 214, 215, 216, 222–3, 224–6; social character of, 228–34, 235, 239, 240
"Time and the Observer" (Dennett and Kinsbourne), 147–8
Tom's moustache example, 119, 120, 130

283

Printed in the United Kingdom
by Lightning Source UK Ltd.
119805UK00001BA/249